MW01049684

NAN S 2083
12/9 95/ firm

The Collector's Encyclopedia of

Russel Wright

Designs

Ann Kerr

COLLECTOR BOOKS
A Division of Schroeder Publishing Co., Inc.

The current values in this book should be used only as a guide. They are not intended to set prices, which vary from one section of the country to another. Auction prices as well as dealer prices vary greatly and are affected by condition as well as demand. Neither the Author nor the Publisher assumes responsibility for any losses that might be incurred as a result of consulting this guide.

Additional copies of this book may be ordered from:

Collector Books
P.O. Box 3009
Paducah, KY 42002-3009

or

Ann Kerr
P.O. Box 437
124 Leisure Court
Sidney, OH 45365

@ $19.95. Add $2.00 for postage and handling.

Copyright: Ann Kerr, 1990
Values updated 1993

This book or any part thereof may not be reproduced without the written consent of the Author and Publisher.

This book is dedicated to those of us who made our way to Joplin, Missouri in 1978 for the first APEC show. It all started there. To Jo, BA, Jan, Gus, Naomi, Sharon and Bob, Terry, Maxine and others, to those others who joined us quickly and who represent the APEC family, so important to the collecting of American Pottery, Earthenware and China.

In Appreciation

I have so many to thank for their help as I have studied these Russel Wright designs. From the first, friends were supportive, adding their experience with these designs to the study I was making. Many dealers loaned me items to study and photograph; others have sent marks, pictures and pricing. Collectors shared their finds, and their questions pointed the way to necessary inquiry, providing a sound base for examination of facts.

Jean Hutchison of Toronto, Ohio helped me with American Modern dinnerware details at a time when the Wright papers had not yet been available at Syracuse University. Michael Smith at Depression Modern in New York City outlined the Iroquois information as he had come to know it first-hand. That stands as the basis for our Iroquois information since the Syracuse files are incomplete on this line. Stanley Cohen at Beige in New York helped me with early studies on Spun Aluminum. Diane Petipas at Mood Indigo in New York has consistently found examples of the unproduced Theme groups. Irving Richards, who, with the Wrights formed Raymor, has been helpful and his recollections have made our story here more complete. Lou Barbieri, a cousin of Guido Barbieri, a Wright associate, loaned me pictures, adding recall of his own years working with Wright. The late Arthur Harshman, who worked with Wright for many years, took an early interest in this project. Ed Fitzwater, another associate, gave me early details. The late Ben Seibel, himself an outstanding designer, added insight into the introduction of Modern design in this country.

My first study of Wright's furniture was a Master's Thesis by Barbara Brody. Her work made the whole of Wright's furniture less complicated and her bibliography led me to other writings which were important.

J.R. Miller and Ed Stump at Racoon's Tail were my eastern photograph connection, and made it possible for me to take a van load of dishes into New York for photos. BA Wellman and Bob Diggs, both with a good eye for these designs, often alerted me to new findings and new facts.

Naomi at Naomi's Antiques-To-Go in San Francisco has been our expert on Sterling, consistently coming up with surprises. Jo Cunningham's friendship and support have meant so much to me. Her contribution to this work and to the study of American dinnerware remains singularly important. Carolyn Davis at the George Ahrents Research Library in Syracuse, New York went out of her way to add what she could to this study. Herb Honig, Wright's business manager and personal friend, was always "on call" and was always helpful. Ann Wright has encouraged me and her sharing has allowed us to know more of Russel Wright personally. Her husband, Adam Anik, took a holiday from his work as a photographer at the Museum of Natural History and shot most of the pictures here. His work speaks for itself, and I am grateful.

Steve Quertermous at Collector Books has been supportive and has never hurried this study. That has meant a great deal to me. All of those who represent the Collector Books family cannot be mentioned individually, but their efforts were so helpful. I am especially grateful to Jane White for the personal care she afforded me while at work

In Appreciation

on this writing.

My own family has contributed above and beyond. They are not collectors and have often shaken their heads as I studied, shopped, wrote and traveled. Our cars do not always stop at antique shows or garage sales but they always stop for a "quick look" when I am a passenger. My daughter, Ann Peirce, and her husband, Greg, did the marks section here as they did with the dinnerware book. My daughter, Susan, has encouraged me without questioning the bizarre pattern of a collector's experience. My son, David, shows early signs of becoming an active collector. My husband, while not understanding my consuming interest in all this, does understand that it is important to me and makes it possible for me to travel and keep a busy schedule, knowing that all is well at home.

My friendship with Pam Garber has allowed me to put these studies at the top of my priorities and our friendship has been a forum where I could climb on the nearest soap box, sure of an impartial and sound judgment.

But there were many more and a list is not only incomplete, it says in a word what amounted to a very great deal of help. These persons loaned items for study and photography, added mark information, and often added to our information with their findings. I must thank: Christopher Wilk, Steve Healy, Robert Wutke, Hugh Schreive, Eason Eige, Bill Nixon, Joe Keller, John Roberts, Howard Foster, Marcia Weaver, Carol R. Bailey, Beryl Wright, William Gaines, Katie Woodson, Paul Beedenbender, Trudy Lavelle,

The Lickerts, Brad Mobley, Ann Swanson, Larry McAllen, Bruce Adams, Audrey Trowbridge, Dennis Boyd, Ruth Budge, Rick Hudson, Jack Brooks, J.R. Smith, William Tanner, Gail Krause, Pat Begrin, Paul Fisher, Alvin Schell, Jose Machardo, Shirley King, Karen and Hal Silvermintz, Doris and Burdell Hall, Jack Chipman, Charles Alexander, Ralph Clifford, Ted Haun, Kent Mathews, David Findlay, Randy Jones, Steve McMaster, Bill Eppard, Paul Walter, John Moses, Pete Palm, Barbara Siemsen, William Strauss, Jack Williams, Leo Wetzel, and Frank Wiedman. All these people and more have been helpful in many ways.

I apologize if I have not listed you here. Any oversight is caused by the shuffling of a great deal of paperwork, and it does not mean that your contribution is less important.

I want to thank those of you who have written such wonderful letters to me. Had I had any idea that I would receive such kindness, I would have saved all your letters. They have given me encouragement and confidence.

In addition, many show promoters, organizations and other groups have asked me to be a guest at their shows. That has been such an honor and privilege for me, and I want to thank them here. Those shows have been wonderfully rewarding to me for they have given me opportunities to add to this information, to "talk dishes" and to put faces to the letters which are my lifeline to the collecting world. These experiences have enriched our study and embroidered my life. My gratitude is sincere.

As We Begin

Beginning this book means turning back 10 years or so to the days when many of us were first collecting Russel Wright designs. We joined others who had never stopped and who had started their own collecting in the mid-1930's when Wright's name became a household word.

Collecting "Russel Wright" has been a 50 or more years of a love affair with modernism. Today the circle has come full, and those who search for Wright's designs are a wonderful group of collectors, supporting each other's efforts and studies, guiding each other through large amounts of documented material, reporting hands-on finds so important to study and verification. By our collective efforts, our understanding of Wright and his work has been enriched, and it is our good fortune that the study continues.

My interest in Wright's designs was an early interest, never quite put aside, and in 1979 others joined me when "The New York Times" printed an article on Andy Warhol and his Russel Wright collection. The following day it seemed everyone in New York became a Russel Wright collector, and they be-

came hungry for information. The time, however, was not quite right. The Wright papers were not yet at Syracuse University, and the only avenue open to research his dinnerware was to look at what information could be obtained by studying the Steubenville Pottery which had produced American Modern dinnerware. Some concrete information on this early dinnerware was documented by the Steubenville study, and the large body of that information stands as the basis of our American Modern Information. Workers in Steubenville shared what they could recall. They shared historical information, examples of dinnerware, printed sales brochures and offered their good counsel. But I was never to meet a person who had known Wright nor were there any existing pottery records. The Steubenville approach was misguided as most of Steubenville's other production has not become collectible. A beginning had been made, but it was shaky.

Soon after the publication of "The Steubenville Saga" it was announced that Wright's papers were available at the George Ahrents Research Library at Syracuse University and I made immediate plans to go there for my research. There was SO much and I was overwhelmed and enthused. Back home, my mail begged for any details I could add to the little that had been available and before I had time to really digest this new material, it became apparent that collectors had forged ahead of information and were finding things we had not known existed. They wanted to know what they had found, where it fit into Wright's work story, when was it made and how much was it worth. So many questions flew, and I knew I must share what information I could verify with certainty and get it out to collectors at once. A price guide outlining Wright's dinnerware lines and reflecting prices that friends and dealers were finding as right for Wright followed in short order. Our facts were catching up with our findings.

The collectors' appetite was satisfied for a short time, and it seemed we could take time for a longer, slower, more careful look at Wright's work. The time bought with the price guide gave us running room, and I was able to work on the 1985 Dinnerware Design book. That work took me again to Syracuse University for another review of the files there. "Russel Wright Dinnerware, Designs for the American Table," published by Collector Books, culminated that study. This book is an outgrowth of that work and the interest it generated. A third Syracuse trip allowed for an even more in-depth study, but totally new information obtained from Russel Wright's personal files made available by Wright's daughter, Ann, has added substantially to what we have known. These files answered many questions and that, combined with the shared experience of collectors' findings, adds to the story of the Wright designs presented here. It has been a long study but even so, questions remain. While this writing is intended to add to your collecting "possibilities," your own findings continue to be important to our information. Much remains to be found and documented.

From the first, "Russel Wright" collectors have been "different." They have sought out where this or that fit into the body of his work and philosophy. They reached out to know the significance of their findings. Though cup handles were important to them, they wanted story as well. Collections, often started with a partial set of American Modern dinnerware, went on to another. Soon we became "Russel Wright Collectors," and we wanted it all, including an understanding of Wright's social concepts and the details of his life and work. Those differences have made our study more involved, but my mail tells me that your interests continue as do my own.

These 10 years of study have established some guidelines which should be established or altered for our understanding. Some consistencies have been recognized, some parallels noted, some discrepancies acknowledged and some omissions found. We would do well to take a longer look at the body of material which interests us as collectors.

Early on we used the word "prototype" in a less than accurate way. Our understanding should be narrowed to define the word "prototype" to pertain to a model, an illustrative piece. These pieces could be one of a sort, perhaps with several variations, each for the purposes of our study, a model made by Wright or approved by him, to illustrate his design for a client. An "experimental item," on the other hand, could better describe the items produced by a client according to Wright's specification for the purpose of examination to determine whether or not production should continue. With our understanding of Wright's contractual clause which provided for redesign or restyle if items met client or customer resistance, we must be aware that the numbers of prototypes and experimental items could add substantially to the numbers that such a term suggests. Prototypes and experimental items could be done at any time during the life of a product. A "sampling" or "run" would indicate a small amount made to specifications for show or limited distribution in advance of actual production. In this writing we have used these terms with what accuracy has been allowed by the information available.

Actual dates are too often not available to us as we study all this. Many of the Wright papers are not dated, and this applies to correspondence between Wright and clients as well as inter-office notations. Some dates which are important to collectors are not certain, and we can only approximate these.

Both the Syracuse files and the photograph files are difficult to work with. Wright was a scribbler, note writer, saver, and we are fortunate that much of that has come down to us. Neither archivists or students, however, can utilize the material to its best advantage since it is not always clear where notes, drawings and papers should have been placed. Where possible, data from the files has been verified by Wright's associates. Recall of the minute detail which collectors seek is difficult and, in some instances, findings offer the most conclusive information. We must remind ourselves that no one ever expected these details to be as important as they are to collectors today.

We had previously believed that the existence of a contract indicated that a product followed. That is not necessarily true. For many reasons, clients were not always able to follow through with production. In such cases, there still exists the possibility that prototypes, experimental items, runs or samplings, as we have defined them here, may exist. Most of those items add to our list of rarities which would also include limited production items. Scarcities which have developed because of collector demand should not be considered rare for our purposes.

Care should be taken in drawing conclusions from sales brochures or original advertising. Often brochures changed according to the date as well as the store which gave them out. Not all items will be found on each brochure, and not all colors are necessarily listed on all. Inventories changed from time to time and store to store. Advertising photographs of the day cannot be studied and considered reliable for identification purposes. Photographers use the best material they can obtain in order to achieve effect. A table set with Wright dishes could easily show another's glassware, wood ware or the like. Later advertising, while more detailed, is still suspect. Stores advertised that part of Wright's work which they carried, and that may or may not have been all of the line in all of the colors.

The term "underglaze" must be approached with care. We often hear of a pattern, design or motif and are told that it is "underglaze," suggesting that if so, it must be a Wright feature. Ceramists now and then have been able to decorate on top of a glaze and re-glaze with skill. Be cautious! Be cautious also if you are new to collecting and find a two- or three-tier tidbit tray which will not be listed. These were favorite pieces with pottery workers and home ceramists who adapted many different dinnerware lines to this use. The holes which were bored into the plates or bowls were often glazed. New collectors, not acquainted with this phenomenon of the pottery industry often feel they have found a rare unlisted item. Other adaptations, using metal in combination with pottery to make serving items fall into the same category. These items surface with regularity and too often are priced beyond their value.

The new material made available to us is extensive and a large body of new information is added to that which we had known before. In this writing, wherever possible, original descriptive wording is used in the interest of accuracy. Wright's own words, used in various speeches, advertising, articles and other forums add to our conceptual understanding and they are used with as much detail as is possible. We must remember that Wright designed the product, conceived the descriptive material to be presented to the client, refined both and approved advertising. He gave speeches, wrote articles, made personal appearances - all in the interest of the product of his design firm. The amount of personal involvement cannot be discounted. His act may not have been a one-man show, but it was presented as such.

Those of us who have collected for these 10 years must define our collecting from time to time, establishing limits, changing them and more often than not, enlarging them. We question ourselves: Does our collecting limit itself to Russel Wright work? Do we collect Mary Wright designs also? Do we include American Way work in our collections? If so, to what extent? Do we seek only Wright designed American Way items or do we accept American Way items which Wright had juried and approved? Does our collection have a limit or does it push its own limits with regularity? Wright's influence on the work of his contemporaries was considerable, and it must be recognized that he was influenced by them. Our collecting often becomes open-ended and unstructured as we examine and admire the Modern movement from many directions. Our new view leads us to new findings, better understandings, more appreciations and greater pleasures. Our collecting takes on a new dimension.

I must not leave this foreword without emphasizing your importance to this study. You have been patient when my efforts produced little information, and you have constantly urged me to dig deeper and report more. With you, it has been a wonderful 10 years, and I look forward to more.

I encourage you to write me or call me. I love to talk dishes. I welcome your findings, especially where they add to the information which we have. It thrills me when you find a bargain. The stories about how your mother packed the dishes away and you have unpacked them, warm my heart and prove to me that our common interest in preserving this information is important.

Let us make another beginning then into a review of what has become familiar and a journey into new findings to add to our understanding of the many splendored world of Russel Wright American designs.

Pricing

Collecting Russel Wright designs became popular when Andy Warhol's collecting was described by the press in 1979. Prices established soon after that became the base line for what has evolved as our pricing information today. Prices have gone higher as new collectors entered the market and as scarcities developed. The recent sale of Warhol's estate has had an effect of all items which he collected. That influence contributes to some degree to the prices we are seeing today.

No attempt has been made to individually price some of the lines listed here. Lamps are too numerous, too varied and too seldom seen to have established a price pattern. For the same reason, furniture is not valued here. Additionally, geographic distances between the Eastern and Western markets involve transportation costs which have a direct bearing on the prices of large items. This is our first look at some of these lines and collector activity will determine values based on recognition and comparison.

Many things enter into pricing not the least of which is to whom it is being priced and where that may be. From sale to sale, dealer to dealer, and from region to region, wide variances are to be expected. It is important to understand that the value of an item depends upon its value to you. If you have looked for an item, finally found it and paid its price, the next one you see will not be worth the same amount to you. Those who have taken sets out of storage would do well to remember the limits of their own sales capabilities. If you know someone who collects these things, you can expect to charge any amount which you and the buyer agree upon. If, on the other hand, you do not know collectors and are not in a position to advertise and ship things, you may be left with your local dealers. In that case, you must expect that they will not be able to pay you full price for your things. Dealers must reflect a profit and since they assume the risk of sales, they usually can pay only half of value.

Neither the author nor the publisher assumes responsibility for any losses which might be incurred as a result of consulting this guide.

As He Lived It

The personal history of Russel Wright remains as we have known it, but new findings add to our understanding of the development of his work, his social concepts and the influences which he began early in this century and which concern us today. This complex man and the complexity of his work are important to America's early acceptance of Modernism as we know it.

Wright was born April 3, 1904 in Lebanon, Ohio. He claimed two signers of the Declaration of Independence as forebearers, and there are some who feel that spirit may have been reflected in the social consciousness which became such an important part of his life. His father was a local judge and, with his mother and his sister made up the small family to which Wright felt strong ties. This family affection and concern was always a part of his life regardless of where success took him. He never lost touch with his family or with Lebanon. His concerns for fellow Americans were reflected in early family correspondence as he touched on prejudices of his time and told of his reading - fictional and nonfictional.

From his earliest years, Wright was to show dedication to work, more than a measure of determination and real artistic tendencies. At 17, with a part-time job in a munitions factory, he spent Saturday afternoons at the Cincinnati Art Academy with Frank Duveneck. After high school graduation, he spent a year in New York City in the study of art and won the first and second Tiffany prizes for the outstanding war memorial of 1929. The following year he entered Princeton to study law in which he was expected to excel and to carry on the legal profession as had others in his family. He soon neglected his law studies, but it was at Princeton where his talents were first recognized. His father had written to the Dean with concern for Russel's grades. The reply came that marks could be better, should be better, but the faculty recognized and they hoped the father would see that Wright was to have a brilliant future, however different than in the law. His ability, skills, dedication to work and a no-nonsense attitude stood out as exceptional to his instructors, and his parents were reassured that he was not being led into a loose Eastern city life. He seemed to have set his sights with new direction. His new goals were different goals, the family was told, but that did not make them of lesser importance. This good advice came at exactly the right time, and his family allowed his talent to take its course. He had become interested in set and production work in the Triangle Shows, and as early as his sophomore year in school the New York theatre world became interested in him. He soon was working for and with Norman Bel Geddes and his legal studies ended as he made a place for himself in the artistic community in New York. He was later to say that studio sculpture or painting would not have satisfied him as he was blessed with a social conscience and working in a lonely studio would have made him feel "left out and misunderstood." Stage design, however, would not hold his interest either, for he felt too much of being a cog in a wheel and quickly realized that his real interest was in home furnishings.

It was Wright's good fortune to meet and marry Mary Small Einstein. She was to make many significant contributions to his future work and life, none more important than her love and support of him during these early years. She championed his creed from the first and her social and financial contacts permitted her to open many doors at a time when her husband had no work background.

In 1930, Russel Wright was making masks of stage and political personalities. Greta Garbo, Herbert Hoover, and Mary Pickford were examples, but within a year he was turning chromium products as well as aluminum and pewter out of his own shop in the converted coach house on E. 53rd Street in New York City. The couple lived upstairs, and Mary supervised sales and production. Neighbors were mystified at the wares displayed in a big glass window inviting customers to look at the strange new things this "Wright fellow" was making. The chrome work done here is not the Chase chrome but work of his own. The aluminum work as we know it had its beginnings here, however. Both chrome and pewter were short-lived for the Wrights had learned that it was easier and cheaper to work with aluminum.

Herbert Hoover caricature mask, 1930.

Out of this home/workshop came Wright's Circus Animals. They and the masks brought him attention and orders but these were few, and Mary urged him to concentrate his work on metal home accessories - things which seemed to be easier to sell. Mary Ryan in New York had revolutionized the gift industry and was the acknowledged guru of it for some time. An early supporter, her endorsement was significant and complimentary. Ryan and the Wright's formed an arrangement which sold Wright's work as well as his cause. She advertised that Wright was an American craftsman, working for the American market and paying American taxes. Modern production, she said, allowed him to place his artisanship at the disposal of the many in contradistinction to the craftsmanship of the past which worked to serve the needs of the few. She called him a modern Paul Revere and sold his avant-garde things on a commission basis.

By 1934, the Depression had left most people with too little to spend on these whimsies. Wright's home accessory line was still developing and in spite of its popularity, sales were falling. These "hard times" were to become better times for the Wrights, however. Observant department store buyers looked carefully at the emerging home accessory lines and questioned him about increasing the volume to permit them to order and stock the line. Those buyers had recognized that the new usages combined with affordable pricing could stimulate their own sluggish sales. Almost at once the Spun Aluminum pieces expanded to what amounted to an astounding number of items and they were to be his spring board to fortune, fame and success. The transition from boutique to department store sales

was a leap into a new market. Orders quickly came from across the country, and the Wrights found themselves in the middle of phenomenal success with many highs and only a few lows. He was making a name for himself as a pace-setter, introducing America to home furnishings geared to informal living and entertaining.

In 1935 a new way of life was in the air, and Wright's kite flew high. Soon the Wrights were to meet and form a friendship as well as a working relationship with Irving Richards who operated a very successful business in Manhattan. Richards joined forces with the Wrights in the business side of Russel Wright Inc., renamed Russel Wright Accessories. Both Wright and Richards believed that a newness of design was appearing in this country, and they believed it to be a distinctive American functional design. The unique Raymor firm developed out of this business relationship. It is important to understand exactly what Raymor was and how it operated to be able to understand Wright's relationship with it and Raymor's own relationship with many fine designers and firms of our times.

Raymor was a company formed to sell and distribute Wright designs as well as the work of others. Mary and Richards were to have the voting stock in Raymor and make business decisions. Wright was to design exclusively for Raymor for a five year period. Profits would be paid to all as dividends. After the original five years, the Wrights sold their stock to Richards who then was in charge of the Raymor firm. It continued to pay Wright royalty on his American Modern line as well as on his other work which they distributed. His exclusive contract had ended, but he was to contribute work on a royalty basis as would others. Raymor went on to become a legend in the marketing industry under Richards, representing the best of designed work done by many firms and artist/designers from all over the world. These business arrangements have been problematic for Wright collectors and misunderstanding of the affair causes confusion on the part of those who see the word "Raymor" on items and believe that it must be of Wright design. Wright's work with Raymor was only a fraction of the many excellent products which the firm marketed over a long and prosperous period. While not exactly synonymous, we may consider the name "Richards Morganthau" to be interchangeable with Raymor. That name reflects a working arrangement and does not affect our understanding of the Wright/Richards/Raymor relationship.

Neither Wright nor Richards lived in a vacuum, and they were well aware of the exciting new work which had come out of the recent Bauhaus movement in Europe and the Arts and Crafts program in England. Wright believed that Americans were not ready to accept the sterility of the Bauhaus lines, but he found similar qualities in the functional lines of that school and work done in earlier America. Refining and reworking these two similar influences while keeping an eye on the way average Amercans live, think and felt rather than on sophisticated metropolitan fads and modernistic cliches was important to Wright. Where traces of the Oriental appear in his work, it reflected his early and continuing admiration for sparse Oriental lines. His work was sprinkled with these qualities from the start.

Texture and construction, stressed to the degree where they substitute for surface decoration, were primary to Wright's design concept. He felt the dramatic exaggerated use of material plus an equally exaggerated construction consciousness would result in a handcrafted look. He further believed that in this way functionalism was best served, paving the way for machine perfection. Informal modern, as Wright saw it, reached ahead into the American future, cutting ties with the formal European concepts of the past and serving the needs of a casual relaxed society of average means. Great social changes called for an adaptation to a new way of life, one in which art was a part of the daily life of Americans. Our everyday tools, he told us, should be artistically functional. The best things in life should be free, or sell for a reasonable price. Our art education, he said, had been imitative and we were insecure with any concept which was not generated years before in Europe. We must overcome such self doubt and be proud of our own heritage, our own skills, our own tastes and most importantly, our own instincts.

Wright expressed it best: "The fear that casual living is sloppy living and that we had better hang on to traditions underestimates a lot of the things that are going on. How can you hold on to the traditions in times that are changing so fast and so radically? In adapting ourselves to this big social revolution we are naturally going through a transitional period. Our new way of living will not be tasteless. Fed by industry and the press which serves it, we have accomplished greater comfort on a larger scale than any previous civilization. Science and industry helped. Traditionalists headed by the great evangelist and leader, Emily Post, were afraid." Our own rules were the best rules, he told us. Living, borrowed from others, would not fit our needs. We needed creative and spontaneous ways, more warmth and friendships. It seemed so right and he proved his point again and again.

Spreading the gospel became a business ritual also. With his reputation now solidly in place, his name a household word, and with magazines and newspapers selling him and his wares, Wright entered every new field that he was able to enter. He soon closed the Russel Wright Accessory Company, which had manufactured his metal, in order to devote all his time to design work. He could afford to write the score to which others danced. The new Russel Wright Associates Company became the design firm and business practices became more uniform, especially his contracts.

All contracts became standard with few exceptions. Wright was to receive 5% royalty on goods sold, a lesser amount on second quality sales. These royalties continued until sales fell below a specified figure after which the contract was dissolved by both parties and the designs returned to Wright. The manufacturer or retailer was to assume advertising costs, and they were free to use the endorsing Wright signature in all but specified cases. It was always to be the largest printing on the page. This advertising was watched and guarded by Wright and his staff and no infraction of this contract clause was allowed to pass unnoticed. Clients were warned when this situation occurred and surveillance was constant. No detail, either business-wise or design-wise was too small to deserve his personal attention and we see here more than an artist. He kept a tight hold on daily practical concerns and that allowed him to make generous concessions contractually. If any part of a client's design met customer resistance or if sales people reported that sales were slow on an item, Wright agreed to redesign the line or restyle items. If there appeared to be a need for an addition to the line, he agreed to do that design.

Business promoters selling his designs to clients received a commission of 15% less certain expenses if they were solely responsible for a sale. Wright furnished salesmen with desk space, a phone, secretarial assistance, calling cards, research assistance, training in industrial design selling techniques and access to his records of potential customers. These salesmen received 5% to 50% commission depending upon the account which they obtained and the terms of that account. They were not salaried but received $25.00 a week as pocket expense money. Wright could restrict their use of an already established house account, however.

Russel Wright Associates included a few designers and a small support group of very skilled managers. A list of the associates should contain at least these names: Herbert Honig, Ed Fitzwater, Don Yellin, Hector Leonardi and Guido Barbierbi. A small staff which he could oversee with a minimum of effort worked best for Wright. Approving all work done by Wright Associates, he watched this work with a religious intensity and, as time allowed, worked on every account and each item which carried his name. He rejected many offers which would have permitted his name to be used on production by firms with which he had no contract. Manufacturers offered fees for blanket use of his name on their products. All were refused, and there is no known instance in which he compromised the intregrity of his name or his designs.

He was a hard man to work for or with, but his demands on his staff, his clients and himself produced uniformly high-quality products. For a time, he occupied two city houses, living in one and using the other as his studio where his staff of 10 or 12 worked. The adjoining back yards were thrown together and work was done at the side of windows facing out on a garden planted with flowers. The staff lunched there in good weather, and it was believed that the atmosphere of tranquility, so close to the city streets gave ease to the work done, and the pace became less hurried. From the first, his homes, penthouses and apartments became magazine showplaces, the background for any new product or design. His life was never a private life.

Wright practiced economy in all ways and time was never wasted. He drew as he waited even though his own drawings did not please him. His papers show many rough drafts saved against some future time when they might apply.

Surely all worked for the best. During this period he was the first to design many things: a portable radio, a radio and phonograph console, sectional upholstered furniture, Spun Aluminum accessories, stove to table accessories, the first to use rattan, hemp rope or wood in informal serving pieces. His blonde wood furniture became the model for furniture of Modern design. Aluminum blinds, stainless steel flatware and Melamine used for synthetic dinnerware were all Wright "firsts." If this were not enough, he was doing a great deal of custom work which included showrooms for manufacturers, room displays for department stores and whole restaurant concepts. He was in charge of the Food Exhibit Building at the World's Fair in 1939, and his work on that attracted national as well as international attention. His contributions were in five areas: Focal Food, Focal Fashion, Guiness Stout, Mental Hygiene and various store exhibits. A whimsical portrayal of dancing vegetables in the Campbell Food exhibit attracted many and a model room exhibited was similar in concept to one he would design for his own use later at Dragon Rock. Wright attended national and international exhibits often and his notes show enthusiasm and respect for many projects presented in such affairs. The coming-together of the design community on such a large scale expressed the efficiency he so admired.

By this time his work had earned many awards and was widely shown in museums here and abroad, none more important to him than the

acceptance of his Cowhide chair as the only American chair to be part of the Museum of Modern Art International Chair Exhibit in 1938. He wrote countless articles, gave many speeches at all sorts of meetings and conventions. He addressed new graduates, made store appearances when new products were introduced. He was in charge of an exhibit at the Metropolitan Museum of Art which was to show the work of contemporary American Industrial Designers. The plans he arranged included rooms done by such impressive names as Deskey, Rhode, Van Nessen, Teague, Bel Geddes, Loewy and more. It was an honor to be part of such a group, even more to have planned the occasion. The tremendous records set by his Steubenville American Modern dinnerware sent reverberations through the design community, the pottery industry and the business world. There could be no mistake, America had embraced Modernism!

The Wright name was selling as fast as his products, and the Wrights had catapulted it to an endorsement of quality, another first in the business world. Their choices were the choices of the day's homemaker, and if the Wrights said beef and beans looked best on certain colors, those colors became the fashion's latest statement. They were recoloring and reshaping the home furnishings field with a national campaign directed toward the manufacturer and the retailer as well as the customer. We were delighted to learn that Nelson Rockefeller ate off of the same dishes we did! Market research showed that young, white collar people were Wright's chief enthusiasts and surveys showed that his name was recognized many times more than that of older, more established names.

In 1941, the Wright's organized a new merchandising concept called American Way. So important to those who collect, this program deserves a chapter of its own, but it should be noted here that it was a group of talented artists and designers who formed a system of merchandising the best of their works. Its early failure was partly because of wartime shortages, but also because it was too difficult to manage sales and distribution of production so diverse and so geographically distant. This was a Wright restatement of the Arts and Crafts movement in his own American version.

In 1951, throwing aside others "isms and "ologies," the Wrights were to spell their ideas out through their book, "Guide To Easier Living," which addressed efficient housekeeping and resulting leisure through the application of business techniques and motion management. It was Wright's idea of how housework could be put on a 40-hour week and featured 1,000 ways to make housework easier, more rewarding and faster. Outlining a plan for building a home, living in it and working in it made the book a best seller and women from all across the country rushed to learn how to do all this and still lead the easy life. The book was to show us how to make a bed in three minutes, how to make a child's room "childproof" and how to make a living room a "self-tidying room." Charts, check-lists and diagrams plotted the way through the promised ease of the plan. It went into three printings and became the Bible of housework. Some of us came to recognize it as a "woman killer" for it left no dust unturned. It is difficult to explain Wright's influence on young homemakers, but we were a textbook-oriented society then. The government had sent a generation to college after World War II and the academic approach seemed right. We read Gilbreath's "Cheaper By The Dozen" and our children were measured by Dr. Spock's standards. The Wrights challenged our housework. It was true that our world was much different from that of our parents, and we needed new experts to show us the way. We were to find our own focus later, to laugh a bit at our intensity, but some of us still practice bits and pieces of those early lessons.

Dust jacket front to "Guide to Easier Living" by Mary and Russel Wright.

That same year Wright became the President of the Society of Industrial Designers, an impressive new honor. To be so recognized by his peers was high praise - praise that was so important to him. His personal lot was not an easy one. It is true that his self perception did not match actuality. Never really a part of any group, he had always turned to his work, for his anxieties and enthusiasms found outlet there. It seemed to not win him friends. He was an opportunist with no negative connotations, and he seized opportunities and ideas with equal fervor. He had never taken on the protective coloration of New York. Perhaps his rejection of the values of the wealthy social group there accounted for the fact that he had never been able to make a place for himself in that group. He was not urbane or socially polished. High society ignored him as a person while it furnished its homes with his work. Other designers accused him of being "too commercial" and that criticism stung. The immensity of his work set him apart from the fraternity of designers and they felt him to be too profit-oriented to be a good designer. They believed him to be a "gate crasher," and it was hard to find a friend among them. A loner, an outsider in his own profession, he held himself apart from every group except those whose cause he defended. In revolt for most of his years, he was iconoclastic and complicated. His disposition was variable, hard to forecast and seldom serene. Things did make a difference to him and that difference set him apart from satisfying relationships. With some personal suffering, he remained apart from his contemporaries and was not allowed the easier life he proclaimed.

His continuing friendships with Herbert Honig and Irving Richards are in contradiction to most of his personal associations. Herbert Honig, as business manager, took charge of the coordination of business details so diverse that they defy description. Only a close friend and mind reader could have brought order to his affairs. With a sense of relief, Wright had turned over these matters of commerce to Honig in 1950. It was difficult for him to relax his attention and the research material shows that Honig was skilled at bringing order to constantly changing details. Richards proved to be a good friend with a good sense of intuition, knowledgeable insights and a willingness to deal with Wright as he found him. His was a life-long friendship, and in many ways Richards brought stability to Wright's fragile disposition. Mary's early death in 1952 left a void at a time when he had much more work to do. His focus was to change. Still working at marathon speed, he was to redirect some of his energies in a personal way.

It seemed a personal rejection when his followers turned to others. He became embittered, a petulant law unto himself. Sure that others were using his work, or parts of it, he became even more withdrawn, and those who worked with him needed patience in increasing amounts. The center of his own world, he had never kept up with life in any area except those which involved his own work. When at last he found that there was no longer room for him in the design world, he said that he felt he had left American design at a time when it was in worse shape than he had found it. Discouraged, he regrouped and redirected his life in ways that surprised those who knew him best.

In 1955, Wright had been retained by the U.S. Department of State to survey the possibilities for developing cottage industries in Southeast Asia. Traveling widely through Japan, Taiwan, Cambodia and Vietnam, he explored native handicrafts, advising workers on ways to perfect their work and to export it. He established centers for the manufacturing of these products and made important contributions to the emerging industries. He was restating his old social concerns, this time on an international scale. It was not surprising when in 1965 he was invited back to Japan to work for more than 100 companies. Later he would work with the Johnson administration to establish a Park Beautification Program, forming an association with public land and its reclamation for public use. Never compromising his own principles, he once refused to work on a beautification project when he saw that housing and food were being neglected. His work in Washington won him several awards and he was never far from involvement with public lands from that time on.

Wright turned to a personal project also, and at last retreated to a place he had loved for many years. In 1941 he and Mary had wished for a retreat home, a weekend place, and had bought 79 acres of wooded mountainside in Garrison, New York, 50 miles from the city. This was abused quarry land, and Wright made a personal project of it for many years, working alone, felling trees, cleaning logging sites, replanting quarry roads and feeling spiritually renewed for this work. He approached this land from the same focus he had all his life. He studied the area as it existed and allowed his imagination to entertain all possibilities which would heal the ground and contrive beauty where he could improve upon that which was natural. He plotted nature trails with unexpected beauty spots. He softened the quarry walls with moss and fern plantings to make rock outcroppings less severe. He redirected a stream and achieved a magnificent waterfall into the quarry pool.

The house and grounds were a world of his own creation, all he had admired as he had lived a lifetime with the best of American design. It was "part pavillion, part cave." It remains an exagger-

ated, impractical, difficult to maintain, breath-takingly beautiful dream home, if not functional, perfectly suited to his desires, not his creed. The walls are hewn from the rock of the quarry as are the floors and steps. Glass walls overlook the quarry pool, a large cascading waterfall, the woods and a grassy area which he named "Mary's Meadow." Wildflowers are everywhere and a four-acre laurel field is beautiful. The interior is an extension of these views, literally a "temple of earthly delight" with many surprises. The fireplace seems to come in from the exterior rock formation. A bathtub fills from a wall of rock as would a waterfall. The walls are a forest green, and there are hemlock needles pressed in, uniting them with the hemlock grove across the way. Butterflies and ferns are embedded in panels and sliding doors. Wildflowers bloom in pockets in the steps which lead to the lower level where a tree grows to the top of the house. Rya rugs resembling pads of moss covered the floors when Wright furnished it. Those who share Wright's love affair with nature will love the memorial to it which he built.

He cared for these grounds with a loving care over all of his later years. He had found personal satisfaction and a never-before known ease in his life. We see here a Wright who had at last found himself able to experience his own pleasure and work outside the marketplace. He had a second chance, and he found contentment in it. You will find pictures of the house in the March 16, 1962 issue of "Life" magazine.

He closed his studio in 1967, but he could never separate himself completely from his work. He continued to be involved in land projects, and he became interested in the reclamation of groundfill areas. Using his old theatrical experience, he designed and directed two local festivals at Garrison to show that beauty could result from restoration. A new sense of community unified him with others of similar interests. He had taken his own medicine, turned his attention and found a sense of belonging.

Russel Wright died of a heart attack in 1976 and did not live to see the "second time around" of his designs. As it happened, they seem never to have been out of favor. He had been too important to his generation. He touched our lives as few others do and with an art that conceals art he had brought beauty and joy to unexpected times and places. Our lives had lost the sameness, and the changes were permanent. We had packed it all away for a short while, certain that it was special - and it was.

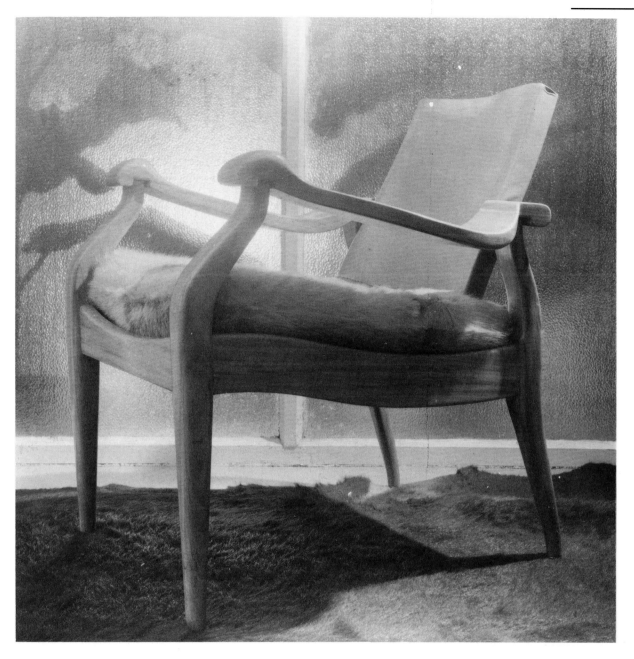

Russel Wright Cowhide Chair. Exhibited in Museum of Modern Art International Chair Exhibit, 1938.

More On Marks

Our new study of marks adds much to what we have known, so much that we must develop a new set of guides to allow for new marks to be included in the numbered series which were shown in the 1985 dinnerware book. In an attempt to preserve the order which was previously established, the newly added marks will be shown with the 1985 mark, but will be listed with an alphabetic sign. For example, if mark #1 is an American Modern Steubenville mark shown before as mark 1, any additional marks would be 1a, 1b, 1c. This may not be the most concise way to give you this information, but I do not want to destroy the sequence of information which has been memorized by those who have been collecting for 10 years or so.

Dating marks and understanding the information in them is made even more challenging by the introduction of so many new marks presented here. There remain minor differences in some of the marks - the addition of U.S.A. or the presence of a period, trivial to some, very important to others. I am pleased that your search has yielded so many additions for it indicates the depth of your interest and involvement.

In 1985, we felt safe in the position that there was only one Steubenville, American Modern mark. We were wrong. Added here is 1a, a new mark incorporating USA as part of the mark. Another, 1b, shows a variance in size and placement of "USA." There is said to be a slight variation in the letters "S" in Russel and that letter in Steubenville, but the variance is so small that it does not reproduce as I would like it to do. Be aware, as you study these marks, that some minor variation can be accounted for by mold ware. Both marks are incised and some irregularity may have resulted from that process. The pottery was handmade, and glazes often ran into the incised mark, all but obscuring parts of it. Not all marks are as pristine as we would like.

Most American Modern is marked - unless the item was too small for a mark. Mark 1c is a mark not shown before and it identifies Wright's American Modern glassware, made by Old Morgantown. It is a gold sticker. In the American Modern photographs you will find a bowl with an experimental glaze and mark. Several of these in different colors have been found but none were clear enough to reproduce here. They were numbered with meanings only to those concerned at the time. If you find one, treat it gently for they are rare. I should be careful not to assume that there are no other American Modern/Steubenville marks. As I write, I expect to hear from some mark researcher who has found a Steubenville mark with periods after the "USA." It is predictable.

Mark 1

Mark 1a

Mark 1b

Mark 1c

The Harker Mark 2 remains the only mark reported. It also is an incised mark and glaze runs did alter signature and company name. Harker had a short history and it is possible that our findings may be limited to the mark. Let me know if you can add to this information.

Mark 2

Surely, I thought, the six marks we had seen on Iroquois would be the total, but they are not. There is a new 4a which is very close to the 4 mark but has a slightly different "I" in Iroquois. This difference adds to seven, still counting, Iroquois marks. The 3 through 8 marks are as we have known them, and it seems that we have placed them in the order of their production. The first two marks appear identical except for the letter "I" in Iroquois. The 3 mark with the "Loopy I" as we have named it, is the earlier of the two and the 4 mark with the straight "I" followed soon after. These will be found in dark blue and brown on the heavier, foamy early ware. Later marks, including the word "Casual" have been found in varying sizes even on identically sized pieces. Additionally they are found in several colors, usually pink, green, or brown. Not only the redesigned ware carries this late "Casual" mark. Any piece made late in production, even of original design may have been so marked. The small code numbers contain manufacturing information which we still cannot decipher. Comments in the files which refer to marks mention "eye appeal," and that may be more of a factor with these marks than we had first thought. Only the smallest of the Iroquois items are not marked, but they are difficult to read on some of the darker colors.

In 1985, we had three Paden City/Justin Tharaud/Highlight marks. Now there are three more. Because there seems to be no better place to present it, 9a is added to show the sticker on the Paden City Snow Glass. 10a shows no period after Pat. and shows the abbreviation for "pending" to be more uniform. 11a eliminates all information below Wright's signature.

Mark 9

Mark 9a

Mark 3

Mark 4

Mark 5

P-1

Mark 6

Rw

PAT PEND

Mark 10

Mark 10a

Mark 7

Mark 8

P.C.B

Mark 11

Mark 11a

The 12 Sterling mark is usually found incised but we know that it is also found in raised relief as is the 13 mark. Much Sterling is not marked and some of that which is marked is done so imperfectly that glaze fills the incised letters. Paper stickers replaced marks in some cases, appearing on items that were known to have had the incised mark. Both marks 12 and 13 are marks which Sterling used on the early line done for their customers. Our new mark 13a is the mark which Wright used in patterns which he did as part of his whole concept theme for his own customers. This 13a is used on the Polynesian shape. Other stamps used in the Wright/Client concept as opposed to Wright/Sterling may be found.

STERLING CHINA
by
Russel Wright

Mark 12

STERLING
by
Russel Wright
CHINA

Mark 13

Mark 13a

Knowles patterns are marked with a gold stamp and identification is made easier because of this. photographic image, so central to the survival of the Knowles line is problematic for those who research it. Remember that the pattern name is usually named in the mark. Our Knowles markings remain as we have known them.

Russel Wright
by
Knowles
Queen Annes Lace
MADE IN U.S.A.

Mark 14

Knowing that little Yamato Theme Formal and Informal was made lulled me into a not-so-safe position for we now have more Yamato marks. The mark 15 Stoneware/Informal shown here lines-up Wright's signature. Our new 15a may be a rejected mark for it does not emphasize the signature as Wright would have required. 16a is the raised mark found on the Shinko Shikki enameled Bakelite which was part of the Theme Formal line. 16b is the stickered mark found on Yamato glassware in the Theme Formal line.

YAMATO designed
Russel Wright
STONEWARE
in Japan

Mark 15

made in
Russel Wright
Yamato Stoneware
JAPAN

Mark 15a

Yamato
Russel Wright
porcelain   **Mark 16**
DESIGNED in Japan

design for
Russell Wright
S I P JAPAN   **Mark 16b**

DESIGNED
SHINKO *Russel Wright* SHIKKI
IN JAPAN

Mark 16a

Mary Wright's signature changed from item to item, time to time, and it seems that she was developing her own marks. Do not be suspicious if you find a signature different from the one shown in mark 17. We can expect, however, that this mark 17 signature is the one which she had come to use as standard.

Country Gardens

Mary Wright

Mark 17

The 18a signature is an early one, used on wood items done out of Wright's own workshop in addition to its use on Oceana. Both 18 and 19 are Klise Oceana marks. Signatures on these wood items may not be all-inclusive. They all represent early work and much of it came at a time when Wright was developing his signature as integral to his designs.

Russel Wright

Mark 18

Russel Wright

Mark 18a

Mark 19

The marks on Wright's synthetic dinnerware, 20, 21, 22, and 23 seem standard - for now. We should add two Ideal Ware marks, both found on the child's toy pieces and name them 23a and b.

ture, the words "Hull Stainless" and a patent number. All are the same Pinch line, reflecting only a change of location for Hull.

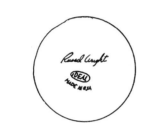

Mark 20

Mark 21

Mark 22

Mark 23

Mark 23a

Mark 23b

Mark 25

Marks 26, 27 and 28 are marks used on Imperial Glassware made to accompany the Iroquois line. As late as this, 1946, the signature was still developing as shown here. Marks 26 and 27 are black, with gold metallic printing on Mark 26 and a gold-colored printing on Mark 27. Mark 28 is a bright red with white lettering and banner. All are enlarged for clarity.

Mark 26

Mark 27

Mark 28

Mark 29

Bauer items are marked as shown in mark 24, lightly incised with the signature sometimes filled in with the extremely heavy glaze. Look for vase bottoms to be heavily irregular, Wright's concept of a built-in flower frog. That often left little room for the signature but is an identifiable feature.

Heywood Wakefield Furniture, made for only a year, was marked in various ways, all incorporating the Mark 30 which was a standard mark of the company. All was to show Wright's name but we should study any highly styled veneered furniture for the Heywood Wakefield mark.

Russel Wright
BAUER

Mark 24

Mark 25 is the Hull Stainless Steel mark as shown on the Hull Pinch line made by them in Japan. That ware made by Hull in this country shows the signa-

Mark 30

The Conant Ball mark is shown here as Mark 31. This is burnt into the wood, perhaps inside a drawer or in an otherwise inconspicuous place.

Mark 31

Mark 32 is the Statton Furniture mark and is found in very small amounts due to limited production.

Mark 32

A bright blue sticker, the American Way mark incorporated the name of the designer in each product. This 33 mark was used in several sizes in proportion to the product. It dates from 1941.

Mark 33

The Sovereign Pottery Mark 34 identifies the pottery made in the "Wright Shape" as first designed for Knowles. Some time after Knowles production was discontinued, Wright gave this shape to Sovereign Potteries in Canada, a firm with family connections. The glazes were Sovereign's, not Knowles, and probably not Wright's.

Mark 34

The ware only now being found and marked as International China Company is in the Knowles Esquire shape. It is identified as Mark 35. This is believed to represent remainders taken by Wright when his contract with Knowles ended. It does not amount to any large sum, nor does it imply a different line than we have known it in the Knowles patterns. This seems to have been a convenient way of rescuing stock for which there were no orders.

Mark 35

The variant Mark 36 signature is as found on early Century Metalcraft items. It shows clearly that Wright was changing his signature/trademark as he developed his products. Contrast it with the early 18a and the polished 37 which became the most popular signature of the 1940's.

Mark 36

Mark 37

The square printed sticker which is englarged here is Mark 38, one of the earliest of all these marks. It is a 1⅛" square, used on several different items all produced from early Russel Wright Inc. or Russel Wright Accessory Company. It followed a mark which was the initials "RW," as well as Wright's name spelled in block letters.

Mark 38

It Started Here

From the first, collectors have cast long and longing looks at the work which Russel Wright did in the metals chrome, pewter, copper, brass and spun aluminum. While we are most familiar with the work done for the Chase Chrome and Brass Company in the 1930's, we must consider the other dimension of Wright's early metal work, that done out of his own workshop and sold as part of Russel Wright Inc. and Russel Wright Accessory Company. It was exciting work and came at an exciting time for the Wrights.

For several reasons, our search will be a difficult one and some of the reasons are intrinsic to the metals themselves. They came at a bad time for metal work. In 1930, the Great Depression and rumors of war combined to limit usage of any metal but it is also true that these metals were difficult for the young Wright to fabricate. His own manufacturing abilities were limited. In addition, most of these early sales were from his coach house door straight across city streets to a Manhattan boutique. The line was a large one with little depth. The concentrated market called for many items with a few of each.

Collectors find less of this metal work than they would like. We cannot be sure of marks on this early metal work, but we will do well to guide ourselves to the modern look as opposed to the Deco look. Wright's metal work was a departure from the chromium work of the Art Deco period. He had rejected that design theme, and his metal work is in direct contradiction to it, moving instead to the emerging modernism.

Early marketing questioned whether this chrome, this new fresh metal would replace silver in the home. Easy to care for, with sleek and soft lines, it was a departure from what had gone before. It quickly made a name for itself in the accessory field. Putting silver "in its place," it was even more usable than silver had been. Wright's shop turned out candle holders, vases, bookends, ashtrays, boxes of every description, serving trays and more. Never meant to actually replace silver, it did instead replace its use in many cases where the older, more expensive silver had not caught up with contemporary designs.

These were promising days for the Wrights. De-signing was not difficult for him and Mary's sales were limited only by production and the practicality of the items she offered. Enthused over the welcome which buyers were giving his work, The Wrights blue-skyed those days. Manufacturing in such a limited space and with such limited equipment was difficult, and that accounts for the limited numbers of these items which come to us today.

The earliest work was that which included the masks and the small animals we so wish to find. We picture some examples of the animals as well as the accessory line hoping that you will notice trends and find identification easier. The animals are marked with the initials "RW" but you will not need to look for that mark. You will recognize it as "special."

Even the work was fun as we can see from the items made at this time. The circus animals and the use of animal forms in accessory items show that Wright could orchestrate with a light touch. The names of the circus animals are whimsical and are an early indication that he would use innovative descriptive words in his work. The circus was wonderful, the performers: a trapezist bottle opener joined a full cast; Bobo the clown, made of nickle, was a bookend as were Libbiloo (his sister's name) horses made of nickle and colors. Rodeo the bull in chrome or gun metal charged into books, as did Moaninlo, a lordly lion made in nickle and colors. A well-antlered fire deer in iron guarded the hearth. Whoozoo was a seal paperweight in nickle and gold; Whoopee was a bottle stop with cork in chrome and colors. Arabella the snake charmer corkscrew was made of chrome. Hotdog, a multi-pieced desk set came in copper. Hokus, a nickle and colored elephant doorstop and Dizzy, a pair of reversible candlesticks, heads up or down, completed the circus except for the Calliope scroll bookends which were widely copied. Other animals were a Noah's Ark assortment, an elephant, seal, lion, a hippo with a cigarette holder in his stomach and seal bookends sitting on a black glass sea. These two animal lines were the earlier animals, and they were soon joined by others made from pressed aluminum. Not as wonderful as the earlier animals, they are almost as difficult to find. Among these are: Tropical birds for centerpieces, Horse and Turtle Dove placecard holders, a Dachshund desk set, and a Perky Penguin. Swan nut cups seem to have survived in more numbers than the other animals, but they are often found in poor condition, the salt from the nuts having damaged the finish. All or any of these animals are precious to collectors, made in such limited amounts as to be rare. Our photos following are "as is" photographs of photographs.

Wright's contract with Chase, widely accepted as the leader in the industry, joined him with other prominent designers who made up an impressive roster. Chase policy was to use only their own mark on their production. That policy has caused confusion and speculation with collectors today. Wright worked with Chase on yearly contracts from 1935 until 1946, but it is safe to assume that some of those years were not years when production resulted. The war restricted Chase work also. By contract he was to submit designs from which 10 items would be selected. Agreeing that he would not design this sort of work for another manufacturer, he reserved the right to work with lamps, already in his own chrome line. Chase held the patents for all the designs which they approved. All rejected designs were to revert to Wright. They gave Wright their standard contract, renewable yearly. Our specific information on the Chase work is still murky. We have known that his work included the 28003 Pancake/Popcorn set on the tray and their #28002 Ice Bowl as well as a beer pitcher. We now can add the #90048 Electric Snack Server, more commonly named the Petite Marmite or Bain Marie, to our known items. Wright had first designed this piece in Spun Aluminum with a griddle base. The chrome model does not have this feature. Chase's #90096 Electric Buffet Warming Oven is suspect. This warmer is not pictured in his files, but a very similar one is there. The concept is the same but we cannot positively identify this as his production. In other work, advertising has given us positive information, but because of the nature of his association with Chase that material is not available to us. We do have a short list which Chase gave to Wright in the early days of his association with them. They expressed an interest in the following: Candleholder Mint Julep set, Baby Cactus pot, deep casserole, flower bowl, hanging flower vase, over bed lamp, desk lamp with side arm, curved bed lamp with side arm of brass or pewter, a vanity lamp described as tall and thin, ashtray, fish tank and bamboo vase. This list would include rejected designs as well as accepted ones.

Early custom work dates from the animal/coach house workshop period at the same time. Done for wealthy clients or firms with specific needs, the extent of Wright's custom work may never be known.

Some accessory items were done for Century Metalcraft while he was under contract to them from 1940-1944. It seems unlikely that much product work would have been done during those years, but tumblers, Old Fashioned glasses, punch cups and bowl, pilsners, a cheese board, an ice bucket, a 10" salad bowl, ashtray, an 8¼" salad plate, an 11" centerpiece as well as a tall cocktail shaker were proposed, all with white glass liners. We should consider the possibility that some or all of these were prototyped or even experimented with to the end that war-time production would have allowed.

We should look at this metal work as significant in Wright's design, for it was through the accessory items that the new modern style was introduced in the United States. Soon it would appear in many areas of home furnishings but the first sightings were in this early metal production done by Russel Wright. World War II ended it all, of course.

We will need a good eye combined with a sense of humor and an appreciation for the modern if we are to find Wright's early metal work. Given the number of experimental items, rejected items, samples and unmarked pieces, our own judgments are important. Much of our information has come to us because of collector's findings, later verified by data. There are still surprises in this work and collectors will find rewards in Wright's metal. Good luck!

Front of pamphlet featuring the Circus Animals.

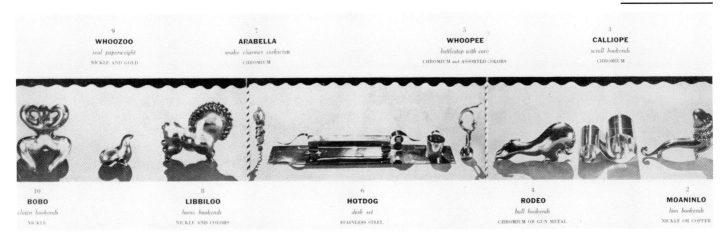

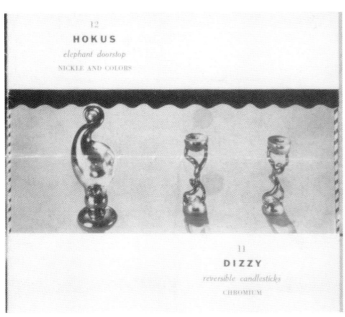

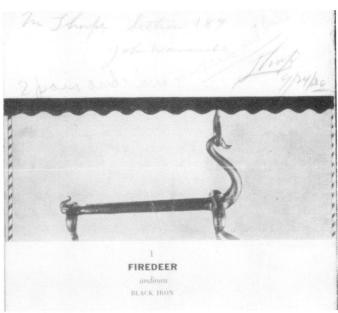

From the Circus Animals pamphlet.

#196 "Tantalus" set: 11½" high, chromium and crystal. Two frosted crystal decanters have vertical ½" lines left clear to show remaining quantity of liquor. Tiny chromium lock to secure use. Decanters sold separately with capacity of one fifth. Chromium caps.

#24 Chromium plated vase, 9" high.

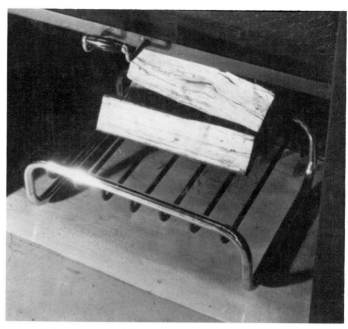

Chrome and iron andirons, custom work.

Chrome electrical server (Bain Marie), Chase ice bowl, Chase corn set includes shakers, oil pitchers, tray, Spun Aluminum peanut scoop.

Service plates, finger bowls and candlestick in chrome and glass. Custom designed for Selma Robinson's office.

Pewter cocktail items. Early items made by Russel Wright Accessories. This set was also made in chrome lined with silver.

Gold aluminite by Everlast. Dinner plates, beaker, 8½" pitcher, bowls: 10", 8", 6".

Left: Early Russel Wright accessories. Chrome combined with cork and Bakelite.

Below left: #119 Chrome accessories: Bar stool with chrome legs, red enamel ring, woven seat. #88 Aluminum wastebasket. Inside lacquered red, green, black or blue.

Below right: #130 Early Russel Wright chrome accessory lamp. Adjustable rod allows various heights.

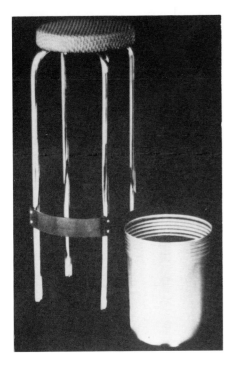

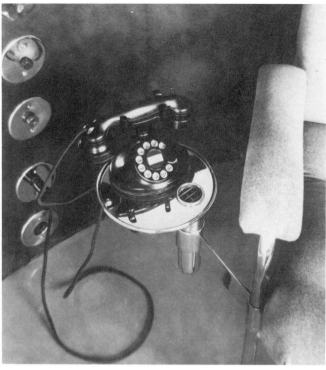

Custom chrome work done for Wright's own use but available for clients.

Calliope chromium bookends sold as part of Circus Animal group or separately.

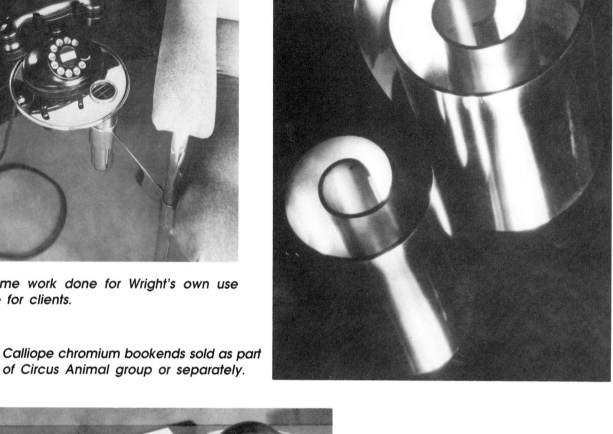

Chrome and Bakelite desk accessories. Pencil tray, pen holder and ashtray. Made by Russel Wright Accessories.

Chromium smoking stands. Made by Russel Wright Accessories.

#318 Copper tray.

#308 Aluminum vase, also made in copper.

Chrome accessories from early Russel Wright catalogue.

Russel Wright hanging ball aquarium, 8" diameter, chromium top fixture with air holes.

Russel Wright cylindrical aquarium. Bowl is 20" long x 5½" high, supported by chromium ends.

The New Metal

Our story of Russel Wright's Spun Aluminum is now a larger story than we have seen before. While an overwhelming number of items were produced, they were made over a short time span and that fact combined with the fragility of the easily bent and scratched metal limits what we find today. This early Spun Aluminum was made by his Russel Wright Inc. and Russel Wright Accessory Company/coach house/workshop with the Wrights living above it. We have many pictures and will show what is possible to include. Do not assume that this is a complete listing.

The basic story behind the Spun Aluminum production is that Wright took this metal, much less expensive than the silver, chrome, copper and brass that it replaced, brought it out of the kitchen and formed it into an informal accessory line of huge proportions. Production was somewhat limited due to the war shortages which curtailed the use of metals for civilian use.

In the 1930's, Wright's inner drummer was beating strong. His work had been accepted by the wealthy to whom he had sold his animals as well as his other metal accessories and he was confident that he could please the consuming world if he could produce accessory items in larger amounts at lower costs. Having served his apprenticeship, he was eager to get on with his work, and was quoted "Before, the idea of acquiring clients or working for a large producer or factory seemed so impossible that we gave little thought to it." His Spun Aluminum was to take him into an even larger world than he could have anticipated.

It would be a team effort. Rejecting other metals, he, Mary and Richards concentrated their efforts on the easier-to-use aluminum.

With the purchase of a spinning lathe, the Wrights were in business in a new and bigger way. Wright's production seemed limited only by his imagination and the more items he produced, the more orders came his way. He was quickly established. From the first, this new line was divided into three categories. They included a stove to tableware group, an informal serving accessory group and an interior accessory group which included items such as bookends, smoking materials, lamps and the like.

With Wright given free reign to exercise his many ideas, Mary attended to sales as she had done in the past, but she soon found that this new aluminum sold itself. Orders came from every direction. Most important were orders from department stores for those were large orders. The Aluminum Company of America sent their people to observe and in no time they entered the market with their own Kensington Company. The Wrights were the uncontested leaders, however, with others following their successful path. The name they were making for themselves was remembered and in the future many observers became clients.

Developing sales allowed Wright to enlarge the variety of items often but production could not keep up with sales. Wearing the manufacturer's hat, seeing this business from that angle gave Wright experience which would help him in future dealings. It shows clearly in his restyle and redesign clauses in his standard contracts which followed.

All this came about at a fortuitous time. There was nothing on the market between paper plates and gold-embossed china. Spun Aluminum, an entirely new material, gave users a choice. Its use was based upon the concept that Americans were living and entertaining in a new informal way. Teas and luncheons, formal dinners and the like were being replaced by spur of the moment affairs, "before dinner drinks," "after dinner dessert," cocktail parties, brunches. Out of the kitchen and on the buffet, Spun Aluminum seemed just right for the new life and it was affordable. Some sort of a "catalog" was needed and that first catalog was a collective effort, a new sales tool.

Modern in every sense, the shapes which this new material took on were typical of the slightly exaggerated forms which Wright would use later in his ceramics. Spherical shapes, circular lines and curvaceous corners were limited only by the workability of the material. Extreme, they were not so radical as the Art Deco designs which were difficult to adapt to already owned furnishings. The new aluminum pieces, colorless, pleasingly shaped and often oversized, blended well. The use of wood, ceramics, glass, cane, cork and rattan combined with the aluminum made for interesting new pieces.

The line was to grow larger and larger, but it all started with a cheese board. That was the original item produced and from then on it seemed they could never produce enough cheese boards or enough variations of them. All were sold as fast as they could be made for cheese was an early favorite at these early cocktail parties. New items were added as quickly as Wright could design them and Mary and Richards could ship them.

From the first, this new line was conceived as "open stock" with interchangeable usage but the ensemble concept was promoted and used with good success - one of the business details that would carry over into other Wright lines. A "Sixtette" group was offered at a savings for the customer. Since this reduced the retailer's profit (while enlarging the designer's), retailers were given a 60¢ incentive refund on all Sixtette sales to guarantee their mark-up. These Sixtette sets were composed of a bun warmer, ice pail set, ring canape tray, buffet platter, sandwich humidor and a double decker stand. Sold as a group they were priced at $10.95; individually, $1.95. Other "sets" sold were called Sunday Supper, Beer Buffets, Cocktail Hour, Midnight Snack, Popcorn Picnic, Sunday Breakfast, After Bridge. Mary's concepts, these groupings were put to test early and were basic in later merchandising by the Wrights and others.

The customer was told that plain steel wool rubbed in the direction of the spinning grooves would erase stratching and keep the aluminum bright. It dented easily and bent alarmingly and those properties have caused less of this to come to us in good condition.

Typical items were: ice buckets, casseroles with ceramic inserts, fruit bowls, lamps, ashtrays, cannister sets, bun warmers, vases - the list goes on. Each piece had variations - as many as the Wrights could conceive. The line grew and sales grew, but World War II came and the material was no longer available for consumer use. After the war the aluminum items seemed never to be so popular. Wright had met the market at just the right time.

These Spun Aluminum pieces are signed with the Russel Wright name in block letters but that mark may be difficult to locate. On some covered items the mark may be on the underside of the cover - but if that cover and the bottom have been separated, collectors are left wondering. A red inked stamp is sometimes found on the wood and there were navy and white labels as well as string tags. Separation of parts and the disposable tags add to confusion for the collector.

The Samovar and the Bain Marie remain special pieces. The Samovar was a modern adaptation of the old Russian Samovar and was well insulated to protect furniture. It brewed 50 cups of coffee (by means of a "scientific percolator contraption") or 30 cups of tea and it did so quickly. This piece was done for Emaline Johnson of the pharmaceutical

family. The Bain Marie was designed for a member of the Vanderbilt family and came with or without a base which could be used as a buffet table griddle. These pieces were typical of a very small amount of custom work done in Spun Aluminum. They date from about 1935 and the work on both is believed to have been more complicated than the Wright's own shop could produce.

In addition to this regular Spun Aluminum line, Wright was to work with a line which he called "Plantene." Ripple finished, It was an altogether new line, of uneven circular lines, deeply engraved upon heavy gauge aluminum. The surface was then burnished to a very bright sheen giving it a "liquid glow resembling quicksilver." Sales literature said that given the same care as Spun Aluminum, the lustre of these pieces would last indefinitely. Included in this line were:

> 6½" Chinese bowl w/cane handle
> Syrup set w/1½ pint pitcher and 7½" tray
> Ball pitcher w/reed handle 2¼ quart
> Thermos, 1½ quart w/cover and bowl
> Four-piece casserole - pot and cover, liner
>   and cover, walnut handles, 1½ quart
> Fruit basket, 11" w/light reed handle
> 15" Round tray w/reed handle
> 12" Round tray w/reed handle
> Ice bucket and tongs, w/light reed handle
> Bamboo handled salad fork and spoon
> Two-tiered tidbit tray w/rattan handles
> Cheese and cracker board w/13" maple
>   center
> 11" large ball vase
> Beverage set w/6-cup pitcher, 16" tray,
>   light cane handles
> Nested bowl set - 10", 9", 7", sold separately
>   or as a set. All with light cane handles.

All of these Plantene pieces have duplicates in Wright's Spun Aluminum line. If you find it you will feel and see that it is different.

Post-war designs done in the 1945-1949 period for other clients are discussed in the metal chapter and the ending summary chapter. Any work done for others was very limited.

This Spun Aluminum work, started in the coach house with little more than a work bench, mushroomed into the concept and the project which would launch Wright's career. That it was his "beginning" is important, of course, but it has further significance. It joined his other metals which first introduced Modernism to the consumers of the 1930's. In a short time Wright and many others would turn and return to these new concepts but in the early 1930's Spun Aluminum was introducing all that was to follow. Life seemed good and what was to come seemed limited only by what the Wrights could make of it. The best years were ahead.

Birchwood and aluminum beverage set.

Dark reed and aluminum sherry pitcher, 2¼ qt., 10".

Hot relish server with two pans, reed frame, Pans, 7" each, 16" overall.

Flower ring.

Double flare vase, reed trim, 12" tall, 5½" diameter.

Gravy/sauce boat with walnut handle.

Cheese board variant.

Humidor for appetizers. Perforations in rings for toothpicks.

All pieces could come off stove on to table. Tray has asbestos center. Double boiler held food in top section, hot water in lower section. Large tureen and server, smaller casserole. Tablecloth is red and white Russel Wright Bandana.

Two-tier tidbit and cork ball tray.

Raffia handled bowl.

9" casserole, pottery inset. Gravy set, hand carved walnut handle, copy of early pewter set. 6½" Ice pail, made in three sizes. Sandwich humidor.

Sandwich humidor shown with top open and closed.

Spaghetti set.

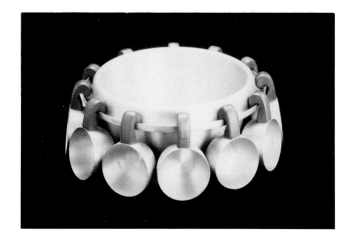

Punch set.

Punch set.

Bain Marie electric server.

Samovar.

Thermo drink holder with reed trim.

Beer set, natural reed trim on keg container and mugs.

Aluminum and cork mint julep set consisting of tray and six tumblers.

Portable bar.

Red lacquered Ballyhoo ice bucket. Detachable aluminum ring for holding and serving aluminum glasses, bamboo handle and aluminum tongs.

Relish Rosette variation and tea set.

Raffia handled serving accessory group.

Six-piece relish basket consisting of basket and 5 removable pottery inserts. Natural reed and cane with rust colored pottery, 12½" diameter.

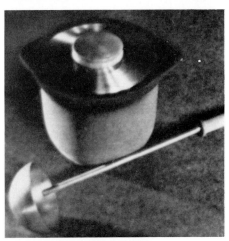

Tureen and ladle - pot, cover and spoon, rust, 3½ pints, 6" high.

20-piece old fashioned set. 21" tray, 12 cups, 4 crystal inserts, bitters bottle, muddler and serving fork.

Smoking stand with detachable base, 22" tall, 4½" diameter.

Casserole, frame and cover held 3 pints, rust colored pottery bisque outside, glazed inside, aluminum and maple, 8¼".

Triple snack server with bamboo trim.

Aluminum candelabra with lacquered holders.

Sheet from early advertising material.

Top row: Flare vase, 10¼" tall, top diameter, 10". Round flower ball vase, 10" or 7", also in copper.

Bottom row: Flower pot, red lacquer base, 6½" tall, top diameter 6¼". Flower pot, same as previous one except all aluminum. Wastebasket lined in chinese red lacquer, 10" tall, 7" diameter.

Early advertising.

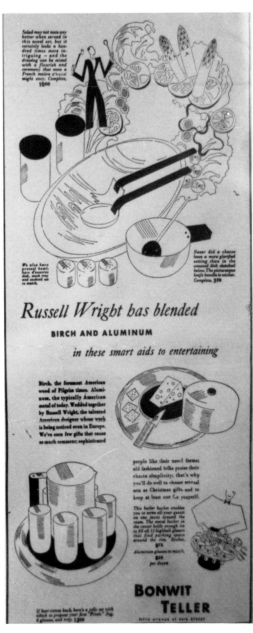

Aluminum cart with bamboo trim.

Roly Poly cart with bamboo hoops and rubber wheels. Trays lacquered chinese red. Punch bowl set on top has ring which is detachable and can be passed to guests. Large ice bucket on bottom.

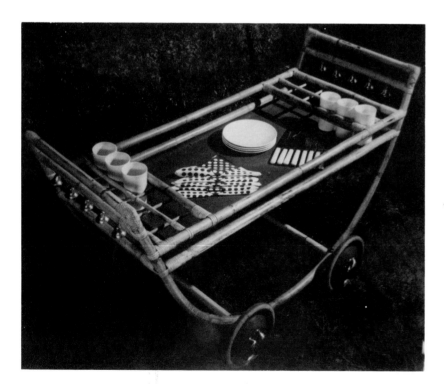

Jingle cart. Bells ring as cart is pushed.

Furniture According To Wright

In the 1930 time reference, with war-time interruptions in the European furniture industry, Wright saw an important opportunity for growth in our domestic production. Our own market had been in a continual state of depression with many homemakers using second-hand family furniture as they first accumulated furnishings, never changing those pieces more than once after that. We "made do," knowing little of furniture styles. While the wealthy used European furnishings, our own acquaintance with those influences had been limited to chance encounters in home furnishings magazines and what came to our experience through auctions and other such limited opportunities. Our use of good quality furnishings was confined to the use of what hand-me-down items our families had preserved, our own changes infrequent ones. The war in Europe played into the hands of those in America who hoped for change in that situation.

The European furniture market was suspended, perhaps never to recover. American technology was teaching new lessons to old industries and the possibility of healing the American furniture community while advancing American modernism in design was a rare opportunity for Wright. Surely European production would be slow to recover and American manufacturers would sieze the chance to, at last, capture a good portion of that market. If the American public could be encouraged to demand a functional design of its own, it would revolutionize the furniture industry in this country, perhaps even in Europe. Wright saw that the situation had many possibilities and the chance to influence good design in home furnishings could be significantly altered by American buyers who would demand modernism from the only source available in the post-war market. Wright saw this not only as a new step, but a new approach which would extend itself in ways not even he could estimate. Wright meant to influence the mass-produced furniture field, sure that other products would demand the same qualities, and that the entire home furnishings field would be altered.

Wright was not an island unto himself. He acquainted himself with the changing styles of his time, attending international exhibits and expositions, eager to explore, interested in new ideas and adapting them to his own work. His modern furniture evolved out of that comparative study. Not imitative, it borrowed trends which Wright believed to belong to the design community as a whole. He admired the work done in this country by Gustav Stickley and Elbert Hubbard who, influenced by the Morris Arts and Crafts movement in England, brought to Americans furniture so simple and still so distinctive that it quickly made a position for itself in American styles. Called "Mission," it was made of oak and made by hand with a minimum of machine work. Wright's own concepts of art put to use in everyday life owed much to this early concept of simplicity of design, little surface ornamentation and "Less is More."

Also influencing American styles was the work done in Europe by the Bauhaus, a group of artists who taught that art and industry had common ground and who advocated the "Form Follows Function" theory. These Bauhaus designs were sharp, crisp, without decoration or ornamentation save for the lines of the piece.

Presented here simply and briefly, we should not minimize the influence of these movements on those who were working to bring good design into American homes. They believed that Americans would accept these new concepts and the pieces which evolved from them, in part; the whole would come later after a transition period. Wright, part scholar, part teacher, seemed to know intuitively where America stood in relation to these new ideas.

In 1934 the Depression had added to the slowness of the furniture business as we have discussed it. It was that year when Wright contracted to do a sixty-piece line for Heywood Wakefield. Offered first at Bloomingdale's in New York, it would be shown in room-like settings, using Wright's own accessory line to complement the furniture. It was to be sold "open stock," a new concept which allowed the buyer to choose furniture items as individual pieces. "Sets" or "suites" would be replaced by a large number of items from which the buyer would select items which suited his own needs and tastes rather than forcing the user to fit those needs into a preconceived "set" which had little relation to the way in which it would be used.

Unfortunately the line was not popular. Heywood Wakefield had insisted that this new line be veneered, believing that the popularity of a new veneer treatment being done in Europe would be duplicated here. It was not to be. The veneers proved difficult to work with, more difficult to care for and customer resistance was joined by customer complaint. Upholstered pieces were oversized and overdone with a solid fabric and printed fabric both used on the same item. It was an attempt to give upholstered furniture a flexible form and the beginning of sectional furniture for mass production. Distribution became problematic because of slow sales and both designer and Heywood Wakefield were concerned. Wright, who had never been pleased with the concept, offered to design a line of contemporary solid maple furniture which he felt would be attractive to those who were already Heywood Wakefield customers. The firm had established a good reputation for solid wood furniture in their Early American line and Wright felt that the same principles, applied to a modern design would be saleable. The firm rejected his proposal and terminated his contract after the first year. With less time than was needed to prepare for the spring furniture shows, Wright was left with no client and no outlet for the large line he had hoped to send into production.

These contracts, agreements and proposals have direct meanings for collectors and they clarify the confusing Heywood Wakefield production. The important word here is "veneer." Heywood Wakefield Russel Wright furniture was veneered, not solid maple. That solid maple furniture, styled much the same as we would expect Wright's furniture to be, is later work by the firm, done after Wright's contract had been terminated. Clearly imitative of the styles he made popular, they later came to make the very work they refused to manufacture in 1935. Be especially cautious of Heywood Wakefield furniture items signed "Honey," "Amber" or other descriptive names. They are not Wright's work. We are able to picture some of Wright's veneered line done for HW. Not well received when it was made, it illustrates his feel for the best of the European work which Heywood Wakefield first hoped to popularize in this country. As collectors, we would do well not to reject this work for 1935 reasons. It is, for the most part, highly styled elegance, a memorial to the respect which American manufacturers still held for European products. You will find it marked by HW and with Wright's name.

Wright found himself without options and all but out of time. Fortunately for all concerned, Macy's, the department store, stepped into the breach and with a guaranteed order, succeeded in persuading the Conant Ball Company to produce Wright's work - to even enlarge their facilities in order to do so. Obviously, the interests of all were served by this hurried agreement. Macy's sponsorship and the good sales contracts which Wright made through this line gave him a firm position in the furniture field.

Of good proportion and fine finish, this new Northern Rock Maple needed no surface ornament. The woodgrain, combined with soft lines eased its own niche in the furniture world in record time. During the first year it was made in the wood's tawny red tone but later it was made in the blonde finish. Mary named it Blonde Maple. It was the most important furniture of the 1930's. The line divided itself into two groups. The first, while at home with modern furnishings, had a conservative quality which allowed it to blend with already owned things. The other group, with slightly different qualities, was newer, more modern in design.

Originally called "Modern Living," this very new furniture was introduced at Macy's in what they called a "Modern Maple House" with every item a Wright design. On the tide of good fortune, Wright tossed convention aside and allowed Macy's to use his name in mass market promotion on a national scale. It set a precedent and you should expect to see his name on each piece of the line.

This "Modern Living" line soon became "American Modern," a new beginning for all involved. Simple, direct, clean lined with rounded edges and corners, the shapes were said to be "Cushion edged," a feature quickly established as important to the new look. Lines were soft and natural, vertical or horizontal, with honesty, no decorative "tricks" or sharp "cuteness." Legs were replaced by sheets of wood to accomplish functional use of every inch. Upholstery was kept to a minimum and then, used largely on loose cushions. A lighter look resulted. This was transitional furniture at its best in America. It was new but not shoddy, borrowing from the best of what had come before. This light but sturdy furniture was geared to the way Americans lived. Modular groups with eye appeal replaced sets and the buyers ran to meet Wright. From the first, American Modern sold at Macy's in New York and Marshall Field's in Chicago. Transportation costs all but prohibited its distribution on the West Coast. Time, no doubt, has mingled households and collectors find it in likely and unlikely places.

We picture later in this chapter the listing of the original items as they were in 1935 with a supplemental listing of items added the next year. This is not all-inclusive, of course. Items had lives of their own, being redesigned, added, dropped or otherwise changed.

A later line, done in 1949 and called "Modern Mates/American Modern" was offered in eight Birch finishes. Black or Black Birch was available at an extra cost. Those items as presented in a 1949 catalog are shown here. Wright's association with Conant Ball was a long one and the influence of the work done for them had a measurable effect on furniture then and now.

The work which Wright did for The Old Hickory Furniture Company is surprising. Wright claimed that hickory was as tough as Old Hickory Andrew Jackson and, as it happened, a hickory chair was a favorite piece of furniture belonging to that president. That had been 150 years before Wright's Old Hickory production in 1941. Making the most of its origins, Wright claimed that it was indigenous to America, strong and resistant. It had been the hickory sapling that had held our covered wagons together, he said, and hickory made the spokes on spinning wheels as well as other useful furniture. It deserved our attention, we were told.

The Old Hickory Furniture Company of Martinsville, Indiana was an old established firm when Wright met it. It had for many years produced the bulk of the hickory furniture made in this country and the company was said to have been the direct outgrowth of a band of pioneer craftsmen. By 1941 Wright knew the advantages that accrued from that reference. Native materials, design and workmanship made this new furniture a "Truly American Product," claimed the advertisements. Wright named it "Americana."

We must look at this Old Hickory production as entirely different in both concept and purpose when compared with Wright's other work. It is a rustic country furniture, honest in its use as an informal outdoor or summer porch-style furniture. Wright had loved the outdoors and he believed that the tubular metal furniture so popular in the 1940's was out of character in the uses for which it was being sold. His competion was formidable.

With an Indoor Group and an Outdoor Group, it was said to be a complete informal furniture line. Unadorned and light in weight, the outdoor group was left the natural color of hickory, treated with an insect and rain repellent. The line was to have been: a sofa, love seat, a tavern chair with arms, bridge chair with no arms, a dining extension table, a bridge table and a coffee table. The Indoor Group was very similar with sailcloth upholstery or muslin cover to be replaced with the fabric of one's choice. Indoor pieces were: love seat, sofa, matching chair, wing chair, coffee table, chaise lounge, bridge table, bridge chair with or without arms and a low chair.

This "Americana," rustic and strong, an altogether different furniture from the painted aluminum and wrought iron which seemed superficial in the outdoors, was joined by another Old Hickory line, "American Provincial," made of chestnut. Still another was a "Modern Maple" line. Much of this

information comes to us from American Way files, but we know that after the short life of that program, these new pieces became a part of Old Hickory's production. We are able to offer some pictures of the sort of designs which were typical of it. You may find some marked or stickered with the American Way sticker but we would do well to examine pieces for possible manufacturer's marking also.

Wright's association with the Statton Furniture Company was detailed and involved. Statton was a furniture manufacturing concern who hoped to open a New York City retail store. The year was 1950. Helen and Philo Statton contracted with Wright for designs of living room and dining room groups. Wright found them to be interested, involved people with a good sense of the needs of the customers they served as well as a feeling for the furniture industry as a whole. Wright was challenged for they had an exciting concept of the future, willing to entertain any innovative and interesting idea. The Stattons did market research, obtained comparative literature, studied furniture trends, collected antique furniture and pursued any avenue which would guide them in the preparation of the line which they proposed. They favored "Satin Sycamore" and "Golden Griege" (beige with a muted grey undertone.) Open minded, they were willing to incorporate solid colored veneers, marble, glass, terrazzo and other laminates. Called "Modern Age," it was to be part of a large line called "Easier Living" which the Stattons were promoting. They were willing and eager to give Wright the exclusive production of their factory and the resultant work would have amounted to a different furniture than we have looked at here. Joints were pegged, slipcovered pieces were standard. Night stands held drawers, a chair had an arm with a magazine holder, the buffet had adjustable shelving, and a wood-topped coffee table had sliding or moving trays for extensions. A card table expanded to seat eight for dinner. Each piece had as much versatility "built in" as was conceivable to Wright or the Stattons.

Much work was involved in the Statton project and Helen Statton required at least two samples of each piece before acceptance. After that consideration and approval, the item was given a stock number and became included in the line. We are left with that information and little else. There is mention of the Statton line in household magazines, but we have no manufacturing details to share. Conversations with Wright associates tell us that the retail store never developed as the Stattons had expected and that production, while planned so carefully, was much less extensive than the files indicate. We have pictures, however, and these surely represent a respectable amount of furniture since so many pieces were made for the Statton's approval.

Our furniture study cannot end without the mention of other American Way lines. These would include a small group of dinette items, table and chairs and a sun room assortment of chairs, sofa and four coffee table styles, rectangular and round. This line, made by Sprague and Carleton in Keene, N.H. was made in maple with a new finish called "Sun tan." A larger line would have been developed if the program had continued. There are no photographs of this work nor are there pictures of another line to have been manufactured by The Company of Master Craftsmen, Flushing, N.J. Another solid maple group, it consisted of a bedroom unit bed, dresser, chest, vanity, night table and bench as well as a living room group of a kneehole desk, straight bookcase, secretary top, buffet base, corner bookcase and secretary case.

Produced for Sears in the American Way group was a line of knock down, assemble-yourself furniture for the living room, dining room and bedroom. This "do it yourself" furniture, so common today, was a new concept in 1941 and Wright gave it no less respect than he had done with other lines. It was another "first." Later, references indicate that a black Japanned furniture was considered for Sears, but there is no other information.

Wright's furniture story is a complicated, involved study and it is one we have not examined before. Your findings will add to this first study and information will become more complete as we are able to find examples. Warnings are repeated: Be very careful with unmarked items, even when they are similar to Wright's work. His designs set the standard for the industry which adopted it with open arms. This is one area where our "good eye" could lead us astray.

The following six photos are 1934 Heywood Wakefield ensembles.

This next section features pages from the 1935 Conant Ball catalog

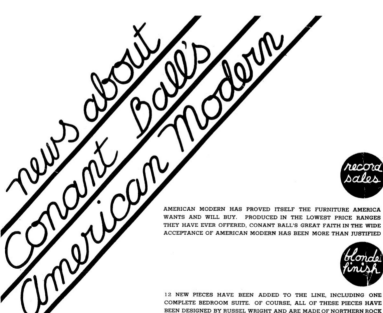

AMERICAN MODERN HAS PROVED ITSELF THE FURNITURE AMERICA WANTS AND WILL BUY. PRODUCED IN THE LOWEST PRICE RANGES THEY HAVE EVER OFFERED, CONANT BALL'S GREAT FAITH IN THE WIDE ACCEPTANCE OF AMERICAN MODERN HAS BEEN MORE THAN JUSTIFIED

12 NEW PIECES HAVE BEEN ADDED TO THE LINE, INCLUDING ONE COMPLETE BEDROOM SUITE. OF COURSE, ALL OF THESE PIECES HAVE BEEN DESIGNED BY RUSSEL WRIGHT AND ARE MADE OF NORTHERN ROCK MAPLE ACCORDING TO THE HIGHEST STANDARDS OF CRAFTSMANSHIP

IN ADDITION TO THE REGULAR MAPLE FINISH, THE ENTIRE LINE IS NOW OFFERED IN A NEW "BLONDE" OR HONEY-COLOR FINISH, MADE OF STOCK ESPECIALLY SELECTED FOR ITS CLEAR GRAIN AND UNIFORM LIGHT COLOR. THIS FINISH WAS THE "SENSATION" OF THE RECENT FURNITURE MARKET

Cover from Conant Ball's American Modern catalog.

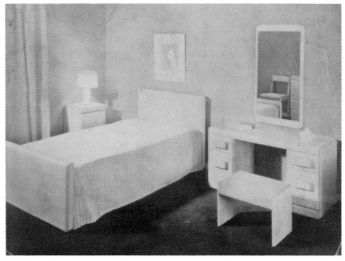

No. 3060 OTTOMAN Upholstered Reversible cushion Height 15½. Top 15 x 21.

No. 3070 CORNER CUPBOARD. Cabinet Below with adjustable shelves. Ht. 66½, depth 16, width and front 29.

No. 3071 DAY BED END TABLE. Two shelves. Height 23. Top 10½ x 30.

No. 3069 COCKTAIL TABLE. Height 16. Top 17 x 36.

MODERNMATES
by CONANT BALL

This insert contains sketches of our complete modern line with style numbers, dimensions and page references for quick identification.

All pieces made of **SOLID BIRCH.** They are available in number eight brushed birch finish. Some items also available with brass hardware and black or black-birch combination finish at additional cost.

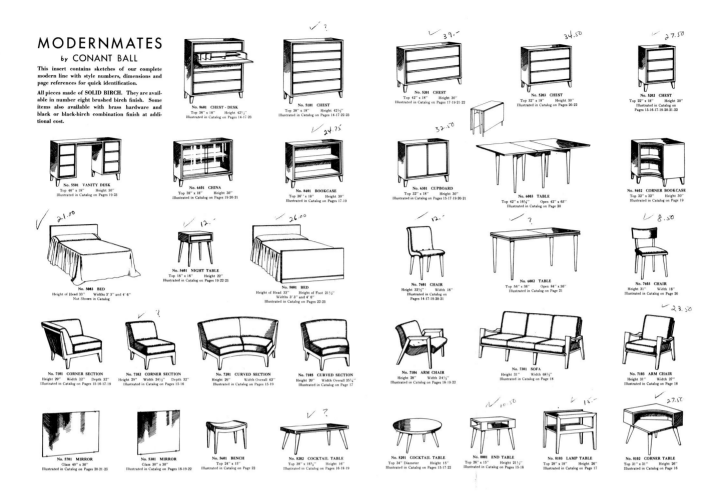

No. 8601 CHEST - DESK
Top 38" x 18"   Height 42½"
Illustrated in Catalog on Pages 14-17-23

No. 5101 CHEST
Top 38" x 18"   Height 42½"
Illustrated in Catalog on Pages 14-17-22-23

No. 5201 CHEST
Top 42" x 18"   Height 30"
Illustrated in Catalog Pages 17-19-21-22

No. 5203 CHEST
Top 32" x 18"   Height 30"
Illustrated in Catalog on Pages 20-22

No. 5202 CHEST
Top 22" x 18"   Height 30"
Illustrated in Catalog on Pages 15-16-17-19-20-21-22

No. 5501 VANITY DESK
Top 46" x 18"   Height 30"
Illustrated in Catalog on Pages 19-23

No. 6401 CHINA
Top 38" x 18"   Height 30"
Illustrated in Catalog on Pages 19-20-21

No. 8401 BOOKCASE
Top 36" x 18"   Height 30"
Illustrated in Catalog on Pages 17-19

No. 6301 CUPBOARD
Top 32" x 18"   Height 30"
Illustrated in Catalog on Pages 15-17-19-20-21

No. 6003 TABLE
Top 42" x 16¼"   Open 42" x 65"
Illustrated in Catalog on Page 20

No. 8402 CORNER BOOKCASE
Top 32" x 32"   Height 30"
Illustrated in Catalog on Page 19

No. 5003 BED
Height of Head 33"   Widths 3' 3" and 4' 6"
Not Shown in Catalog

No. 5401 NIGHT TABLE
Top 18" x 16"   Height 22"
Illustrated in Catalog on Pages 19-22-23

No. 5001 BED
Height of Head 33"   Height of Foot 21½"
Widths 3' 3" and 4' 6"
Illustrated in Catalog on Pages 22-23

No. 7401 CHAIR
Height 32½"   Width 18"
Illustrated in Catalog on Pages 14-17-19-20-21

No. 6002 TABLE
Top 56" x 36"   Open 84" x 36"
Illustrated in Catalog on Page 21

No. 7403 CHAIR
Height 31"   Width 18"
Illustrated in Catalog on Page 20

No. 7101 CORNER SECTION
Height 29"   Width 32"   Depth 32"
Illustrated in Catalog on Pages 15-16-17-19

No. 7102 CORNER SECTION
Height 29"   Width 24½"   Depth 32"
Illustrated in Catalog on Pages 15-16

No. 7201 CURVED SECTION
Height 29"   Width Overall 62"
Illustrated in Catalog on Pages 15-19

No. 7105 CURVED SECTION
Height 29"   Width Overall 35½"
Illustrated in Catalog on Page 17

No. 7104 ARM CHAIR
Height 28"   Width 24½"
Illustrated in Catalog on Pages 18-19-22

No. 7301 SOFA
Height 31"   Width 68½"
Illustrated in Catalog on Page 18

No. 7103 ARM CHAIR
Height 31"   Width 27"
Illustrated in Catalog on Page 18

No. 5701 MIRROR
Glass 40" x 30"
Illustrated in Catalog on Pages 20-21-23

No. 5301 MIRROR
Glass 30" x 30"
Illustrated in Catalog on Pages 18-19-22

No. 5601 BENCH
Top 24" x 15"
Illustrated in Catalog on Page 23

No. 8202 COCKTAIL TABLE
Top 38" x 18½"   Height 16"
Illustrated in Catalog on Pages 16-18-19

No. 8201 COCKTAIL TABLE
Top 34" Diameter   Height 15"
Illustrated in Catalog on Pages 15-17-22

No. 8001 END TABLE
Top 26" x 15"   Height 21½"
Illustrated in Catalog on Pages 15-18

No. 8103 LAMP TABLE
Top 28" x 18"   Height 26"
Illustrated in Catalog on Page 17

No. 8102 CORNER TABLE
Top 31" x 31"   Height 26"
Illustrated in Catalog on Page 16

Modernmates by Conant Ball.

The following five photos are Russel Wright's Old Hickory Americana.

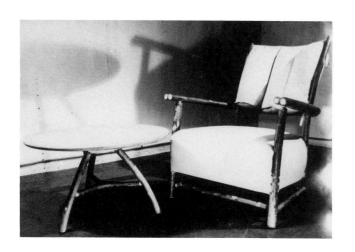

This next section features Statton Furniture.

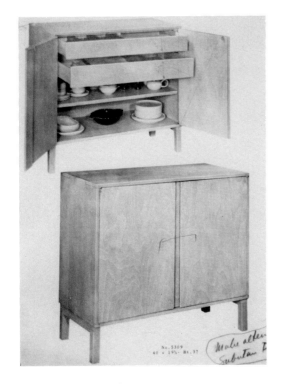

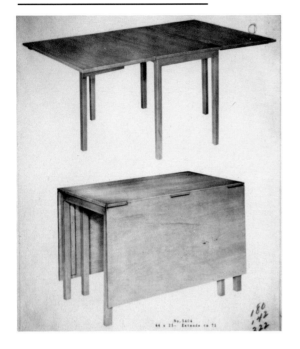

No. 5404
44 x 25. Extends to 71

No. 5514
13½ x 19½. Ht. 30
2- Pull Outs 18 x 14

No. 5404
32 x 55. Extends to 71

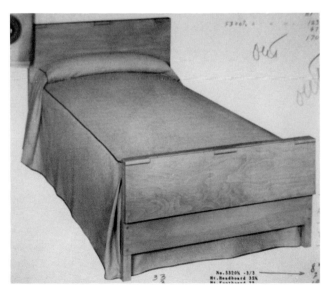

THIS ATTRACTIVE SERVING TABLE-CART HAS MANY USES IN THE HOME

This ingeniously designed serving table-cart can be used as a buffet table, a tea table, a movable bar, or a dining table for an intimate party of two. When not in use, it adds a decorative note as a side table in the most finely furnished room.

As planned here, power tools are needed to cut the miters and grooves. The setting of blind dowels also calls for a certain amount of experience. Although this is the ideal way to build a table of this quality, these construction methods can be modified so they can be done without power tools. The shelf box, for instance, instead of being put together by a mitered-and-feathered joint, can be made with a simple butt joint, with the shelf placed down on the side panels. The grooved drawer-slide cut into the sides of the shelf box can be replaced by hardwood nailing strips fastened by screws and glue to the bottoms of the side panels. And the blind-dowel construction can be replaced by dowels bored through or even by long screws countersunk in ⅜-inch holes and then covered over with ⅜-inch plugs cut from the actual wood from which the table is made.

No matter which method you choose for the construction, you will be able to make a beautiful and useful table of which you and your family can be proud. It will cost you only a fraction of what you would have to pay for such a table in a retail store.

Mr. Wright recommends that this "Do-It-Yourself" table be made from Weldwood African Mahogany plywood with legs of solid Mahogany and a drawer bottom of green Micarta No. 732. You may, of course, use any of the other beautifully grained Weldwood panels such as Walnut, Korina, Rift Oak, or Birch.

Your local lumber dealer will be glad to help you select the *right* Weldwood panel for the job. Make sure that the panel you select carries the Weldwood label. It's your *guarantee* that you are buying a *top-quality* plywood panel.

Gluing the table frame together with long clamps

Front cover of pamphlet for Do-It-Yourself Plans.

Inside of pamphlet showing construction for the table-cart.

Lighting The Way

If there has been obvious sequence in our collecting of Wright's work, it has seemed that collectors have started with dinnerware, more often than not, American Modern. Sets follow sets for a time but we have become collectors in a broader sense. Often we turn to lamps. Our search, for several reasons, is more difficult than was the tracking of cups and plates and the absence of marks and signatures on lamps has discouraged many. With no guidelines but our own intuitions, it has been difficult to add lamps to our collections. It will be so for a time, for while we are able to answer some of our questions, most of the Wright lamps were tagged or paper stickered, with no permanent markings to identify Wright with the product. For now, the measurement of a lamp should include the name of the manufacturer and the characteristics of Wright's lamp work. That look would incorporate an exaggerated use of texture substituted for surface ornamenation, adding interest. The combination of materials in a single lamp was and remains a good guide for our identification of these lamps. He combined various metals, woods and pottery in a large amount of this work and that usage sets his work apart from most of that which was on the market of the day. As we familiarize ourselves with qualities of his lamps, we will identify them more easily for they stand out as different from the lamps which they followed. We have a number of photographs which will be helpful, pointing you to the sort of work which Wright did.

The first lamps were made in his own shop under the Russel Wright Accessory line and these set the standard which he would return to as he worked with lamps. The line was to become a large one and what we picture here are representative items. Made first in the early 1930's, the time span was not a long one, but it was sprinkled with a wonderful assortment of lamps limited, it seems, only by the Wrights' imagination.

An early listing of these lamps would include table lamps made of cork, wood, ceramic material, as well as metals, chrome, Spun Aluminum, brass and copper. Student lamps, desk lamps, bridge lamps, reading lamps of all descriptions as well as reflector or torchier lamps served every purpose.

Having entered the field, Wright was determined to leave his mark in a big way. Signatures were not permanent, of course, and only the large metal lamps seem to have been signed. These will show the Wright name in block letters on the underside of the base.

Early work by The Accessory Company was followed by work done for clients and that work not only adds to the number of lamps which we may find, it also adds the name of the manufacturers which may mark the lamps.

A working agreement existed between Wright and the Mutual Sunset Lamp Company in 1946. He was to design 20 or 30 lamps within a specified price range and he was to agree not to accept other clients with production competitively priced for the duration of his contract with them. He could, however, keep the accounts to whom he was already selling. Mutual was not pleased with his samples and returned them at once, telling him that they were releasing him from his contract. Wright, stung, felt that he had done a considerable amount of work for them, had submitted a good sampling of his proposed work and that they had a contractual agreement to produce. As was not uncommon, the matter went to arbitration and then to the Supreme Court of New York State for Mutual Sunset appealed the matter. In the end the decision was in his favor and they settled with him, paying him for his work. The designs reverted to Wright but we have no information as to where they were used. It is very possible that these sampled lamps are still around, unmarked. This is a situation typical of "empty contracts" where some limited amount of the product may exist, though actually not produced.

In that same year, Wright was still working with Bauer and he proposed two lamps for their consideration as part of his art pottery line. They were sampled along with that ware at the Atlanta show. No orders were taken and with uniformity of glaze not achievable, Bauer did not put these in production. Some few surely exist, as we have seen the rest of the Bauer line. Look for these in Atlanta Brick, Stone Mountain Grey and Bybee Brown. What a prize a Bauer lamp would be!

A contract with the Acme Lamps Company dated from 1946-48 indicated that they would manufacture and distribute, through Sears, six or eight Wright designed lamps. He was to submit 12 for consideration and was to allow his name to be used. Our information ends there with no photos or descriptions. Those who tell us that they bought a Russel Wright lamp at Sears are to be believed. Sears catalogs do not help us with identification.

Another short-lived line was one contracted for by the Colonial Premier Lamp Company in 1949. Wright was to design 16 lamps of glass and ceramic materials. The agreement was a strange one, however. He allowed them to use his name on tags for some of the production and they could use his name in advertising for some of it, but he was to supply them with other lamps which could not be marked with his name or advertised as his. Premier agreed to pay standard royalties, even on second quality items but if lamps were sold at price reductions, the contract would have to be reviewed. They were to have his exclusive service and he was to "refresh" the designs as requested, making yearly additions. With only a year into the production, and for reasons not explained, they wrote that they were unable to proceed. They paid him for services to that time and it was agreed that when they were able to produce, his contract would be resumed. Both parties appeared to have parted with good feelings. Some of these Premier lamps are around, of course, and your guide should be their name combined with the Wright look.

An extensive line of lamps was done for the American Way program and distributed by Raymor. These would include table lamps, floor lamps and bridge lamps all combining wood or bamboo with rattan, brass or copper and reflector lamps combining oak with brass, copper or "white brass." Early Raymor catalogs will not reproduce and we are left with those descriptions.

In 1951 Raymor was to distribute lamps made by the Fairmont Lamp Company and the Statton Furniture Company was to have been an early customer of the extensive line which Fairmont would make. The line, called "Lamps for Easier Living" was to have been made in several metallic colors and combined materials such as split bamboo, brass, copper, walnut, oak, pewter, ribbed plaster and glass. This large assortment was at first limited to 10 designs but was to increase often. While there was a considerable amount of work done by Fairmont, the work is less documented than we would like. Examples are known for we have many pictures of this line and will show here what space will allow.

Ceramic lamps in designs which seem to represent the style of the 1950's but not the style of Russel Wright are known to have been made with the Steubenville glazes. The Wright files do not mention this work and it seems likely that these may be lamps upon which Wright drew royalty because of the use of his glaze, but which he did not design. Recently, we heard of a lamp which combines the Steubenville child's bowl with Spun Aluminum and were told that the threading column hole is glazed, suggesting that this may have been done at the pottery. This may be an example of the sort of work done by a pottery worker in his own time, to his own specification and for his own use.

In spite of our 1980's interest in Russel Wright lamps, there seemed to be no real market for them in their time. These lamps have a look of sameness to our 1990 eyes, but they were "different" in their day and they did not sell well, customers finding that they did not fit in well with the home furnishings already owned. Trade journals of the day tell us that lamps are the most difficult items to design and test the skill of a designer. Wright's lamp line, not really popular with customers was regarded as fine work by those who knew the complexity of his task and his work was regarded by them as unaffected and practical. The lamp industry as a whole was slow to adapt to modernism but Wright had made a beginning.

Those who search for these lamps today find the torchier and reflector lamps most easily but that may be because they are more easily recognized, reflecting a fashion in lamps which fell from favor for some years but which is "high styled" today.

Wright's lamps were very different, very modern and most of the 1940's lamps could not hold a candle to them.

Russel Wright Accessory Company Lamps

#474 Bamboo lamp. 23" high, 17½" widest shade diameter, 2 light. Light colored natural bamboo, brushed brass, shade of rough textured ivory colored fabric over parchment.

#961 Earthenware lamp. 20" high, 12" widest shade diameter, 1 light. Highly glazed rust toned pottery and waxed maple, shade of maple veneer over parchment, trimmed with brown leatherette.

#960 Diamond boudoir lamp. 17" high, 9" shade depth, 1 light. Brushed brass and faceted crystal, shade of white moire over parchment, trimmed with gold and white silk braid.

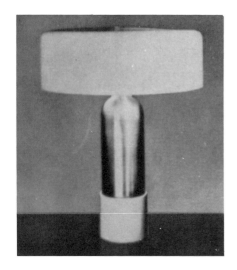

#935 All metal lamp. 21" high, 18" widest shade diameter, 2 light. Oyster white enamel, finial and small stem at bottom are brushed aluminum.

#916 Glass and metal lamp. 14" high, 13" shade diameter, 1 light. Brushed copper, glass, white baked enamel.
#975 Same with brushed brass, glass, with blonde maple stem.
#976 Same with aluminum, glass, with walnut stem.

#917 Glass shade lamp. 15" high, 12" shade diameter, 2 light. Oxidized gunmetal and white baked enamel.
#977 Same with brushed brass.

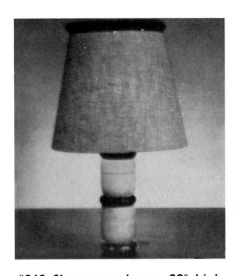

#481 Pottery and reed lamp. 17" high, 15½" widest shade diameter, 1 light. Highly glazed sand colored pottery, dark brown reed, shade of coarse beige crash over parchment.

#962 Stoneware lamp. 20" high, 11" widest shade diameter, 1 light. Putty colored unglazed pottery and walnut, shade of ecru yarn over parchment with brown trim.

#427 All reed lamp. 16" high, 14" shade diameter, 2 light. Brown reed with white baked enamel eyeplate. #426 Same but in light natural colored reed.

#930 Desk lamp. 14" high, 13" shade diameter, 2 light. Aluminum and walnut.

#914 Walnut fin lamp. 20" high, 13" widest shade diameter, 2 light. Walnut and aluminum, shade of brown and ivory woven luggage material over parchment, trimmed with flat brown leatherette. #972 Same in walnut and brushed copper, tan colored luggage cloth shade.

#700 Table reflector. 14" high, 10" reflector diameter. Aluminum and walnut.

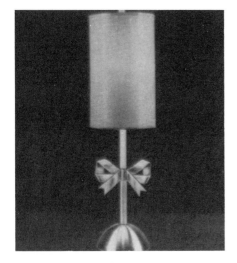

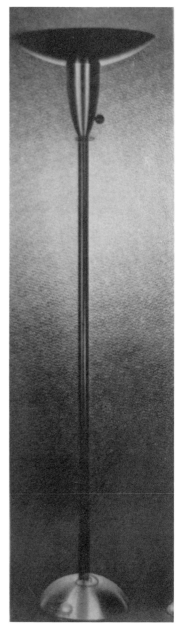

#924 Bowknot boudoir lamp. 14" high, 9" shade depth, 1 light. Brushed copper, white baked enamel, shade of peach toned parchment covered with net. #978 Same with brushed brass base and bow, ribbed net shade over white parchment. #979 Same with aluminum base and bow.

#926 Copper and reed lamp. 18" high, 17" widest shade diameter, 2 light. Brushed copper, natural light colored reed, tan shade of rough flecked cotton fabric over parchment, trimmed with heavy white braid.

#921 Bull's eye lamp. 17" high, 12" shade diameter, 2 light. Aluminum and chocolate brown baked enamel, shade of natural colored pongee over parchment, trimmed with flat brown leatherette and topped by aluminum cover.

#929 Reflector. 65" tall, 18" reflector diameter. Brushed copper socket-housing and base, shade and stem in baked ivory enamel. #928 Same in brushed copper and baked brown enamel. #702 Same in brushed aluminum and baked brown enamel. #725 Same in brushed aluminum and baked white enamel.

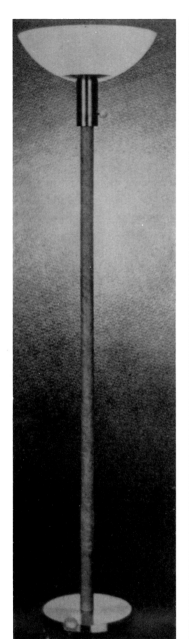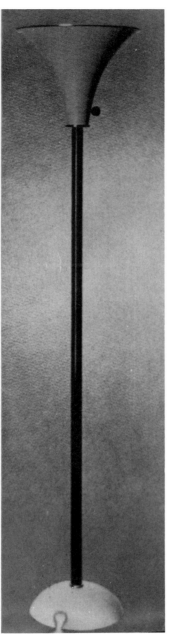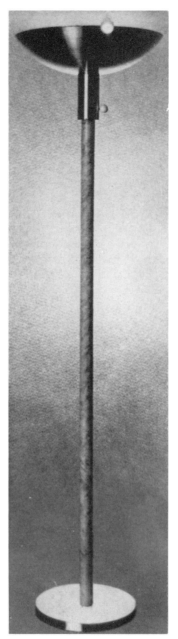

Left to Right:

#488 Reflector. 65" tall, 17" reflector diameter. Maple, brushed brass, ivory glass reflector. #708 Same with walnut and brushed copper with ivory glass reflector. #726 Same with maple and brushed copper with ivory glass reflector.

#915 Reflector. 63" tall, 13½" reflector diameter. Baked white and brown enamel, aluminum trim, walnut switch. #973 Same with baked white and terra cotta, aluminum trim and walnut switch.

#478 Reflector, 65" tall, 18" reflector diameter. Walnut stem with brushed aluminum base, reflector and socket housing. #707 Same with walnut stem, brushed copper base, reflector and socket housing. #927 Same with maple stem, brushed brass base, reflector and socket housing.

#913 Reflector. 63" tall, 11" reflector diameter. Brown and ivory baked enamel, ivory catalin switch. #971 Same with blue and white baked enamel with red catalin switch.

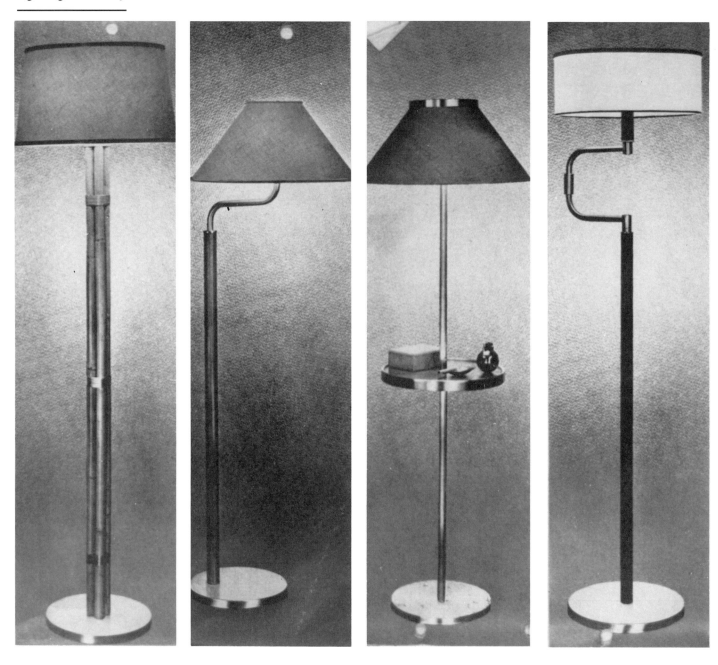

Left to Right:

#473 Bamboo lamp. 61" tall, 20" widest shade diameter, 12" shade depth. Bamboo, brushed brass, shade of rough textured ivory fabric over parchment with brass wire trim.

#933 Swinging bridge lamp. 54" tall, 18" widest shade diameter, 2 light. Mat finished cadmium base and arm, walnut stem, shade of tan pongee over parchment, bordered with brown leatherette.

#957 Shelf lamp. 45" tall, 17" widest shade diameter, 12½" shelf diameter, 2 light. Brushed aluminum base and shade cover, walnut shelf, baked brown enamel stem, shade of beige pongee over parchment.

#923 Adjustable reading lamp. 52" tall, 14½" shade diameter, 2 light. Mat cadmium arm and base, baked brown enamel stem and cover for shade of clear frosted "clair de lune."

Russel Wright Fairmont Lamps

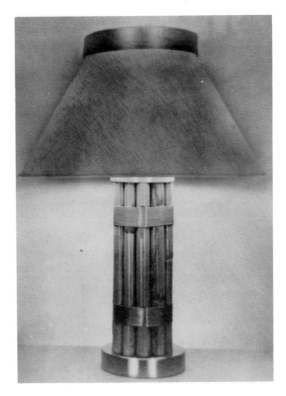

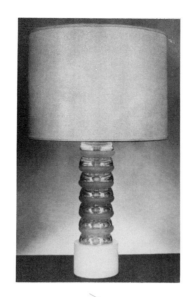

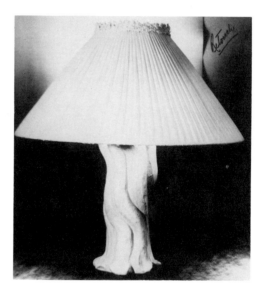

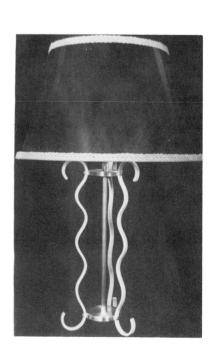

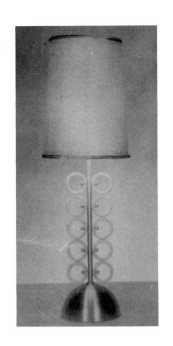

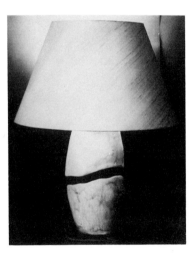

1007-X

1009

1077

1050

1020

1031

1071

1067

Wonderful Wood

As early as 1932, in his own workshop and with Mary as his salesperson, Wright had worked with wood serving items which attracted the attention of "House and Field" (now "House Beautiful.") These were informal serving items of simple shape, not especially "right" looking. Simple to the point of being almost plain, these early items were sold from shop to store, with no real catalog. Without that, and with no means to improve upon the product, Wright abandoned his plans for wood and claimed to have been forced out of the field by intensive competition of his own ideas in the hands of others, a position he was to return to often during his working life.

Three years later, with a completely new product, one which others could not imitate, he again entered the wooden accessory market. Working with Klise Wood Working Company of Grand Rapids, Michigan, he developed his Oceana line. A marine motif was central to the Klise product which used various woods - cherry, gum, blonde maple and Hazelwood, with a rich dark appearance. This work allowed Wright to experiment with free form. Pieces of Oceana were sculptural in appearance, designed within the limits of woodworking machinery. What appeared to be handmade was not. These designs reached out to the future, "leaving behind the stereotyped geometrical cliches which constitute so much of our present day modern picture." Oceana items drew their shapes from shells and strange sea plants and there was no attempt to achieve faithful reproduction. It was soon found on the pages of the smartest magazines of the day.

The Oceana line was one of Wright's contributions to American Way, and was enlarged for that purpose. When the Way was aborted so quickly, the production of Oceana was halted. Not popular with buyers in 1940, production was limited and that is our loss. It remained a favorite of the Wrights as well as others who designed for the program. The failure of its popularity may well have been that the thematic marine treatment seemed to restrict its use. Buyers felt that its use should be limited to beach or resort homes and never regarded it as appropriate for any use beyond that narrow concept. It was an early marketing failure.

There were some, though, who saw elegant modernism here from the first and the centerpiece bowl which we picture here was used on a cover of a 1940 Museum of Modern Art catalog. It is said to have been the most sculpturally beautiful of all the items.

We cannot list the early wood production beyond the terms of bowls and trays but we do have a listing of Oceana. Do not consider this as an all-inclusive list. Klise was a line with two chances of production and there was much experimental, probably even sample work done. Originally planned items included:

One-handled relish for canapes/snacks, 6¼" x 17½"
Fluted salad bowl, 4½" x 9"
Wing shell bread tray, 6"
Buella shell bowl for fruit or salad, 13" x 8"
Starfish relish, 13½"
Reversible rosette, relish side and cheese/cracker side
Shell candy box, 3" x 9"
Wave salad bowl, 15"
Wave salad bowl, 13"
Wave salad bowl, 11"
Wave salad bowl, 9"
Pearl plate, 9"
Shell plate, 9"
Seaweed relish, 4½" x 19"
Lazy Susan, 15"
Combination serving tray/salad bowl, 10" x 18"
Small nut bowl, 2" x 5"
Small relish dish
Flat shell salad bowl, 12"
Hostess tray with glass inserts, 11" x 24"
Snail salts
Jelly set
Small shell dish
Salad fork and spoon
Leaf tray
Relish, four compartments
Bowl
Two compartment bowl
Deep bowl
Hostess tray

These Oceana items are signed with Wright's signature burnt into the wood. Some turquoise stickers have been found and only recently an American Way sticker was sighted. While most items are thematic, some are less so. Any interesting pieces of wood should be considered since Wright's earlier work joins Oceana and adds variety to the wood production.

We are now able to describe the line which Wright did for Klise later, in the 1950's. These were also buffet serving items for snacks/brunches/cocktails or other informal occasions. Look for cigarette boxes, bowls of various sizes. Lucite, glass or chrome may be combined with Frosted Oak. This popular wood of the 1950's was typical of the "50's look." Once more, careful examination may lead you to a Wright wood piece when you are not expecting it.

Interestingly, in 1957 Wright found himself without the Oceana pieces he had prized and tried to acquire them. The chief officer of Klise answered his letter with the fact that he owned nine items and he would be glad to loan them for a short time, not to sell them. Later Wright considered having the items cast for use in the Formosa Family business, part of his Asian Handicraft program. It was not done.

All the approval from museum, to other designers, to the manufacturers and now to collectors illustrates the importance of this work to Wright's design concept. Produced by machine with a hand done sculptural look, it put art in the dining room. Wright loved it, collectors love it but there is very little of it to be had. Oceana items are very special items.

Russel Wright Oceana items

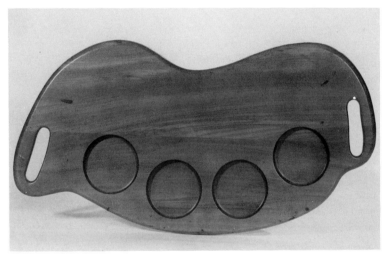

Serving spoon not listed but pictured as Oceana, 14" x 7½". Hostess tray with glass inserts.

Oceana serving tray. Courtesy of Brooklyn Museum, gift of Arthur Drummond.

Oceana Snail relish.

Oceana Leaf relish.

Jelly jar. Serving tray, 10" x 18".

Centerpiece bowl.

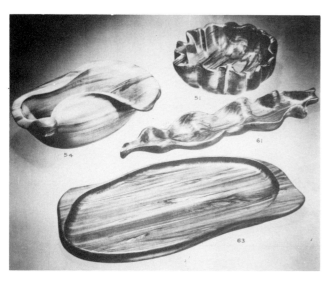

Wave salad bowl, fluted salad bowl, centerpiece bowl and serving tray.

Leaf tray, small snail dish, nut bowl, jelly set, Wing shell bread tray and salad fork and spoon.

Buella shell bowl, four-compartment relish, snail relish, flat shell salad bowl and one-handled bowl.

Late Klise Frosted Oak Deisgns

Giant dice shaker, 3⅜" cube. Steak platter, 18" x 10¼".

Four-compartment relish, 12" square. Three-compartment relish, 11" x 6¾". Jelly jar, 6" high. Nut bowl, 10½" x 8".

Various sized bowls.

Oceana Snail relish.

Fifty Years of Modernism
1939 - 1989
American Modern Dinnerware

1939 became the best of times for Russel Wright. Previous success with his metal work and his furniture had brought him to the center of attention with those who were searching for a new contemporary American style.

That American Modern Dinnerware was mass produced, bringing it into the affordable price range of most people, combined with the fresh newness of the ware meant that art forms, though ceramic art forms, could be a part of everyone's everyday life. America embraced the ware and the idea behind it in unprecedented numbers and our lives were richer for having done so.

Gimbel's in New York was the scene of a near riot in 1946 as the result of a 2" x 4" newspaper ad. When the store opened, a block long queue had formed. Several people were hurt during a rush that was estimated at a constant 100 customers per salesperson. Hundreds of orders were written for which there was no stock. In large department stores such as Altman's, Bloomingdales's and Gimbel's in New York, as well as J.L. Hudson's in Detroit, crowds gathered and it was necessary to establish a supermarket technique to handle the sale of Wright dinnerware. Hudson's orders were shipped in by the boxcar. In Baltimore, Smitty's Fish Market received a carload of "seconds" several times a year. Ware was sold directly from the railroad car with crowds so large that police were necessary to control them. In Middletown, New York, there was a Russel Wright club with bridge players competing for prizes of Wright design only. At least one family of Wrights named their new son Russell. We were caught in a frenzy, but Nelson Rockefeller used American Modern and presidents' wives, form Eleanor to Mamie, bought the dream and the dishes. We were in good company.

The sailing had not been smooth, however. The Ohio River potteries, all staggering from the assault of foreign competition felt this new ware to be too radical, too bold, too much of a departure, too costly to produce and since they felt that they knew the pottery market best, they felt they knew a loser then they saw one. One by one they re-fused to produce it. The Steubenville Pottery finally took a chance on a sure thing. The Wrights agreed to finance production and the giant department store J.L. Hudson's in Detroit made a personal request for it, sure that it could be marketed readily. Steubenville couldn't lose - and they didn't. From the time of its production, 1939-1959, it grossed $150,000,000.00 and went on to become the largest selling dinnerware ever in the history of pottery sales. At a time when most potteries were feeling the chill of possible closings, Steubenville had to expand twice to keep up with their American Modern orders. Other potteries who later added contemporary lines used the Potter's Union description of "Russel Wright shape" to mean any modern dinnerware design.

Selling it first through Russel Wright Accessories, the Wrights soon joined with Irving Richards to market and distribute the dinnerware through the huge Raymor firm which they formed. All who touched American Modern were well paid as it was sold over twenty odd years, breaking all marketing records. Richards and the Wrights agreed that a nationwide advertising program was important and many of the large full-page ads placed in the leading home furnishings magazines were, in themselves, small works of art. This carefully orchestrated advertising kept American Modern before the consumer constantly and the quality of the ads duplicated the quality of the dinnerware. There was no desire, however, to portray American Modern as so "artsy" that the average buyer lost touch with it and large color ads from the Campbell Soup Company showed soup bowls full, reminding us that this was for everyday use. This was art for the masses, not for the classes.

Every aspect of marketing technique was studied to achieve broad appeal. Open stock was a new concept and it appealed to buyers at once. One could buy basic pieces now and add serving items or place settings late. A broken cup could be replaced without the purchase of a new "set." Gift givers could select a serving piece which was sure to please. One's service was never quite complete, but never incomplete either.

At the same time, usages conceived by Wright were suggested at every turn. A Child's Group-- Under 3 or another Child's Group--3-5 were boxed and sold as mini sets in 1953. A group was suggested for all sorts of occasions, some of which were established, and some which were emerging on the changing entertainment scene. Groups included Every-Day, Patio or Barbecue, Television group or Bridge group as well as Buffet, Brunch, and Cocktail groups. A 1951 news release showed a Mug Group, the Covered Pitcher and the Tumbler/Mugs.

Families were looking beyond the kitchen or the dining room as the only places to eat and some of our new concepts of eating areas were prompted by the newness of television viewing for we soon found ourselves eating in front of the set - where ever that might be. The advent of the family room, separate from the kitchen or dining room called for changes in how we ate and what our food was served on. Ours was a changing home in a changing world and Wright had known that before we did.

The style of American Modern has been difficult to conform to a description. Surely it broke with the Art Deco style for there were none of the geometric or angular lines. Certainly it bore a resemblance to the sleek European lines popular in its day, but it was not as cold, not as extreme. Strictly functional, its amorphous shapes conjured the surrealistic influence, but this new American Modern was best described by the name given it by Wright. This was a new Modernism, All-American Modernism. Born out of the influence of the Great Depression, its leanness reflected not only sparseness of detail, but the functionalism just recognized as core to good design. Sprinkle some American primitive with a bit of the abstract, combine all with functionalism and one comes up with the new modern look so admired in 1939 and again this second time around. Those who bought and used it in 1939 were not surprised that it won the American Designer's Award for the best ceramic design of 1941. We knew it was "right" then and we put it away, what was left of it after it was discontinued. We knew it was special, a bit of art in a tea cup, and we saved it. How right was Wright with this special design! Many copied it but American Modern stands alone as the best example of a new movement in style and design.

Wright recolored the rainbow with the new colored glazes of American Modern. Almost muted, softly glowing, the American Modern glazes have an underlying textural feeling with variegated self-tones, all beautifully worked out to intensify the attractiveness of food when served. The original colors were Seafoam Blue, Granite Grey, Chartreuse

Curry, Coral, Bean Brown and White. This palette reflected a real departure from what Wright described as the "paint job" look of the dinnerware it sought to replace. Granite Grey is a stone-like grey in an eggshell finish. Chartreuse, popular color of the day was a new color in dinnerware and Wright often interchanged its name with "Seedless Grape." Bean Brown was really composed of three shades of brown ranging from burnt umber to a dark tete de negre. A rusty shade, it was discontinued during the war and replaced with Black Chutney after the war. Seafoam Blue was a new color to pottery also, slightly darker and bluer than the usual pale turquoise tint. Coral, soft with an earthy warmth blended well with the spectrum. The warm White glaze, a creamy rich white, is under-stated elegance. In 1950 Black Chutney, a foamy glaze more ripe olive than brown, replaced the Bean Brown and Cedar Green, a muted green unlike any color then on the market was added. By 1955, Canteloupe and Glacier Blue, both brightly jeweled pastel colors had appeared and the rainbow of American Modern could interchange to effect any dining mood. The handsome effects achieved by combining these colors is not accidental. Wright accomplished them after long and careful comparisons of combinations resulting from many glaze trials. In January 1956, Seafoam, Chutney and Cedar Green were discontinued but were made available twice a year - if the pottery was able to produce them.

We have not mentioned the variant color which collectors have named Steubenville Blue. This bright, deep blue with no green in it has appeared in enough amounts and with enough regularity that we had to question it. A late piece in this blue led to the understanding of what probably resulted in this color. We now believe that this Steubenville Blue was a color which resulted from changed glaze formulas when World War II restricted cobalt in civilian uses. This came at a time when Seafoam had been discontinued, made only twice a year, in small amounts which added to little more than replacement orders. This substitute color was a poor match for the Seafoam it replaced and that may account for the small amount of it which we see. Little of it was made and a "set" may be an impossible dream but many collectors are happy to locate a piece of this rare blue.

All colors of American Modern were popular when they were introduced and remain popular with collectors today. While Chartreuse is not favored today, we must remind ourselves that it is a color which goes in and out of style and it may still become important to collectors. It crazes as does the White and very hot water should be avoided when using these colors.

Shapes in American Modern are as different as were the colors. The classic coupe-shaped plate was first designed by Wright for the American Modern line. It became a staple in the ceramic industry. The salad bowl breaks away completely from the traditional round shape for salad bowls. Its curved-in sides not only add interest, but serve a practical purpose in keeping the leaves from being tossed out as a salad is mixed. It is just as wonderful holding fruit or Christmas greens. The abstract leaf shape of the celery makes it a favorite piece with collectors. The chop plate, a new item in the dinnerware industry, is a square with rounded handles. From the first, it was a multi-purpose tray and its uses are many. The one-handled sugar bowl was a first of its kind and the miniature Aladdin's lamp creamer remains a small wonder. Wright took his Spun Aluminum relish rosette and adapted it to a ceramic one in this line. The classic water pitcher remains just that - a classic. The fruits and soups break away completely from the small bowl concept and their tab handles add to their ease of use. The stack set serves as a cookie jar, what-not holder or a covered sectional vegetable unit. We saw it first with a deep bottom section, a smaller top section and a cover. It easily suits itself to other uses if another section is added or if one is omitted. Publicity shots show it in combination with a candle warming unit. This was not part of the Wright concept, of course. The small ice box jars nest easily to become individual portion containers. The covered ramekin, in addition to its casserole use, could hold jams or jelly, even candy. The bowl section of this ramekin became the child's bowl. The stoppered jug/carafe with its myrtle wood stopper could hold the drink of your choice. There are two lip versions of this jug, one slightly more ridged than the other, the result of redesign. All these forms are different in that they do not borrow from the past. They are modern in the sense that they are new, designed primarily for their intended use, their function. Perhaps the unseen appeal of this dinnerware lies in the sincerity of the designer's work for he avoids any effort to shock us into forced attention.

Today's collectors are finding many new uses for these pieces. Eating and drinking styles are still evolving and new foods as well as different occasions make for versatility. Sauce boats, small vegetable bowls as first conceived, are sought after as bowls for stews or hearty soups and many collectors want several of these. Platters seem to make good individual steak plates, and will substitute for the hard-to-find hostess plates. A present day use for the coasters turns them into individual sauce dishes for dipping. These have found their way into collections in increasing numbers.

Steubenville dipped its own shapes into American Modern glazes from time to time, paying royalties as they did so. Coasters, unmarked in the Wright set, were adapted for Steubenville custom work, personalized with the customer's name or logo as decoration and marked with the pottery name. This was not Wright's doing, nor were square coasters wtih center rings which Steubenville made in Wright glazes. Some small Steubenville animals may be confused and believed to be his work. They were not. The Woodfield line salad fork and spoon, welcomed from the first as an addition to a Wright set, were really another example of this cross pollination. In addition, workers did make individual items for themselves as "lunch hour" projects and some of those have filtered into today's collecting. Other potteries, anxious for the good fortune that had come to Steubenville, made imitative glazes and pieces. Be aware and wary of luncheon plates, only slightly smaller than the dinner plates similarly glazed. Tab-handled bowls for fruits and soups, an inch or so larger than the American Modern bowls have been found in similar colors. The Chartreuse is a "ringer" and the Chutney so close that it is clearly imitative. Strange as it may be, the Steubenville Woodfield Rust and Wright's Iroquois Brick Red are exactly the same color.

One of the surprises of collecting American Modern has been that we have seen small amounts in a few patterns. Recently, a naturalistic leaf pattern done in Black Chutney on white appeared in a complete set. Serving items were in solid Chutney. This challenged the "experts" and no one could explain its existence. On the heels of that finding, a white plate with a matchstick/straight pin pattern, a coral scroll pattern and a broken grass leaf pattern were found. All of these were done in an underglaze treatment and all were strangers to the line as we have come to know it. More important to collectors is that the new photograph files picture these patterns. It seems certain that Wright had a hand in them, and may have approved of them. The Scroll was named Spencerian, but we have no names for the others. The Chutney leaf pattern was a familiar theme, however, and we find it in linens, paper and other mediums of his work. Monogrammed ware found is known to have been made for customers in large department stores. This involved an overglaze process and probably was done with Wright's permission. Do not assume that there are more patterns. These few, identified by inclusion in the files have verification, but no other patterns are listed or discussed there. Any others which we may find are likely to be the work of a home ceramist or pottery worker. They detract from values and should not be considered as rare or unlisted. Any amount of patterned American Modern is very rare.

With such outstanding design, glazes and shapes, the fact remains that the quality of the Steubenville product was poor. That it broke easily was explained away by its low cost and the open stock option, but these answers did not address the real problem, of course. Wright was to come to grips with this situation soon and his next ceramic line would overcome the fragility of American Modern. The amount of American Modern which has come to us is in direct proportion to this manufacturing factor.

Collecting American Modern today will take effort and expense as items considered plentiful a few years ago have since found their way into private collections. Rarities, experimental pieces and short production all influence availability today. What was everywhere yesterday is nowhere today. Items which seem standard to the line went in and out of a constantly changing production. Sales literature showed variances of colors and pieces from store to store, time to time. Coffee pots, soups, the divided relish, the relish rosette, the child's cup and saucer and the carafe, all went in and out of the line. In 1951 there were new additions and the covered pitcher, stack set, the individual ramekin, coffee cup cover, divided vegetable, hostess plate and the mug were added. While these should not be found in Bean Brown, they are difficult to locate in any color and their late production accounts for the fewer numbers in which they were made. It seems true, also, that the after dinner coffee pot, sauce boat and the children's items as well as the covered butter dish were also later additions coming sometime in the late 1950's. These have been rare since the current collecting began and it is believed that not only were fewer of them made, but that they were not made in all colors. Production, with a list of what appears to be an uncomplicated number of items still was loosely structured and it seems reasonable that the scarcity of some of the items today may be the result of the inability of the pottery to facilitate the manufacture of all items during the long production time. Success was not always easy to handle and in the failing pottery industry, caution often counseled entrenchment even in the face of overwhelming achievement.

American Modern quickly made a place for itself in our 1939 lives and it does so again today. Collectors find themselves challenged, but rewarded as they search for this Modern dinnerware. It is often the first Wright design which we collect and owning a part of Americana, an example of the broad sweep of style that influenced our times is exciting. Wright would have wished it to be so. Our 1990 recognition of this work and our appreciation of the unique place it holds in the annals of good design would have given him pleasure. He knew it would be timeless, however. That quality was also intrinsic.

On Pricing American Modern Dinnerware

American Modern Dinnerware, with prices established by ten years of collecting may be the starting point for collections which go on to include other Wright designs. For that reason, it has a favored position in relation to his other dinnerware lines. None are more popular than American Modern by Steubenville.

Those who collect Wright designs break into two groups when we consider his dinnerware. Some do not consider themselves a part of the collecting world. They have a set, or a partial set which they bought years ago and packed away. They are collectors just long enough to acquire the pieces which they need to make their dishes usable again. Never mind rare pieces with this group. They need enough cups to replace the ones they broke and some salad plates, not purchased with their starter sets would be nice. It is this group who continue to shore up prices on plates, cups and saucers, and the like. They have a continuing need to replace items which become unusable. The true collector, though, wants it all in every color. This group searches for the rarities as well as flatware. It is they who have seen scarcities develop and who have sought out rarities. The pattern they seem to follow is one which starts with an American Modern set, adds an Iroquois set for "every day" and goes on from there.

Both these groups have a direct effect on pricing but it is difficult to fit them into a price scale. In the last analysis, if you must determine value, study color and rarity. Those are generally felt to combine with demand to establish dollars and cents. If you wish to sell you must consider that the value of your things depends upon the buyer. A dealer can offer you only about half of the value. You should establish your price before you offer it for sale. Many dealers will not make you an offer.

Those who helped with pricing were almost unanimous in their opinions as to the value of colors and these reflect changes in demand since the 1985 book. Canteloupe, Glacier Blue, White and Bean Brown are most favored. Black Chutney, Cedar Green, Seafoam and Grey continue to be at the high end of our scale. Seafoam should be watched for it was discontinued early and we are seeing less and less of it. Look for it to change upward in value. Chartreuse is still not popular and must still be placed at lower values. Coral should average out in the price ranges since it seems to be such a common color.

Some pieces have been few from the first and those are rare pieces. Other items which seemed to be plentiful five years ago are gone, new collectors still searching for them. You will find that indicated in the pricing. Those items for which collectors have found double usage are increasingly hard to find and these would include at least the sauce boats, salad plates, platters and coasters. All "pouring pieces" are fewer and now the after dinner coffee pot seems to be more easily found than is the regular coffee pot. The butter dish has been difficult to find from the first, but finding it in good condition complicates our search. It has four unglazed corners and these often have absorbed oil and odor from the butter. The mugs/tumblers are scarce, seeming almost rare. The covered pitcher seems as difficult to find as is the jug/carafe. Coffee cup covers, covered individual ramekins and ice box jars light up a collector's day - but not often.

Not a part of the American Modern line, the Woodfield salad fork and spoon have always been popular with Americna Modern collectors. They are the most fragile of the Steubenville work. Breakage accounts for their scarcity.

One Myrtle wood stopper for the jug/carafe has been found. That may not make the evening news, but those of us who have never found one are encouraged. A carafe with the original stopper would be worth double the suggested pricing.

Not all American Modern is collected as part of a dinnerware group. Some collectors look for water pitchers - one of every color. The same trend applies to celery dishes, coasters, or other items.

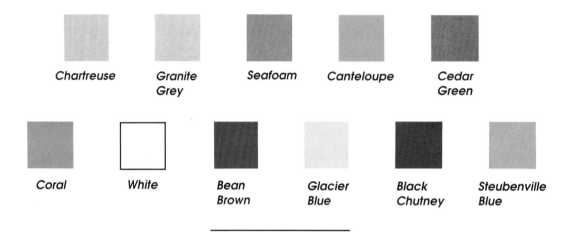

Chartreuse   Granite Grey   Seafoam   Canteloupe   Cedar Green

Coral   White   Bean Brown   Glacier Blue   Black Chutney   Steubenville Blue

Dinner plate, salad plate, bread and butter plate, Woodfield salad fork and spoon.

Cream pitcher, water pitcher, cup and saucer, and covered sugar.

Chop plate, child's plate, relish rosette, covered butter dish, tumbler, salad bowl and after dinner cup and saucer.

Covered pitcher, patterned plate, platter, shakers, child's bowl, child's tumbler and Old Morgantown dessert bowl.

Individual covered ramekin, coffee pot, divided relish, ice box jar.

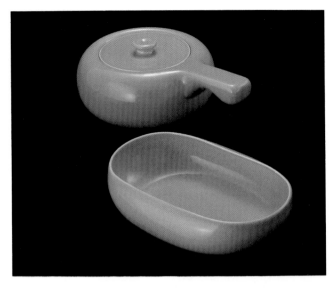

Covered casserole and open vegetable bowl.

Covered vegetable dish.

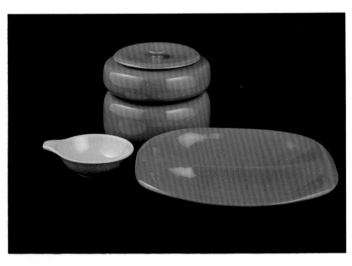

Fruit bowl, divided vegetable bowl and stack set.

Gravy on liner (pickle dish).

Stoppered jug/carafe.

After dinner coffee pot, jug/carafe, teapot.

Gravy on liner (pickle dish), small baker, covered casserole and coaster.

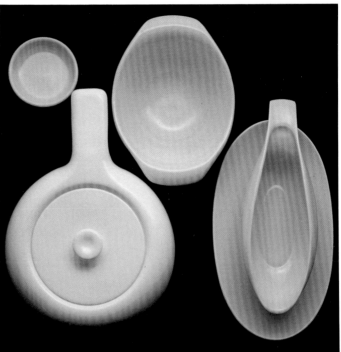

Celery on Simtex cloth.

Hostess plate and cup on Leacock cloth.

Soup on Leacock linen cloth.

Small baker on Leacock linen cloth.

Lug soup and lug fruit.

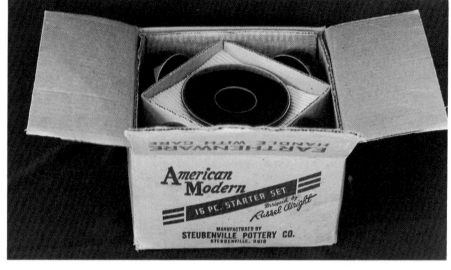

16-piece starter in original box.

Child's set in original box.

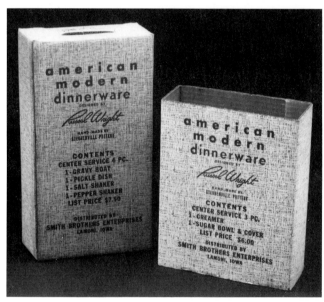

American Modern original boxes.

Rare American Modern patterns. Pitcher is typical of work done by home ceramist. Bowl is experimental color #16.

 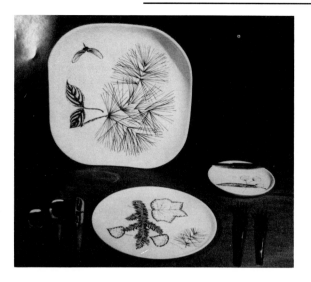

These two photos feature rare patterned American Modern Dinnerware. On the left is Spencerian and on the right is the Chutney Leaf pattern.

AMERICAN MODERN

hand-made by STEUBENVILLE

designed by *Russel Wright*

Left: Original American Modern brochure. Above: Campbell's Soup ad using American Modern Dinnerware.

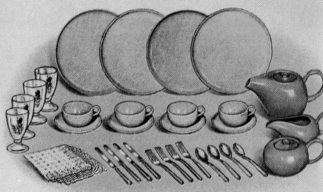

Just like the Russel Wright Set mommy has

52-piece Russel Wright Modern American Dinner Set for Six

Created by a famous designer for little hostesses. Wonderfully tough plastic, takes lots of hard play. Modern mottled pottery colors stay bright. 6 each of plates, cups, saucers, metallized cutlery, goblets, napkins. Creamer, teapot, sugar bowl, gravy boat and stand, casserole with cover, large platter.

49 N 944—Turned-edge plates, 6¼-inch diameter. Shipping weight 2 lbs. 14 oz....... $4.78

33-piece Russel Wright Modern Set for Four

Pottery-colored plastic tea service . . gives little hostesses the "feel" of really fine service like mother's. Consists of 4 cups, 4 saucers, 4 plates, creamer, sugar bowl, teapot, 4 napkins, 4 sets of metallized cutlery, 4 clear goblets. Plates 6¼-in. diameter, others in proportion.

49 N 942—Gift box. Shipping weight 1 pound 10 ounces.................... $2.78

Above: Ads for toy American Modern made by Ideal Toy Company. From Sears 1959 Christmas catalog. Right: Ad for toy American Modern made by Ideal Toy Company. From Sears 1961 Christmas catalog.

Just like mommy's Russel Wright Set $4.44

Dinner Set for six created by a famous designer especially for little hostesses. Wonderfully tough plastic in mottled pottery colors that stay bright. Set includes 6 each turned-edge plates (6¼-in. diam.), cups, saucers, metallized cutlery, clear plastic goblets, napkins. Also sugar bowl with cover, creamer, teapot with cover, gravy boat with stand, large platter and casserole with cover.

49 N 944—58-piece Set. Shipping weight 2 lbs. 14 oz.............. $4.44

Casual China - A New Treatment

Wright's largest dinnerware line, Iroquois Casual, is a favorite with many collectors. There are many colors, many pieces and major redesign means that there is often more than one version of the same item. That it can be used with a minimum of care puts it into everyday use today just as it did the first time around.

In 1946, firmly established now, in the dinnerware field, and with American Modern a classic, Wright had problems less concerned with finding a pottery to produce this line but more to do with finding a pottery which would work to his specifications. Complaints that American Modern broke easily needed answering and in overcoming that problem, manufacturing procedures played into the designers hands. Iroquois was to be a strong china, high-fired to 2300° F. with thermo shock properties. This new line was to be advertised as china, not earthenware and many benefits accrued to it because of the manufacturing details which were shared with consumers. From the beginning, Iroquois was guaranteed not to break or chip with normal use if bought in a service for four people. Signed and numbered certificates were given to buyers and a personal relationship between buyer and seller developed at the time of purchase. Buyers were told that this ware could go from refrigerator to stove to table and back to the refrigerator with no harm to the platters or bowls used. The use of an asbestos pad, they were told, allowed for stove top use and after a time special cooking items were added.

Still promoting efficiency in the home, advertising made much of the fact that minimum space was needed to stack and store the ware. Buyers were told that many pieces had double usage, resulting in less-is-more. The large bowls could be used for hot foods, salads or handsome centerpieces. The small bowls had multiple uses, the carafe could become a vase, the large platter could be a tray to hold coffee service and the gravy liner would line a soup bowl, the carafe or whatever. The large casseroles could be used as soup tureens, bean pots, salad bowls or punch bowls. Today's collectors find the pieces easily adaptable to today's dining uses.

The working agreements between the pottery, Iroquois, the distributor, Garrison, and Wright were so complicated and protracted that the seeds of some of today's questions were planted in the early legal concerns which became binding commitments in the first planning stages. The initial agreement was that Garrison, the distributor, would buy from Iroquois 100,000 pieces of dinnerware on a ratio of 12 to one serving items/flatware. This initial order was to be replaced by monthly orders for retail accounts to add to 8333 dozen pieces. Iroquois promised to produce that amount within a year barring an act of God. Wright allowed the use of his name. He further agreed that he would not develop another line of china or earthenware with a comparable number of pieces at 70% above or below retailers cost. Exceptions were accessory items such as buffet serving items, the Steubenville line, in production, and a proposed earthenware line, not similar and only to be made after December 1947. If, however, billings for Casual fell below 200,000 pieces for any 12 month period, the contract would not apply in all circumstances and Wright would be freed from limits imposed in the original agreement. Additionally, if Garrison became bankrupt or if any other breach of this contract came about, Garrison was obliged to sell the designs and trade-name agreement back to Wright for $1.00. With the stage so set, complaints and accusations began and continued until Garrison wrote: "Keep in mind that I will finance and take the responsibility for the distributing company and must have a considerable area within which to do that job as I see fit. If you do not want me to do that job or if you do not want to allow me the elbow room in which to do it, then our basic set up is wrong and you should finance the distributing company, operate the distributing company and provide the factory to supply the distributing company. I am perfectly satisfied that this is no more your intent than mine." This memorandum points to the Wright characteristics which were troubling to those with whom he worked. He was not able to rise above what often seemed trivial.

By 1948 differences between Wright and Garrison became so numerous that Garrison exercised the option and vacated the position of distributor. A new contract between Wright and Iroquois replaced the first agreement and was more favorable to Wright. Royalties, having been established, were extended to second quality ware. Wright was free to design one earthenware line which would bear his name and one which would not. He could produce a line of thin china if it were priced to sell at retail prices of no less than 50% higher than Iroquois. He agreed to design patterns for the ware when asked to do so and he agreed to redesign as sales indicated need.

As it evolved, Iroquois Casual is classic for researchers complete with clues, evidence, fact and supposition. It is a story of trouble with a happy ending.

Early marks had not pleased Wright and were changed for what appears to be eye appeal only. Dates, which we had hoped would help us with our study seemed not to apply on the earliest marks. Early glaze trials, particularly the Ice Blue glazes did not please Wright. He accused Garrison of releasing a glaze of which he had not approved. Records showed blue was being used over a tan body while he had indicated only a white body was to be used. Collectors have not noticed this difference and it may be a minor detail, but an important one to Wright who must be responsible to his artistic sense. Formulas for all the glazes changed often and these changes are found today in several shades of the same color. Wright had further objections to covers for the teapot, soups, casseroles and vegetable bowls and changes in these resulted in a better "fit," a feature collectors have found. The numerous cup handles (six) and bowls (six) all appear to have evolved from this early period of sorting as well as the later redesign work.

In spite of false starts, Iroquois, called Casual from the beginning, was actively promoted by Garrison and major newspapers carried full-page ads from giant department stores. Home furnishings magazines showed the ware in full color and the Wrights made personal appearances, washing dishes and spilling them on the floors to show durability. The ware was marketed expertly and was so well accepted that 12 years later it was still breaking its own sales records. It was no small happening in the dinnerware field. Small town jewelry stores and quality gift shops joined department stores in featuring this "china" and it was more available than American Modern.

Early Iroquois pieces were almost ⅜" thick with an institutional weight much different from the refined ware which it would become later. The glazes were foamy and irregular, an effect Wright wanted to achieve and which had been formulated by ceramists at Alfred University in New York. A crystallization in the glaze combined with the weight suggested the irregularity often found in handmade

dinnerware, but this was not the case. Wright had contrived formulas to achieve this new look.

The original colors in Iroquois were Sugar White, Lemon Yellow and Ice Blue. Nutmeg, Avocado Yellow and Parsley Green followed soon. Lemon and Parsley were quickly discontinued, but were added again at a later date. Nutmeg was a color often in dispute when Garrison and Wright were at cross points over glaze formulas and this accounts form some of the wide variations in the Nutmeg we see today. Early records of a grey-blue have proven to be Oyster. In 1951 it joined Charcoal, Ripe Apricot, Pink Sherbet, Lettuce Green and Canteloupe. Forest Green was a late name for the earlier Parsley. Both Aqua and Brick Red were late colors. Unsure of dates for them, we are sure that they were made for a short time in short amounts. They represent a challenge to even advanced collectors and many of that group have not seen examples of these wonderful colors. Where color variations appear within the same color, probable cause is that suppliers of color oxides had changed or variant oxide ingredients had been used. Certainly color variations do exist in spite of early established formulas. Buyers from the beginning were told to expect some slight variation but there seemed to be little objection to these differences then. Collectors are more discriminating, however, and caution should be used when mail ordering these Iroquois colors.

Original shapes in Iroquois are of the "Pinch" style. Surfaces are rounded and curved with handles that recess and are molded into the body of the piece, making warm bowls easier to handle and easier to stack in cupboards. There are no rims or grooves, no protruding handles or grips. Both bowls and tea cups were restyled several times and finally were part of the larger redesign work. Sorting bowls and cups is difficult. From the first all lids were sold separately. A coffee pot without a lid became the pitcher. A covered casserole with no lid, obviously, became an open casserole. No items were considered less perfect because of the absence of a lid.

Major redesign did come about in 1951 and by that time a sleeker lighter weight, more refined look prevailed. The mottled glaze had given way to a more sophisticated polished look. Be warned, however, old colors and old items were still being made. Customers used the old with the new with no more objection than they had expressed over color variations. All was sold interchangeable. Stores mixed and matched styles as well as colors and as late as 1952 the pinched look was still being advertised in new additions to production. By that time the number of items available had mushroomed and the large line became even larger.

The redesigned look featured knobs to replace

the older pinch look. Handles were loopy and much different from the five or so handles that preceeded the redesign. Bowls were not so cushioned and the entire line took on an Oriental accent not expressed so obviously in the original style. As before, covers sold separately. Old tops appeared on new bottoms and the customer seemed to care very little.

Interesting variations have been found. A Canteloupe stacking cream and sugar have been found with the sugar not the pinched bowl, but the body of the coffee cup with no indentation. After dinner cups have been found only in Ice Blue, Parsley and Avocado Yellow but they were sold in Ripe Apricot, Oyster and Nutmeg. In any color, these are to be considered a very rare find. Advertisements and sales brochures of the 1940's must be viewed with discretion. Items were added to pictures for effect and these pictures cannot be trusted for identity purposes. We must be cautious with colors also and would do well to remember that brochures given out by stores listed the colors that stores carried, not necessarily all the colors available. There are look-alikes, some even made by Iroquois, and these would include egg cups and bowls which make nice additions to one's collections. Be careful not to stray from the list of Iroquois presented here. Be aware that the original coffee pot was redesigned to become a teapot. Coffee cups as pictured here were discontinued early and a variation of the tea cups replaced it. Family sized stacking cream and sugars are slightly larger than the usual cream and sugar but are much harder to find. For unexplained and illogical reasons, stacking creamers are found more frequently than sugars and one can only suppose that cooks found yet another use for the sugar bowl. The cover for the soup bowl has a steam opening while the gravy cover has a ladle slot, each sold separately from the soup or gravy. The smallest platter is very hard to find.

Some plates bearing late marks have an ever-so-slightly higher foot and this has caused some to believe that all the flatware was redesigned. There is no reference to this in the files but it is true that in a random stack of plates there will be some which do not conform to the neat stack we were to expect. There are several answers, all uncertain, and among them is that new molds replaced old molds from time to time. The fact that these plates with the higher foot consistently have newer marks cannot be explained away, and this adds to the complexity of the lines. Your own comparison will illustrate this slight difference and you will feel it as well as see it. This small almost imperceptible detail repesents the sort of fact finding that has helped us study the development of Casual. Those who study marks may well consider this in their own work and

it may help us with our understanding of the confusion of these marks.

In 1959 redesigned Iroquois with pattern was sold in 45-piece sets composed of eight dinner plates, bread and butter plates, cups, saucers and cereal bowls, a covered sugar and creamer, an open 8" vegetable bowl and a platter. The copper plate engraved, underglazed naturalistic patterns are lovely and much different from the decaled ware which was on the market then. An open-ended listing would include: Shepherd's Purse - white, beige and green flowers on Ripe Apricot; White Violets - violet veining in white blossoms with green leaves on Ice Blue; Orange Flower on a Lemon Yellow base; Woodhue on a Canteloupe base; Nasturtium - orange blossoms with various greens on Ripe Apricot; Gay Wings, a fantasy of pink flowers with deep pink veining on Pink; Pepper Tree - orange flowers and green leaves on Lemon. Babies Breath showed white traced flowers on Pink. The details of these designs were delicate, adding to the Oriental look of the redesigned ware. Buyers were told that no two pieces had the same detail - a cup might feature a flower while the saucer showed a leaf. The plate could show the entire pattern. Interest was added by variation and clearly this late feature was no slip-shod make-shift attempt. The files indicate that some patterns that were very different were done by the Sheffield Pottery Company in Sheffield, Massachusetts. These would be decaled country motif designs, inferior to the Wright floral lines. We must be aware of it, but not consider those decaled Sheffield items as Wright patterns. These Iroquois patterns were not well received when it was introduced but it is important to our understanding of Wright's work. We have come to know that his shapes and colors were very different, very new and modern. Now we see pattern and it also is very new and different. One has only to compare it with other dinnerware from the same time span to see that this Iroquois pattern was a departure. There would be other returns to decorated dinnerware but there was never a conformity to the style of the day. Always divergent, he was always able to find a new statement of an old concept and did so with this work.

Cookware added to the Iroquois line was a late addition and should all be found in the redesigned style. Do not be surprised, however, to find a pinch lid, separated from its bottom and resting on your sauce pan. Over the years parts have been mixed. The redesigned knob, however, is typical of the cookware which came in the later colors as well as white. The Dutch oven, covered fry pan, electric serving tray, percolator, covered sauce pan, hot plate and three casseroles are all signed and care instructions are clearly marked on each piece. These are rare pieces and in spite of the fact that they are "Range-Proof," one should use them with care. The asbestos pad which accompanied them is an absolute necessity if you are to use them on top of a burner. New information in the photograph files indicates that the Imperial Glass Company did work on the coated glazes of this cookware.

Iroquois Casual is a line that has an appeal to all. Its durability makes everyday usage possible and it frequently is the set a collector will turn to after having discovered American Modern. Those who study marks, who enjoy the interaction of color and those who like to cook, to entertain, to make a meal an "occasion," all have favored Iroquois Casual. Its durability adds to our pleasure for it is an easy style that can serve the most formal or informal occasion and can do so in surprising ways if you will compare the effects achieved by contrasting these wonderful colors. Even advanced collectors who are well acquainted with the Iroquois palette surprise themselves with the results of color contrasting.

The world of Russel Wright, so closely examined by collectors continues to challenge those who study it and Iroquois remains the most complicated of Wright's dinnerware lines. He had used this line to alter china table service and the story of the American Table would never be the same.

On Pricing Iroquois Casual

As we examined pricings reported by those who helped with them, some opinions were consistent. All agreed that Aqua and Brick Red should be much higher than we had thought previously and they suggested that these should be double the price of other colors. I was told that cookware prices were far too low and that lids were nowhere near their actual value. I have reflected that thinking here. Some pieces which appeared to be scarce before are now believed to be rare. Some pieces which we had thought to be plentiful have not

proven to be so. The stars in the pricing will guide you on those items.

Color preferences seem to be much the same as they were in 1985, with Aqua and Brick Red seldom seen, highly valued. Oyster, White, Charcoal and Canteloupe continue to be at the high end of our scale, Avocado at the low end. Ice Blue and Pink Sherbet remain the colors found most often but that seems to make them no less desirable. Lemon Yellow and Lettuce Green do not come our way often. Both Ripe Apricot and Nutmeg, good mix and match colors, are popular. Parsley and Forest Green are the same color.

The good news on piece identification is that we seem to have counted the bowls and tea cups correctly. Their numbers seem not to have changed. The redesigned gravy is an outstanding piece - one that advanced collectors will take in any color that comes their way. The restyled butter dish is much harder to locate than the original half-pound one. The single salt and pepper (pepper mill) are unmarked and rare. The 1½ quart water pitcher is scarce, the redesigned one is rare. Both the original mug and the redesigned mug are hard to find. The gumbo (a flat soup) has all but disappeared and we are all surprised. It seemed there were many and now there are none. The carafes have found their way into carafe collections. The after dinner coffee cups are just NOT found and may be the rarest item you will collect. All cookware is desirable and seldom seen.

Keep in mind that all items are considered wholes whether or not you find the lid. NEVER reject a lid.

Those who are new to Iroquois Casual will find their way through the Original/Restyle/Redesign sequence soon. It falls into place quickly though it may seem overwhelming at first. For identification, try measurements listed in the price guide combined with the pinch OR redesign look as well as the lid/no lid practice. You will learn to love Casual and you will be in good company. Many of us start the day with an Iroquois cup and saucer.

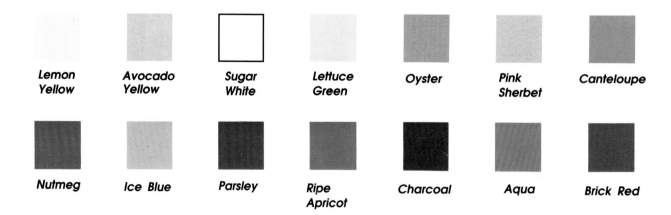

Lemon Yellow   Avocado Yellow   Sugar White   Lettuce Green   Oyster   Pink Sherbet   Canteloupe

Nutmeg   Ice Blue   Parsley   Ripe Apricot   Charcoal   Aqua   Brick Red

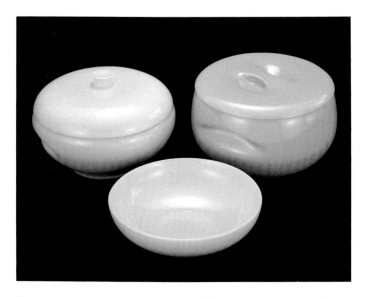

Two quart covered casserole, 8". Four quart cookware casserole, 8". 36 ounce open vegetable bowl.

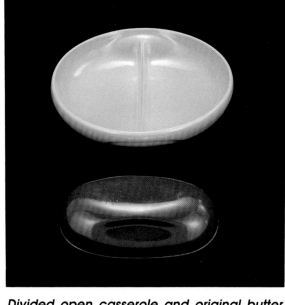

Divided open casserole and original butter dish.

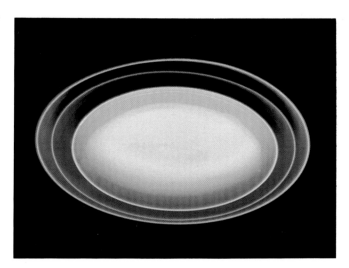

Plates: dinner, luncheon, salad.

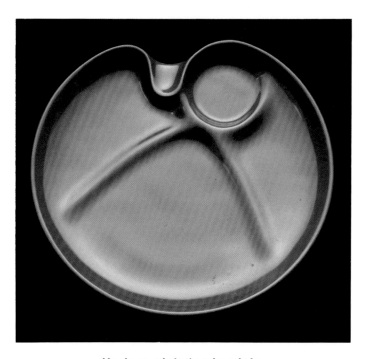

Hostess plate/party plate.

Original coffee pot.

Gravy with fast stand and covered gravy bowl on liner.

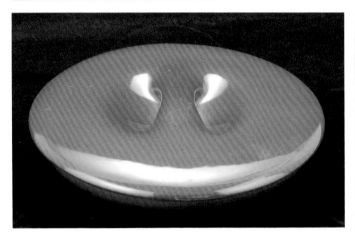

10" original covered casserole.

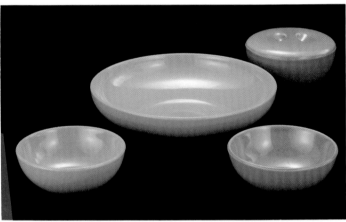

Open vegetable bowl, 10", covered soup and cereal bowls.

Stacking shakers, single salt, pepper mill, tea cup/ saucer, coffee cup/saucer, after dinner cup/saucer.

Stacking cream and sugar, family size cream and sugar.

Below: Advertising sign with original brochure and cookware. Left: Iroquois advertising ashtray used as holiday greeting in 1952. Very rare.

Redesigned mug.

Redesigned teapot, carafe and gumbo soup bowl.

Redesigned covered casserole, fruit and redesigned fruit.

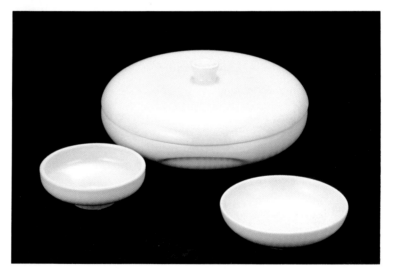

Restyled water pitcher, family size cream and after dinner coffee pot. All rare.

Iroquois Casual platter, redesigned teapot, advertising ashtray, covered pitcher, original mug, redesigned butter dish, gravy with stand cover, and redesigned covered sugar.

Iroquois Casual gravy with top which becomes a stand.

Left to right: Three early cup handles in what appears to be the order of production. Cup #4 is the coffee cup, discontinued early and rare. Cup #5 is late redesigned tea cup.

Cooking is Fun...

Entertaining Easy with Iroquois Casual

A roast is magnificent (tasty warm, too) served complete with garnish on the **electric platter**. Buffet fare can be cooked on the **china stove** and kept hot between helpings. These and the **saucepan** will serve you so many ways . . . . and eliminate the extra-pots-and-pans-cleanup from your household routine forever!

america's
most
versatile
true
china

FAMOUS
Iroquois
CASUAL CHINA
by Russel Wright

◆ COOK, BAKE 'N SERVE CHINA ◆ REPLACED IF IT CHIPS OR BREAKS* ◆ SOLID COLORS ◆ DECORATIONS ON COLOR

Front and back of Iroquois brochure. Back shows cookware.

THE ALL-OCCASION GENUINE CHINA

FAMOUS IROQUOIS CASUAL CHINA BY RUSSEL WRIGHT
GUARANTEED 3 YEARS AGAINST BREAKING, CRACKING...EVEN CHIPPING!*

Original advertising bro-chure.

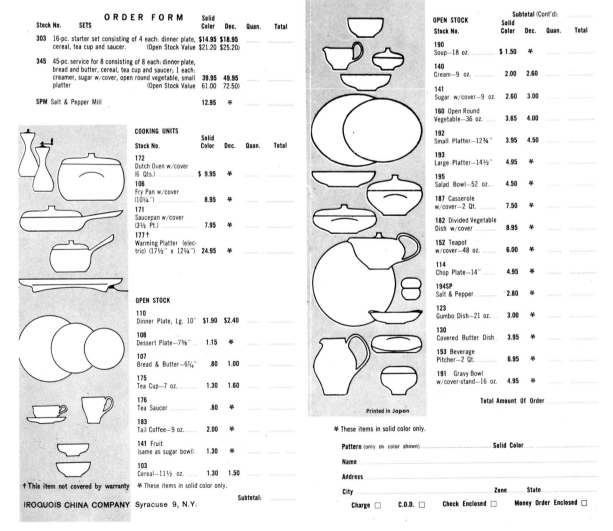

ORDER FORM

Stock No.	SETS	Solid Color	Dec.	Quan.	Total
303	16-pc. starter set consisting of 4 each: dinner plate, cereal, tea cup and saucer. (Open Stock Value $21.20 $25.20)	$14.95	$18.95		
345	45-pc. service for 8 consisting of 8 each: dinner plate, bread and butter, cereal, tea cup and saucer; 1 each: creamer, sugar w/cover, open round vegetable, small platter (Open Stock Value 61.00 72.50)	39.95	49.95		
SPM	Salt & Pepper Mill	12.95	*		

COOKING UNITS

Stock No.		Solid Color	Dec.	Quan.	Total
172	Dutch Oven w/cover (6 Qts.)	$ 9.95	*		
106	Fry Pan w/cover (10¼")	8.95	*		
171	Saucepan w/cover (3½ Pt.)	7.95	*		
177†	Warming Platter (electric) (17½" x 12¼")	24.95	*		

OPEN STOCK

Stock No.		Solid Color	Dec.	Quan.	Total
110	Dinner Plate, Lg. 10"	$1.90	$2.40		
108	Dessert Plate—7⅜"	1.15	*		
107	Bread & Butter—6⁷⁄₁₆"	.80	1.00		
175	Tea Cup—7 oz.	1.30	1.60		
176	Tea Saucer	.80	*		
183	Tall Coffee—9 oz.	2.00	*		
141	Fruit (same as sugar bowl)	1.30	*		
103	Cereal—11½ oz.	1.30	1.50		

† This item not covered by warranty   * These items in solid color only.

Subtotal: _____

IROQUOIS CHINA COMPANY Syracuse 9, N.Y.

OPEN STOCK

		Solid Color	Dec.	Quan.	Total
	Subtotal (Cont'd):				
190	Soup—18 oz.	$ 1.50	*		
140	Cream—9 oz.	2.00	2.60		
141	Sugar w/cover—9 oz.	2.60	3.00		
160	Open Round Vegetable—36 oz.	3.65	4.00		
192	Small Platter—12¾"	3.95	4.50		
193	Large Platter—14½"	4.95	*		
195	Salad Bowl—52 oz.	4.50	*		
187	Casserole w/cover—2 Qt.	7.50	*		
182	Divided Vegetable Dish w/cover	8.95	*		
152	Teapot w/cover—48 oz.	6.00	*		
114	Chop Plate—14"	4.95	*		
194SP	Salt & Pepper	2.80	*		
123	Gumbo Dish—21 oz.	3.00	*		
130	Covered Butter Dish	3.95	*		
153	Beverage Pitcher—2 Qt.	6.95	*		
191	Gravy Bowl w/cover-stand—16 oz.	4.95	*		

Total Amount Of Order _____

Printed in Japan

* These items in solid color only.

Pattern (only on color shown) .... Solid Color ....
Name ....
Address ....
City .... Zone ...... State ......
Charge ☐   C.O.D. ☐   Check Enclosed ☐   Money Order Enclosed ☐

Brochure pages showing Iroquois shapes.

The Many Faces of Sterling

The Sterling China Company, Wellsville, Ohio and Russel Wright reached mutual agreement in 1949 when Wright was asked to design a dinnerware line for this leader in restaurant/hotel/institution ware. It is very obvious that this was a multi-faceted challenge for Wright. Wright's shape line for Sterling would be basic but it was to be based on the existing standards of the institutional field. Glazes were also Wright's concern and some of the most interesting restaurant/institutional colored glazes then or now came from work done for Sterling during this period.

Perhaps we should not be surprised that problems in finding the correct glaze formulas occurred at once. Doris Coutant, Wright's expert on glaze experimentation made a trip to the Ohio River area to personally arrange glazes which would please both Wright and Sterling. It was a difficult assignment but Coutant was, by this time, an old hand at dealing with Wright's demanding instructions and client relationship was well within her expertise. Over and over simple colors were fired and most often refused, repeatedly falling short of Wright's requirements. In spite of this, Wright felt that excessive testing was being done and that the "right" colors were so simple that they should have been achieved at once. After many delays the colors were approved: Ivy Green, Straw Yellow, Suede Grey, Cedar Brown, Shell Pink and White. These were to be made in solid colored dinnerware only. If Sterling's customers wanted individual patterns, emblems or logos, those were the responsibility of Sterling and the client. There were some rare exceptions, but these were very few and would be Wright's own customers for whom he was doing custom work. If you are collecting Sterling, be aware of these facts but do not be discouraged by them. Interesting patterns evolved out of the pottery's client relationship and some equally interesting patterns are now known to have been custom work attributable to Wright. He drew royalties on all as the shape and glaze were his design. Any of this patterned ware will be in short supply and a word for today's collector is that when a pleasing pattern is found, buy it for it may well be all you will see.

Sterling, as experienced in the production of this type ware as Wright was with home furnishings, had definite requirements and was not hesitant to take issue with each of the pieces Wright designed if they found them not practical or usable in institutional usage. The company knew the correct serving sizes, needs of restaurants, and equally important, they knew the price range which must be met if they were to operate competitively. Wright's creativity was confined within those limits, but he was willing to grant Sterling the last word on each item for he recognized their judgments as experienced ones. The teapot discussion still represents this situation best. Wright felt the 10 oz. teapot was too small, not generous enough. Sterling wrote that a larger pot would badly weaken the tea and, additionally, "This is the size that sells. All are made but the 10 oz. size is the volume item in teapot size." Wright conformed and the 10 oz. teapot and coffee bottle were approved at once. Increasingly, (Wright believed), Americans were lingering over "another cup, please" and with the Wright creed firmly in place, he hoped to encourage more relaxed dining, at least in "better establishments."

Both the designer and the pottery seemed willing to work out each item in this line with less dispute than had accompanied other Wright dinnerware lines. Both set aside preliminary judgments and tried to achieve a functional design which would work well in the home or institution. What emerged was a design altogether new in appearance and which, at the same time, filled pre-existing standards in an old industry. The "In Home" market was a new one for Sterling also and Wright was pleased with the product as they adapted it to both uses.

Sterling was warm in style, easy to use and with dual uses for items, it fulfilled its potential and met the needs of both areas, remaining popular through its short life span.

Piece identification is a problem for collectors since usages are not the same as home usage. It seems right to list the qualities of the items here since many of the small pieces served a variety of uses and familiar shapes often served unfamiliar needs. Plates were available in 5 sizes: 11½" service plate, 10¼" dinner plate, 9" luncheon plate, 7½" salad plate, and 6¼" bread and butter plate. An almost imperceptible depth was achieved by the slow, curving upward flow of the edges from the center of the plates. The foot of each plate is hidden by the graceful roll of the edge and the underneath side is so shaped that the waitress could get a good, firm grip. The grasp covers little of the eating surface.

The tea cup and saucer are shaped with the unique handle jiggered on as an integral part of the cup. While the cup looks larger than the ordinary hotel cup, it actually is a 7 oz. cup, average in size. The saucer is deep so that any liquid spilled during service had less chance of soiling table linen.

The after dinner coffee cup (demi cup) and saucer are different from pre-Wright a.d. cups, seeming to be of generous capacity while holding the usual 3½ oz. The handle is molded onto the top of the cup and then curves gracefully downward and inward, sloping before reaching the cup body.

The sugar bowl has a lid with the Iroquois pinch look. It features finger grip depressions instead of the traditional knob. This was expected to reduce breakage. The rounded bowl has no handles. The handled cream pitcher follows the lines of the tea cups with the same type of handle integrally molded into the shape. The lip was shaped especially to cut down on dripping. It holds 9 ounces. Individual creamers were available in two sizes. The smaller holds 1 oz. for coffee or tea while the larger, with a 3 oz. capacity was to be used for cereal or dessert. These flow upward and outward in a manner different from the straight sided creamers of the day.

The fruit bowl doubles for a dessert bowl or individual vegetable serving. It featured the cushioned edge which eased serving problems.

The bouillon bowl is round with small lug handles extending outward and slightly downward from the rim to give the grace of a cream soup but still be ruggedly durable. The lugs were molded to the shape for less breakage. These are small items with multiplicity of uses.

The four compartment relish server was especially practical and useful for restaurants and hotels where "extra helpings" were served. It was designed to be carried to the table full of dinner relishes, jams and jellies. High partitions prevented foods from running over and the compartments were deep enough to prevent spoons from falling out. Oval in shape, it is 16½" long and is an exception to the general rule that larger items are signed. This one is not, but it is a popular and useful item as a buffet accessory piece and Russel Wright collectors admire it as such.

Four platters cover a great many uses. They follow the same graceful rolled edge design as the plates, making excellent frames for foods and facilitating handling. The smallest platter is the most difficult to find.

The coffee bottle was a double duty item used for either coffee or tea. 10 oz., but tall and slender, it has an integrally molded handle. The cover which must be removed for pouring, has two finger grip depressions rather than a knob. It takes up less space than an ordinary coffee pot yet it holds two cups of coffee or two cups of hot water for tea. A favorite with both Sterling and the designer, this coffee bottle is another piece which collectors seek out whether or not they collect Sterling.

The teapot was designed for a maximum of durability with the handle molded onto the body and finger grip depressions on the cover in place of knobs. The cover remains securely in place while pouring, the lip specially shaped to reduce dripping. There are no inside rims to hold the cover, making draining and drying easier. It it also a 10 oz. item. With no cover, this item may appear to be a cream pitcher. Not true. If you have no items to compare, be aware that the cream is a 9 oz. item while this teapot is 10 oz.

The Wright sauce boat was a new and more practical design for this piece. The handle curves downward from the top rim, turns slightly toward the cup body and then stops, forming a curved half handle. Usage was for serving sauces, syrups and such. The bowl holds 5 oz. The handle treatment is one that Wright used in his Melamine dinnerware line also and collectors have named it the "pony tail handle." Caution is again urged. This small pouring vessel is not another creamer.

The deep soup bowl was said to keep soup hot for a longer time than was possible in the usual shallow soup bowl. It has the appearance of an extra generous capacity. Holding 14 oz., its usage was for anything requiring a larger helping.

The salad bowl was intended for use for individual salads when salad was served as a main course. It is particularly practical for salads with dressings as it does not allow the dressing to spill over. This piece works equally well as a fruit bowl, holding a generous 23 oz.

The celery server is a slender, graceful boat-shaped piece with the same type of cushion edge rim as appeared in the plates. The edges at either end slope slightly down to form handles. A space-saving piece, it has the reflected memory of the American Modern butter bottom but is 11" long.

The unique ashtray follows the general theme of the entire line with its rounded gentle curves. Even with a match book compartment, this is not a large or cumbersome piece. It also is a favorite with collectors who feel it to be one of Wright's best works.

The water pitcher as originally designed was almost straight sided, bulky and unlike the more popular redesigned item which quickly became part of the Sterling line. Not spherical, this early piece has a molded handle with a two-quart capacity. What followed the redesign was a modified tilt jug style, more graceful and less chunky.

A covered onion soup with finger grip cover makes an attractive piece for an individual casserole or for any food which needs a cover for warmth.

Those who collect Russel Wright Sterling and those who would study it should be aware that much of it is not marked. Stickers alone have been found on items which were known to have had the pressed Wright signature. It is supposed that molds may have worn and the stickers replaced expected marks in those cases. Do not be discouraged if an unmarked, but otherwise known to be Wright design comes your way.

The new files have opened up a new world for Sterling collectors. We had a small amount of verifiable information on the Polynesian Shape and we believed that it was used as a part of a total design concept for The Shun Lee (Li) Dynasty restaurant in New York. Those facts are certain now and we know that Wright's work with Shun Lee was a total design concept in which he was responsible for every detail. With the identification of Polynesian dinnerware verified, it is reasonable to expect that he did work on other table top items, stainless, glass and the like. The Polynesian shape items date from 1965 and would include: sake bottle with stopper, 9" plate, tea cups with handles and without handles, teapot, rice bowl, double sauce server, covered compote, dessert dish, various platter, 15" chop server, soup server, after dinner cups and saucers, a 10 oz. teapot, a 24 oz. teapot, and a 32 oz. teapot. Seen first in black and white with the ruffled edge, it now has been found in Coral and a Seafoam. There may be other colors. No large amount of this should be expected. Wright's customers were much fewer than were Sterlings.

But there are other examples! A patterned line has been found by collectors and verified by the new files. The motif is underglazed showing decaled children and Oriental dancers. These have been found in an unfamiliar shape but references in an old undated Sterling catalog show a shape which

Sterling called "Chinese." We are tempted to consider this a problem solved by putting two and two together, but all the parts do not fit. Some examples found do not conform to the shapes shown here, nor are sizes exactly as we would expect them to be. Do not confuse this with Sterling's Blue Willow line. This is a simple line decal on a white ground, randomly spaced. Let me know what you find. We have pictures to guide you.

Before we leave Sterling's land of conjecture, I must add another Wright shape/design. The same Sterling catalog shows a shape which is named "Newport." With no reference, a picture in the new files shows this same shape, decorated with a stylized tree pattern. We show the picture as well as the catalog information with the warning that this is new information with no supporting facts and no findings.

We will do well to remind ourselves that Wright's contract with Sterling was in 1949. These new shapes, Polynesian, Chinese and Newport date from 1965, long after Wright's contract with Sterling had expired. All these lines appear to be Sterling shapes with Wright modifications and decorations, done for his clients as opposed to his own earlier shape which Sterling decorated for their customers.

On Pricing Sterling Dinnerware

Sterling collectors are really Russel Wright collectors. Often the Sterling that we have seen comes our way because a determined collector will locate a great deal of it at a restaurant supply house. He will invest a good bit of money because he most often has to buy it as a "lot." After that, he will invest a good bit of time because he has had to buy more than he wanted to get what he wanted. He has become a dealer in a flash of his checkbook. I urge you to follow his example. His story has been a success story and with probable new lines to be found, there may be good reason to expect more good luck.

The short year-long production of Sterling resulted in less made and limits the success of those who would collect Sterling but we remain hopeful that the excitement of Chinese and Newport will renew collector's search. It should be a good time for those who search for Sterling.

Ivy Green

Shell Pink

Suede Grey

Straw Yellow   *Cedar Brown*

Dinner plate, salad plate and celery.

Sauceboat, bouillon bowl, fruit bowl and cup and saucer.

Ashtray and four-compartment relish.

Platters.

Three oz. cream and one oz. cream.

After dinner cup and saucer, rare.

Redesigned water pitcher, teapot, fruit bowl and coffee bottle.

Covered sugar, sake bottle, original water pitcher and handled cream pitcher.

Large bowl believed to be "Chinese" shape, client-patterned plate and small bowl.

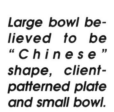

Two Shun Lee platter/plates and popular palm frond plate. Sterling pottery pattern.

Teapot believed to be "Chinese."

PRICE LIST
STERLING-RUSSEL WRIGHT* WARE

Item	Size	Price Per Dozen
Plate	6¼"	$ 5.70
Plate	7½"	8.00
Plate	9"	10.50
Plate	10¼"	13.40
Plate	11½"	17.10
Tea Cup	7-oz.	8.40
Tea Saucer	6¼"	5.10
AD Cup	3½-oz.	6.30
AD Saucer	5⅛"	4.70
Fruit	5"	4.70
Bouillon	7-oz.	7.60
Oval Platter	7⅛"	8.00
Oval Platter	10½"	12.50
Oval Platter	11¾"	15.60
Oval Platter	13⅝"	24.70
Celery	11¼"	25.10
Relish	16½"	each 5.00
Individual Cream	1-oz.	5.70
Individual Cream	3-oz.	6.80
Cream Pitcher	9-oz.	17.10
Covered Sugar	10-oz.	17.10
Sauceboat	5-oz.	17.10
Ash Tray	6"	12.00
Onion Soup	10-oz.	9.50
Onion Soup Cover		7.60
Soup Bowl, 6½"	14-oz.	9.50
Salad, 7½"	23-oz.	11.40
Water Pitcher	2-qt.	22.80
Tea Pot	10-oz.	19.00
Coffee Bottle	10-oz.	17.10

THE STERLING CHINA CO.
EAST LIVERPOOL, OHIO

*PATENTS PENDING   PRINTED IN U.S.A.

Original price list on back of Sterling brochure.

Original Sterling brochure.

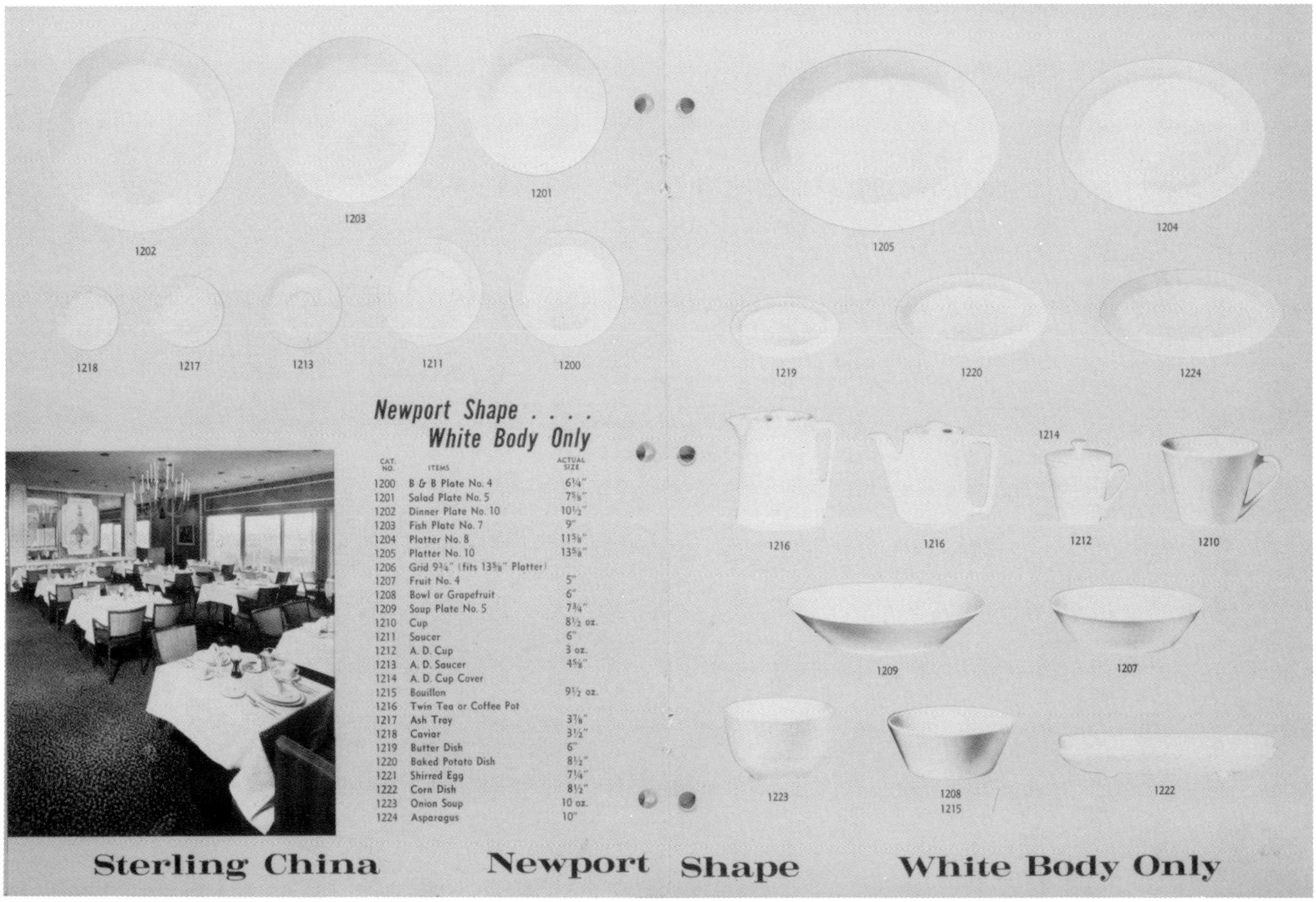

Newport Shape . . . .
White Body Only

CAT. NO.	ITEMS	ACTUAL SIZE
1200	B & B Plate No. 4	6¼"
1201	Salad Plate No. 5	7⅝"
1202	Dinner Plate No. 10	10½"
1203	Fish Plate No. 7	9"
1204	Platter No. 8	11⅝"
1205	Platter No. 10	13⅝"
1206	Grid 9¾" (fits 13⅝" Platter)	
1207	Fruit No. 4	5"
1208	Bowl or Grapefruit	6"
1209	Soup Plate No. 5	7¾"
1210	Cup	8½ oz.
1211	Saucer	6"
1212	A. D. Cup	3 oz.
1213	A. D. Saucer	4⅝"
1214	A. D. Cup Cover	
1215	Bouillon	9½ oz.
1216	Twin Tea or Coffee Pot	
1217	Ash Tray	3⅞"
1218	Caviar	3½"
1219	Butter Dish	6"
1220	Baked Potato Dish	8½"
1221	Shirred Egg	7¼"
1222	Corn Dish	8½"
1223	Onion Soup	10 oz.
1224	Asparagus	10"

Sterling China Newport Shape White Body Only

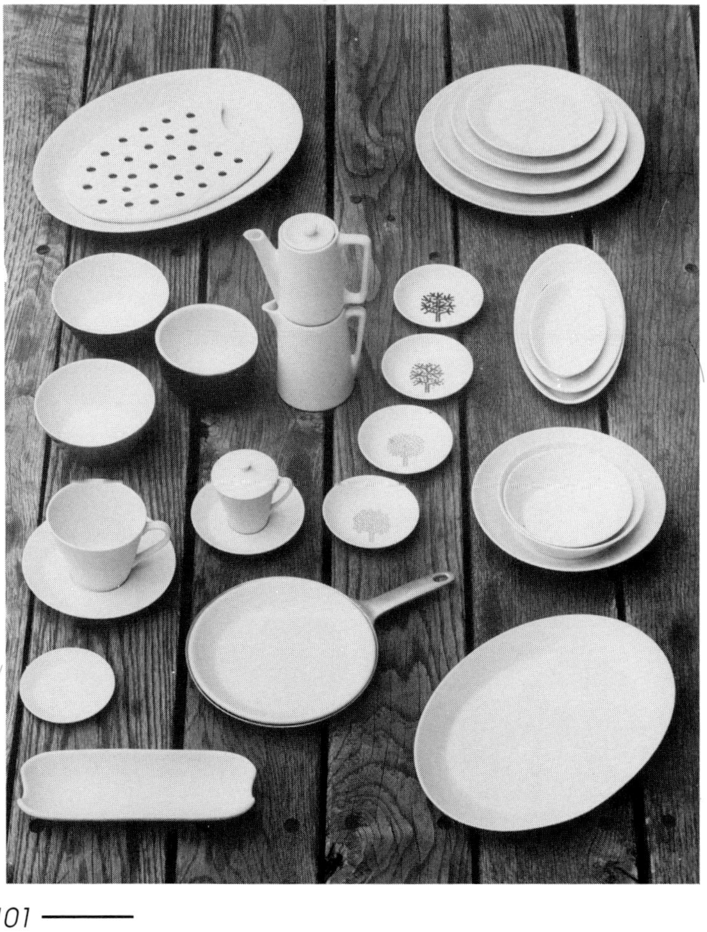

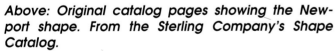

Above: Original catalog pages showing the Newport shape. From the Sterling Company's Shape Catalog.
Right: Newport shapes.

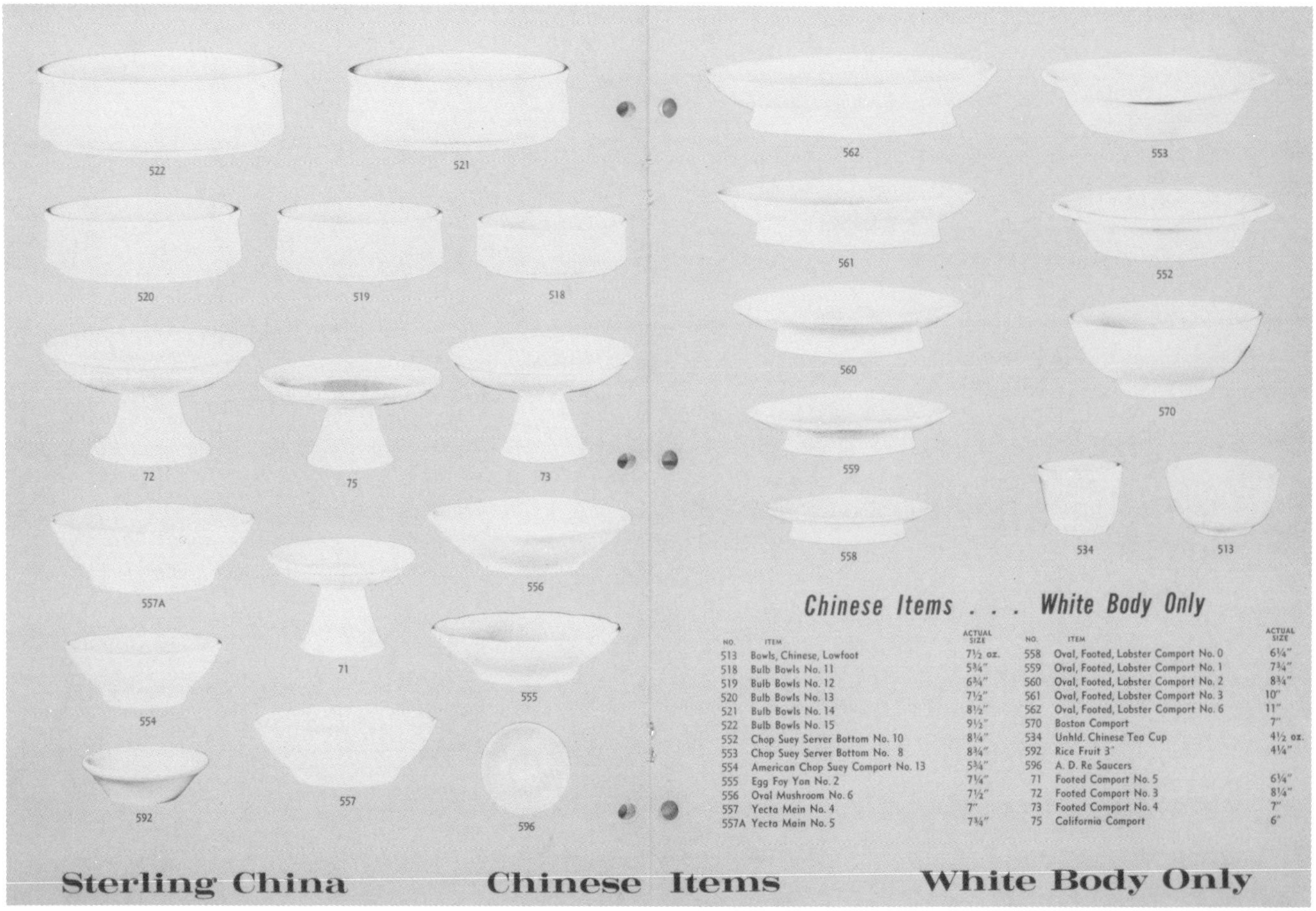

Chinese Items . . . White Body Only

NO.	ITEM	ACTUAL SIZE	NO.	ITEM	ACTUAL SIZE
513	Bowls, Chinese, Lowfoot	7½ oz.	558	Oval, Footed, Lobster Comport No. 0	6¼"
518	Bulb Bowls No. 11	5¾"	559	Oval, Footed, Lobster Comport No. 1	7¾"
519	Bulb Bowls No. 12	6¾"	560	Oval, Footed, Lobster Comport No. 2	8¾"
520	Bulb Bowls No. 13	7½"	561	Oval, Footed, Lobster Comport No. 3	10"
521	Bulb Bowls No. 14	8½"	562	Oval, Footed, Lobster Comport No. 6	11"
522	Bulb Bowls No. 15	9½"	570	Boston Comport	7"
552	Chop Suey Server Bottom No. 10	8¼"	534	Unhld. Chinese Tea Cup	4½ oz.
553	Chop Suey Server Bottom No. 8	8¾"	592	Rice Fruit 3"	4¼"
554	American Chop Suey Comport No. 13	5¾"	596	A. D. Re Saucers	
555	Egg Foy Yon No. 2	7¼"	71	Footed Comport No. 5	6¼"
556	Oval Mushroom No. 6	7½"	72	Footed Comport No. 3	8¼"
557	Yecta Mein No. 4	7"	73	Footed Comport No. 4	7"
557A	Yecta Main No. 5	7¾"	75	California Comport	6"

Sterling China   Chinese Items   White Body Only

Original catalog pages showing the Chinese shape. From the Sterling Company's Shape Catalog.

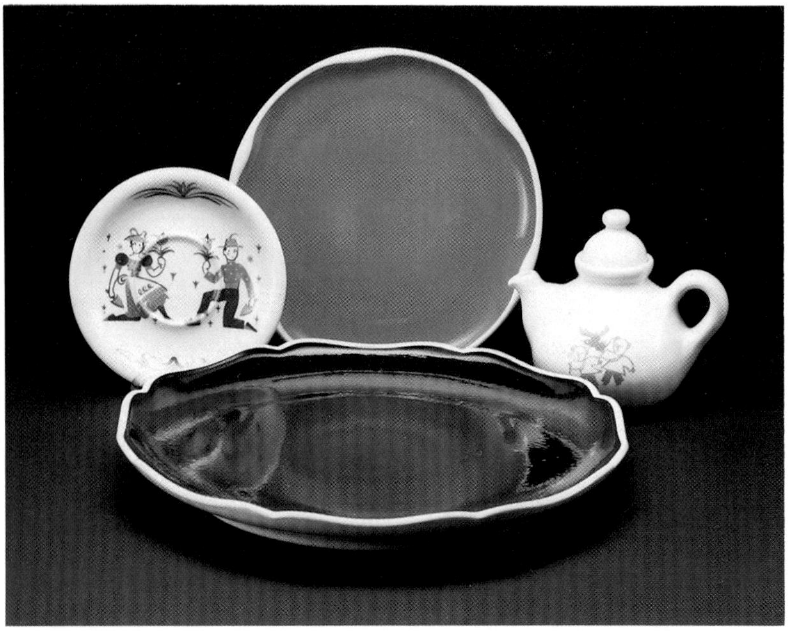

Sterling Polynesian dinner plate, saucer and teapot believed to be Chinese shape, Polynesian chop plate.

Highlight's Elegance

The Paden City/Highlight/Justin Tharaud line of Russel Wright, troubled as it was, resulted in one of the most admired of his works, Highlight has a secure place in the collecting of Wright designs and when found, it is quietly seductive with an attractiveness that is soft and understated to the point of elegance. With such wonderful properties, it is a favorite of almost every Russel Wright collector. It fills a need for fine dinnerware.

In 1948, after seven months of back and forth negotiating between Wright as designer, Justin Tharaud as marketing specialist, and the Paden City Pottery the supplier, production was off to a shaky start.

From the first, business affairs were difficult. Justin Tharaud, Wright's marketing expert in this line had a Wright-sized ego. His name had become associated with high styled merchandise and Wright ignored all signs of what was to come. Tharaud had insisted that a contract clause would allow him to approve each item of the line before production of that item was done. Why Wright agreed is not clear, but the correspondence between the parties is sprinkled with "Let me know when you are serious," "You called me, I didn't call you," and "This is my field of expertise, not yours." Of course, Wright felt that Tharaud involved himself in design detail of which he had little knowledge while business matters went unresolved. Molds needed to be made, new mills to grind glaze colors were to be purchased, new spraying equipment was required and if this ware was as widely accepted as had been American Modern and Iroquois, a new building at the pottery must be erected. All these matters waited, Wright said, while Tharaud concerned himself with the angle of a cup handle, about which he knew little. Accusations flew back and forth and manufacturing functions were not carried out. Advertising, promotion and sales were in client's hands before production began. Dissatisfaction was mutual and unresolved before the clay was in the molds.

Much of the acrimony was the result of the agreements made contractually. In addition to the clause giving Tharaud approval rights for each item, Wright had agreed that Highlight would be made to sell at a lower price than Steubenville's American Modern or Iroquois Casual. Wright was restricted from designing another dinnerware as long as his royalties averaged $10,000.00 a year with the first year to be the start of production. Additionally, Wright was to agree to the production of white, other colors, or patterns if the accepted glaze colors did not meet the approval of the buying public. Not included was a stipulation which Wright had requested and which would have given him a flat fee of $15,000.00 at the time of submission of designs to Tharaud, regardless of approval or rejection.

Predictably, the dinnerware itself was in trouble early on. Costs ran higher than either party had expected and it quickly became more competitive with American Modern and Iroquois than had been expected or hoped for. An early price cut to boost sales was effected by Tharaud and Wright sent reams of correspondence which questioned that necessity and Tharaud's competency. Tharaud felt that some of the fault had accrued from Wright's design and the war raged on. Almost from the first, neither party profited financially as they had expected.

In spite of questions of responsibility between the two parties, the Paden City Pottery turned out another Russel Wright award winner. Highlight won the 1951 Museum of Modern Art Home Furnishings Exhibit award which toured this country and Europe. The Merchandise Mart in Chicago and the Museum of Modern Art in New York City co-sponsored it in their Good Design 1951 Exhibit and it won the Trail Blazer Award given by the Home Furnishings League. These awards reflected well on the line and with such acceptance, the pottery had little cause to complain. Though constant conflict surrounded the line, the pottery remained aloof and the quarreling parties did resolve differences - one at a time.

Highlight was the name given this high-styled dinnerware and that name derives from the appearance of the white clay showing through at the rims and edges of the pieces, giving a highlighted effect. The marvelous colors of Highlight reflect Wright's own favorite earth-toned glazes. Blueberry, Nutmeg, Pepper, Citron, Dark Green and finally, White made for distinctive colors, not seen in dinnerware in this price range. Dark green and White were late 1951 colors and there was less of those made than other colors. White became Snow Glaze but the Dark Green had no descriptive name. These colors were first made in a soft matte glaze but later production was of a glossier sheen, showing less of the highlighted edge. This was a design adjustment, made to stimulate sales. Collectors find their favorite to be the earlier, matte glaze, but the glossier glaze is handsome and was not considered as less fine.

With sleek lines, soft contoured handles, exaggerated lips and cushioned edges, Highlight quickly made a place for itself in Wright designs, a favored place. It appealed to those who asked for a more refined design, carrying art in dinnerware to a new level. Its statement was that of elegance using some of the same features that were in the Sterling line, in a manner completely its own. This was Vintage Wright.

Snow Glass, made by the Paden City Glass Company, joined with the pottery to effect an entirely new dinnerware concept. It added drinking vessels, but also added serving items and flatware pieces made of glass. One's Highlight set was not complete without the use of both pottery and glassware. Wright's name, "Snow Glass," best describes this glass for it appears to be crystaline with minute flakes of opaque white resembling snow flakes scattered randomly in the crystalline body. Textured in feel and appearance, it was a new approach to dinnerware, another Russel Wright "first." You should be guided by one principle: Remember the shapes in which it was made. Other look-alikes, described in the 1985 dinnerware book have now been identified. They are, as we suspected, hand made, hand bent glass of fine quality. They were designed by Paul A. Lobel, sold by Mary Ryan, Wright's early supporter. The line was called Benduro and was advertised as an American Expression in Glass. Similar in concept, this glass was made in several colors but it has been the Snowflake which has confused Snow Glass collectors.

In passing, we must be aware of a Bubble Glass, similar to Snow Glass which was designed and made by Irving Richards in 1942. Made in Mexico, this glass was often confused with Snow Glass. It was made in a 5 oz. juice glass and a 10 oz. cocktail size - no other items, but it was very popular with those who reached for good designs.

In addition, a very small amount of Fostoria Glass, probably a prototype for Snow Glass is part of the collection of The Huntington Museum in Huntington, West Virginia. It has a thinner body, darker than Snow Glass (see glass chapter). Granular free-form bowls/ashtrays are finding their way into the Snow Glass look-alikes. These seem globular, not dinnerware items and not likely to be confused with Wright's designs. They do exist, however and they

should be mentioned with the warning that they are not authentic Wright designs. All of these make good additions to a set of Highlight for they are useful additions, substituting for the rare Snow Glass while collectors search for the authentic shapes.

From the beginning, Snow Glass pieces were three sizes of tumblers, salad plates, saucers, fruit bowls, various lids, a 2-pint pitcher, a round vegetable bowl, shakers and candle holders. Glass lids for the pottery sugar bowl and vegetable bowl did duty as small platters or trays. They are poor "fits," however, and their use is risky.

By 1953, other changes were afoot. The Paden City Glass Company had ended its production and the search for another producer of glass had not met with good results. Animosity between the interested parties once more flared and both held the other responsible for not locating an alternate glass producer. Wright felt that he had worked on this line for five years with little to show for his work and Tharaud was equally dissatisfied. With little choice, the two agreed that Snow Glaze, the white pottery substitute for Snow Glass was their only choice. It did not help, nor did the addition of gloss to the pottery items. Neither additions nor redesigns, as described in the files, had changed the sales slump and the writing on the wall was not good news. Production ended soon, leaving the dinnerware scene the lesser when this lovely line was no more. Wright had found himself in competition with himself through it all, and in spite of planning which was to have eliminated that possibility. In a last effort to sell, Tharaud had cut the price of Highlight below that of American Modern. This was the final indignity, Wright felt. The parties released claims against each other and except for royalties due, their contract and agreements came to an end.

Our study, remains inconclusive because many of the pottery serving pieces, listed here, listed in the files, drawn in the files and described in correspondence have never been found. The 1953 records show that the shakers, butter dish, soups and pitcher were redesigned but collectors, those who search and study these products, have never seen the originals and many are skeptical about their existence. Without explanation, the files give exact sizes. The butter dish, we are told, was made in an Eastern style, 3" x 5", or a Western style, 9" x 5". No one has ever seen either. Nor have we seen the teapot, covered pitcher, mug, casserole and more. In the listings here, I have indicated which pieces are still not found. Every sort of explanation has been considered but no explanation is supported by facts that are acceptable. Those who believe these do not exist find that premise no easier to defend than do those who remain hopeful.

On one hand, the absence of the dishes themselves, after these years of collecting seems to refute their production. On the other hand, files are specific, and we question the detail which describes non-existent items. Would awards be given to a partial set of dinnerware? Interestingly, a pair of shakers were found very recently and that gives hope that the missing pieces may still be found.

The solution may rest somewhere between the opposites, as we have found it to do with other of Wright's work. It seems logical that the discord over Highlight may have hurt its production and that Tharaud with his approval clause may never have approved the designs of these items. We know enough of Wright's nature to know that he would have continued study and work on a design regardless of set-backs and it seems likely that the planning may have gone on while production was brought to a stop. This is conjecture, a try at finding middle ground for this troubled story. In either event, we should keep our expectations high. If there were plans, there were prototypes. Some experimenting and sampling was certain to have been done and it is not beyond our dreams to suppose that a short run many have been done. Any amount of it would be rare, very special, very wonderful. A very recent finding of Highlight in a light powder blue matte glaze is exciting and suggests more surprises. Cups and saucers found in this pastel blue, entirely different from Blueberry, are marked with the Justin Tharaud/Wright signature/USA mark. These suggest a "set," a sampling or short run, at least. Is it possible that other colors may appear now, after all the scrutiny and study which has accompanied Highlights? If this new color is only

now finding its way out of china closets, may we take heart and still find the elusive serving pieces which are so well documented but never seen?

Today, those of us who collect Highlight have very often found it in sets of one color. Not usually mixed or matched, it was also not advertised as stackable, unbreakable, or easy to use or care for. Different from its successful sisters, Highlight was elevated to a position of worth based on beauty and elegance for its own sake. This is functionalism with emotion. Its place in the Russel Wright dinnerware designs is a unique one for the same reasons that it won awards in 1951.

On Pricing Highlight

Highlight's pricing reflects its rarity and new collectors would develop if more were available. One of those who helped with pricing asked "Where, oh where, are you going to find Highlight?" It is rare.

Those who are fortunate enough to have bought Highlight early got the bargains for none of this is inexpensive today. Snow Glass, a rarity from the first, has taken price increases not expected. Replacing Snow Glass, the pottery Snow Glaze is also in short supply. Blueberry and Pepper are the popular colors but all are to be considered desirable. Even Citron, Wright's name for chartreuse is a good color, not so sharp as his other chartreuse. The high gloss glaze is slightly less popular than the original glaze. There is no mix and match with these colors and a collector will do well to buy what he finds if it is priced affordably.

| Green | Pepper | Nutmeg | White | Citron | Blueberry |

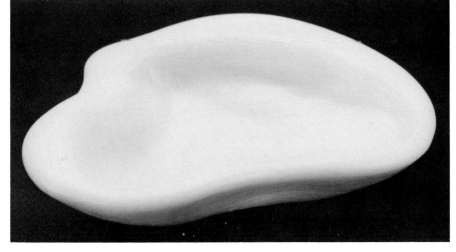

One of several Paden City look-alikes. NOT Wright design.

Sugar and vegetable bowls shown with pottery covers which replaced Snow Glass covers.

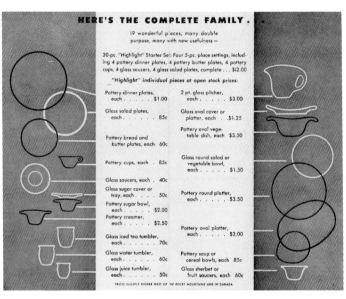

Original brochure showing all 19 pieces.

Top row: Citron lid/tray, oval vegetable bowl.

Middle row: Platter, Snow Glass tumbler and lid/tray, redesigned soup/cereal, cup on Snow Glass saucers.

Bottom row: Soup/cereal bowls.

Top row: *Platter, dinner plate, Snow Glass salad plate, bread and butter plate, shakers, round vegetable bowl, sugar with Snow Glass cover.*

Middle row: *Covered vegetable bowl, sugar with pottery lid/tray.*

Bottom row: *Cream oval vegetable bowl, Snow Glass round vegetable bowl.*

Russel Wright

ADDS NEW SNOW GLAZE
TO *Highlight*
DINNERWARE

OPEN STOCK IN

Black Pepper

Blueberry

Nutmeg

Citron

Snow Glaze

Prompt Delivery

Distributed exclusively by

Justin Tharaud & Son Inc.

129-131 Fifth Avenue, New York 3

Original Highlight advertisement.

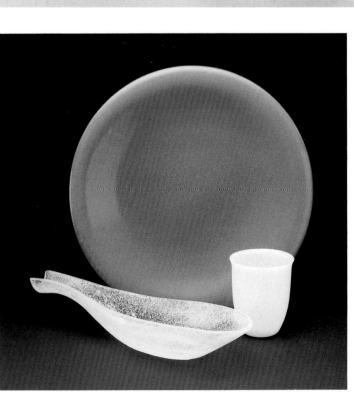

Platter, Snow Glass tumbler, Snow Glass look-alike sauce boat.

Pattern in Dinnerware
Harker White Clover

Wright has been taken to task by writers and collectors for his use of pattern in the White Clover line done for the Harker Pottery. Perhaps we have used the wrong measure. A comparison with other patterns of 1951 shows it to be restrained to the point where he considered it acceptable for use as dinnerware. Our measure should be, perhaps not between his solid colored lines and this patterned line, but between this and other patterns then on the market. Minimally self-patterned, incised to show the white background through the glaze of a different color, it was as innovative as had been his solid colored lines. Clover makes no attempt to use floral patterns in imitative ways, but, rather, uses a light touch, almost whimsical.

White Clover had many of the Wright features which had been so important to buyers of his other lines. It was made of a detergent-proof, craze-proof glaze which would not chip easily. It was designed for easy stacking in cupboards, open shelves or refrigerator and it went into the oven with your favorite recipes. Wright even included a few of his own on some sales brochures. The pattern itself was interesting with various clover forms on different pieces, most with pattern variations, or no pattern.

In 1951 Wright was in a secure position with award winning credentials. American Modern and Iroquois were still breaking records, his Sterling line had met with approval in both the home furnishings fields and institutional markets and Highlight, in spite of the personal problems it had caused him, had also become a very popular line. His work clearly dominated the dinnerware industry.

Wright's choice of a naturalistic theme should not surprise us. By this time, he was spending his weekends at Garrison, New York on the acreage where he relaxed by physical work, clearing the land, reforesting as much as possible and generally planning for the home he was to build there. The property had been quarried and logged so his work there was a restructuring of nature, contriving and re-establishing it to achieve the best and most beautiful results. Increasingly, he had found himself going back into the city on Monday mornings, incorporating his weekend experiences in his work.

He had found a consuming interest in nature and it would be a lifelong love affair with the land. His work reflected that interest.

Wright was confident that White Clover would be well received and, indeed, the design community responded positively. The Museum of Modern Art acquired a set and gave it their Good Design Award almost at once. In the marketplace, however, the story was a different one. Inefficient, inexperienced marketing had resulted in a slow sales start. No national distributor had been named and sales were left to the sales department at the pottery. Harker had not advertised except for flyers and salesmen's samples displayed in their permanent showrooms. In the beginning, they took orders for Meadow Green only and wanted to promote the idea that White Clover was "hard to get." American Modern dealers were always out of stock, always waiting for new orders to come in and buyers stood in line to wait their turns with no complaint. It might be a good position for Harker to take, the pottery told itself. Salesmen were told not to call on all acounts in a town but instead to place it with a choice account and offer that account exclusiveness.

By 1953 when all the colors had been released and all accounts given the opportunity to buy, complaints began. Buyers did not like the fact that the undecorated 9" plate was the largest plate in the starter set. Harker countered that the 10" decorated dinner plate was too costly to make and sell in these 16-piece promotional starter sets. Wright responded that a set claiming to be decorated but with only the cup showing pattern as would be the case, could only result in customer dissatisfaction. The 9" plate was to be decorated and included though it escalated Harker's already soaring costs. In an effort to make the ware cost effective, Wright wanted to develop West Coast accounts but the pottery refused to consider such shipments unless each customer took a boxcar load. This severely limited accounts in the western half of the country. Wright complained about Harker's low-figure advertising budget and proposed new themes, only to have them rejected. Harker claimed kiln space for the plates was more than customary and special cartons added to their costs. They asked for less royalty. He claimed he was not aware of these special needs which had derived from the design and had he known earlier, he would have modified the design to help. Their suggestion, coming as it did, after sales had been made, might force a failure of the whole line, he said.

In 1955, with bankruptcy waiting at the door of the pottery industry, Harker, fighting for its existence, reduced the price of White Clover and Wright's royalties reflected that position. Special prices were given on starter sets, $7.95 in the East and $8.95 on the West coast. At this time, shipments had added up to little more than 60% of expectations on open stock and to slightly under 40% on starter sets. It was a bad year in a bad time. Most potteries were working at 70% of their capacity and most were involved in wage conferences. No one in the industry was proud of the wages earned but they could not improve and be competitive because of imports. It was said, "Averages mean nothing to a man who is working two days a week or laid off." Harker, still at work was forced to admit that optimism on White Clover was far ahead of results and they had few hopes that situation would change. Wright responded by cutting royalites on the General Electric clock which matched the dinnerware.

Of course, the seeds of Clover's fate may have been sown in the profitable soils of American Modern and Iroquois for they continued to dominate the market. White Clover, with higher production costs could not keep up. Advertising costs had mounted and with no national distributor to coordinate the advertising, sales never improved. Industry-wide problems had become critical and all American dinnerware as well as the potteries which produced it was in a fight for its life. Harker discontinued White Clover shortly after reductions were made.

White Clover was made in Golden Spice, Meadow Green, Coral Sand and Charcoal and the companion General Electric clock was made in the same colors. These colors were soft, warm, easy-on-the-eye colors and complemented the svelte shapes. You will not mistake it for any other dinnerware line of its time. Most items are marked but the covering glaze at times fills in the incised mark and may be difficult to see. Try to remember shapes when in doubt. Some color glazed bottoms have been found unsigned in spite of the fact that they were to have been. Not all pieces were intended to be clover decorated and the plain color glazed pieces were meant to add interest when used with decorated pieces. Do not be surprised if you find a piece which is listed here as decorated and you see no decorations. This was not meant to be, of course, but pottery workers had a way with a dish

and some results reflected their own creativity. These cannot be called rarities, but they are unusual. Colors are more uniform in this line than in some of the longer lived lines.

White Clover shapes are distinctly different from other lines of the 1950's. The pitcher has a locking lid which prevents it from spilling when liquid is poured. The shakers were sold with the salt being the tallest. Many 1950 buyers, it appears, had preferences for similar sized shakers and the stores usually allowed choices. From the beginning the sugar bowl did double duty as a covered individual ramekin and was sold as such. The short life span here prevented a larger line of items and the multiplicity of use which would have evolved. With short production time and no redesign work, the line as it has come to us is basic.

Harker used these Wright colors on items of their own production and we have seen cake lifters as well as pieces combined with metal to make servers of several sorts. A salad set using the open vegetable bowl and the cereal bowls is attractive. All of these make nice companion pieces and fill needs not met by the small line. Do not be persuaded that these are rare, unlisted items and overspend, however. They are adaptations of Wright's shapes and glazes. He drew royalties on the original items as single pieces. The adaptation was the work of others.

Surely this Russel Wright White Clover deserves better than it met in the stores of the mid 1950's. It is lovely in every way and because of the short time it survived, it is in scarce supply today. It is most often found in single colored partial sets. This was not a line to mix and match. Partial sets languish for replacements for this line is in short supply and not found with regularity. The serving pieces are almost rare. Demand has not exceeded supply but we would do well to regard this line as a good representative of the sort of patterns which Wright found compatible with good design and expect it to make a place for itself in the collectible dinnerware which he designed.

It was a challenge to the designer, we know, for his daughter, Ann, remembers train rides home from Florida with Wright sketching clovers for this Harker line. A commercial failure, it was not a design failure and it stands out as one of the unique patterned designs in American dinnerware.

On Pricing Harker White Clover

White Clover is a line which should be watched for it has all the qualities which have made other Wright designs popular. Off to a slow start with collectors, probably because so little has been available, it is rare enough to present a challenge and the prices at this time are more reasonable than other lines.

All colors are favored, most collectors trying to add to the partial sets they find first. This is not a mix and match line and when seen, often is for sale as a "lot." That situation makes item pricing chancy, and the breakdown of lot prices may not be the best reflection of piece pricing.

I expect White Clover to increase in value for Russel Wright collectors who have achieved their goals in American Modern and Iroquois sets may want an example of Wright's patterns and White Clover is an excellent example of that work.

Golden Spice

Meadow Green

Coral Sand

Charcoal

Original White Clover advertisement.

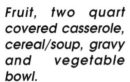

Fruit, two quart covered casserole, cereal/soup, gravy and vegetable bowl.

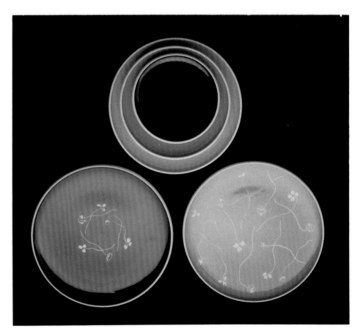

White Clover plates.

Top row: Divided vegetable dish and pitcher.

Bottom row; Vegetable bowl, fruit and cereal/soup.

Water pitcher, shakers, dinner plate and cup/saucer.

Brochure pages showing White Clover pattern and shape.

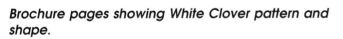

CUP AND SAUCER — CREAMER — COVERED RAMEKIN/SUGAR — CEREAL/SOUP

FRUIT DISH — COVERED VEGETABLE DISH — OPEN VEGETABLE DISH — COVERED CASSEROLE — GRAVY BOWL

BARBECUE PLATE — DINNER PLATE — SALAD PLATE — BREAD & BUTTER PLATE

CHOP PLATE — PLATTER — SALT AND PEPPER SHAKERS — COVERED PITCHER

White Clover shakers, clock, vegetable bowl, cup/saucer, cream, fruit bowl and covered sugar.

Harker showroom display.

The Understated Patterns of Knowles Esquire

Knowles Esquire, the shape and various patterns done on it were Wright's Cinderella line and while findings and discoveries made by collectors are surprising, it seems that the Knowles story is still unfolding and we have much to add to what we once considered complete.

In 1955, with the unfortunate White Clover behind him, Wright at once entered the dinnerware field with his Esquire line. Well aware that the pottery industry was in deep trouble with the flux of Japanese wares, most often available at prices which undercut our domestic prices, it seemed a bold gesture for Knowles as well as Wright. Here we see both the shape and the pattern with clear Oriental influence and we find a positive statement where before we had seen a suggestion. Wright's work in Asia had brought him into close contact with this eastern influence and heightened his interest in the clean spare lines, the efficiency and economy of detail as well as the restraint of work done in the Orient. Having long admired these qualities, he was now to use them with more frequency.

Correcting an error in a study such as this is difficult but it is necessary that readers of the dinnerware book will change the information shown there to include the new facts. The black and white picture shown there and here was mismarked and is not the Esquire shape. I had previously believed that the Knowles line, as it has been found was a redesign of this shape and that differences could be explained by that interpretation. It now seems clear that this understanding was wrong. This black and white pictured shape, while Wright's work, is not the Esquire shape. In this writing and in the future, we will refer to that shape as the "Wright shape."

Given that change, it remains true that shapes and patterns were advanced, rejected and replaced many times during the life of Esquire. Changes were made from the very first and patterns accepted were a few from the many that were offered. What resulted were naturalistic patterns, each on its own color. Grass on blue only,

Botanica on brown only, each on its own color.

In short order after Esquire was introduced, Sears and Montgomery Ward refused to carry the line at any price. It was simply too difficult to depict the decorations and glaze techniques in a catalog format. Their earlier interest had been important as Esquire was to have met a different market from the designer's earlier work. Club plans were investigated as possible outlets for the work and met with no interest. These marketing groups also depended on good photographic representation which could not be achieved with Esquire. The S&H Stamp company achieved the best photo representations but they had to take a price cut on roughly 1,000 sets to move it. Old selling techniques, proven workable with Wright's other lines did not help here and for a time both the pottery and the designer had different ideas about the problem. There were customer complaints about knife scratches. A glaze problem, Knowles said. Wright claimed that poor sales were the fault of sales people who did not actively promote it. Reductions in price, he was told, must be taken since distribution had broken down.

Challenged in every way, Wright offered new designs but Knowles, with overstock and few orders, replied that they had worn out any goodwill that Esquire had accrued and that if Esquire was to be successful, it would have to be an entirely new concept. Ready to do what he could to put life back into the line and to renew Knowles interest in it, Wright sent sketches of many new patterns. Each was carefully planned and suggested glaze colors accompanied each. The large number of experimental patterns made may have resulted in runs and there is the probability that unknown Knowles patterns exist in some of those not accepted. No alternate patterns were approved.

Knowles salesmen reported that while at first they sold the line easily, they found the retailer still had it on hand six to eight months later, called dead inventory. The pottery said it had not done better in direct sales than it had done with catalog sales. They told Wright that new changes would not help this troubled line and that they would be ill-advised to go ahead on any Esquire work. Wright had tried to avoid this consequence in any way he could but the pottery remained firm. The end was delayed for a time and Wright continued to approach the pottery with suggestions. A plain white high gloss glaze as well as a new tan called Fontaine and a plain blue named Mayfair were considered.

It all came to an end in 1962 and Wright found himself with two shape lines, a folder full of patterns, some rejected glaze formulas and no pottery company to bring it all together. Knowles, however, seemed to have taken on a benefit in reputation by virtue of having made a Russel Wright line. They claimed no responsibility in the matter and other potteries sympathized. That made Wright's situation more difficult.

Patterns known to exist include those done on a pastel glaze, a departure from Wright's earth-toned dinnerware. Beige, white, pink, yellow and blue, they were first done in a matte finish with an under-glaze rubber stamped pattern. The overglaze gold stamping included in the pattern was also used to backstamp the pieces. Look for items to be marked by the pattern name where size permits. They would include Seeds, on a yellow ground; Grass, broken stems on a blue base; Queen Anne's Lace on white; Snowflower on pink; Botanica on a beige base; and Solar on white. Be aware that these patterns were to have been put on only the colors listed, but all things are possible and a worker with a favored pattern may have put it on the color of his choice. These patterns are light and delicate, certainly they show the Oriental touch. Low profiled and hard to distinguish, they adapted well to the light body with traceries borrowed from the earth and sky on cool, serene colors. Antique White was architecturally simple, a classic for "modern purists," Fontaine and Mayfair only slightly less sophisticated. These undecorated versions dramatized the symmetry and airy quality of the shapes.

The generous size of this Knowles line adds to many different pieces. It is not a partial line, partially designed. Each piece was studied to obtain the double usage so important to Wright. The deep compote, while planned as a fruit bowl, could serve as a soup tureen, floral centerpiece, or salad bowl. The round serving bowl's cover made a nice hot plate. The sugar does double duty as a server for relishes or jam at the table, candy or cigarettes in the living room. In sets of four or more, they are portion-sized fruit bowls. The Esquire lids were adapted to many uses as were the Paden City lids. The fit is not good.

There are more chapters to this sad story, however. Items made on the Esquire shape as we describe it here, have been found with Knowles designs but the backstamp indicates that they were made by the International China Company in Alliance, Ohio. Wright's associates say this ware probably represents the remainders sold by Knowles after Wright's relations had broken off. The only findings have been in Grass and Botanica, but more are certain to be found.

There is even more to report. The "Wright shape" version of the Knowles work has been found back-stamped "Mary and Russel Wright/Sovereign Potteries." Glazed in a speckled pink or blue, this line is much different from other Wright lines but all thoughts and opinions on Sovereign Potteries were taken out of "hold" and re-examined. It had been known that Wright's sister had connections with this pottery in Canada and the files show a good amount of pottery correspondence between them. Still there was no mention of other lines and no more detail than would be expected under circumstances which showed his concern for his sister's welfare. There were financial discussions and suggestions that Wright was helpful. A considered judgment would suggest that Wright gave this Wright shape to his Canadian family to use and make of it what they could. Certainly that would account for its production and would explain his own lack of involvement. We know that he had earlier turned to Sovereign as a possible supplier for Country Garden and this may have been a way to use Esquire/Country Garden/The Wright Shape. Expect ANYTHING from this Sovereign work. It could incorporate even more aspects of Wright designs than we are aware of at the present. Think of it as a cover-all line and try to be open minded when pottery shopping. This Sovereign work is full of surprises, as the entire Knowles line seems to be.

In spite of the troubles surrounding the production of Esquire, much that is good about the line must be said. The problematic glazes, different from any of Wright's past work, were new to buyers and there was an understated elegance to the designs. Walter Dorwin Teague, respected designer in the mid-1950's borrowed some Esquire for a table setting he was displaying in spite of the fact that he also designed dinnerware. Wright's "company set" was Grass and in 1960, while the ware was still in production, he was not able to find replacements for it. My mail indicates that those who study design, who work in the arts, whose taste runs to "high style" are today's Esquire collectors. We do not find enough to satisfy all who would add this set to their collections and time and patience will be required in the search for this tasteful dinnerware. That it would not photograph well was the worst that could be said about it.

On Pricing Knowles Esquire

All Knowles is difficult to find. Not a popular line when it was made, it has a real position with Russel Wright collectors today and is becoming increasingly popular with new collectors. Each pattern in Knowles is on its own color, of course, and that usually results in the finding of partial sets. If Knowles is on your shopping list, buy it soon for it is one of the dinnerware lines that is increasing in value at a surprising rate. Grass is the pattern of choice. Both Solar and Botanica are seen less than are the other patterns. Antique White, Fontaine and Mayfair, all solid colors, are expected to become hard-to-find favorites. The teapot and the centerpiece are outstanding examples and are prized. The 16" platter, just found, can be considered the most rare of the items, at least for now. This line was short lived. It was not a large line from the beginning, and no approved redesign was done. There is not much Esquire around - but there may be some exciting prototypes, experimental pieces, even short runs. This is another line on which we will hope to hear from you.

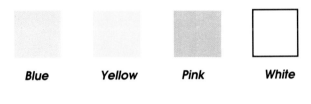

Blue   **Yellow**   **Pink**   **White**

Knowles "Wright shape."

Knowles Wright shape marked Mary and Russel Wright by Sovereign Potters.

Botanica platter.

Solar oval vegetable bowl.

Botanica platter, covered sugar, vegetable bowl, fruit dish marked International China Co.

Antique White shakers, pitcher, deep compote, plates, cup and saucer and covered sugar.

Queen Anne's Lace covered vegetable bowl.

Grass shakers and Snow-flower soup/cereal.

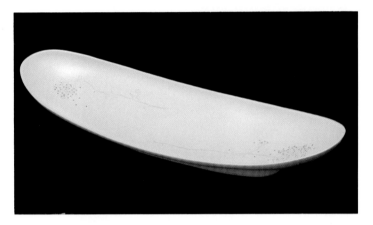

Queen Anne's Lace centerpiece bowl.

Seeds water pitcher.

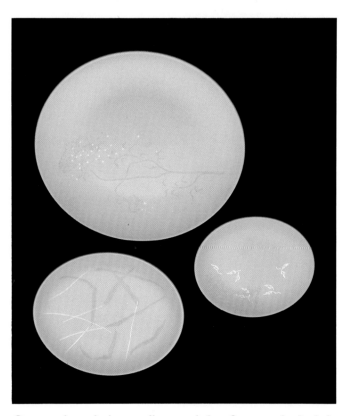

Queen Anne's Lace sugar, creamer and teapot.

Queen Anne's Lace dinner plate, Grass salad plate and Seeds bread and butter plate.

Solar divided vegetable bowl and tea-pot.

Snowflower tidbit server made from three dinner plates. This is an adaptation, not an original design.

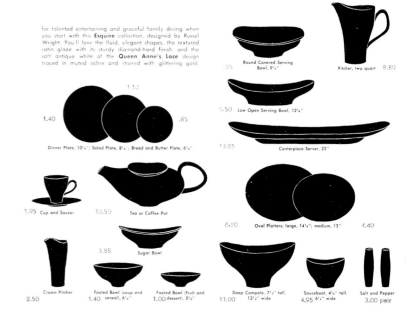

for talented entertaining and graceful family dining when you start with this **Esquire** collection, designed by Russel Wright. You'll love the fluid, elegant shapes, the textured satin glaze with its sturdy, diamond-hard finish, and the soft antique white of the **Queen Anne's Lace** design traced in muted ochre and starred with glittering gold.

Original brochure showing Esquire shapes.

Original brochures for Esquire's Grass, Seeds, Antique White, and Queen Anne's Lace.

Wright's Art Pottery
Bauer

Our narrative account of Wright's art pottery work begins and ends with the work done for the Bauer Company in Atlanta, Georgia. It was 1945 and the project was the first ceramic work done by Wright after his popular Steubenville American Modern line. The Wright/Raymor combination found itself courted from all directions with 27 companies having written to Raymor asking to develop a Russel Wright dinnerware line. American Modern had taken center stage and it was not surprising that Wright found Bauer very interested in working with him. Mary's Country Garden was in experimental stages there and the Wrights were no strangers to Bauer.

No small condition was that Raymor was "in place" to market this art pottery. Bauer did not wish to involve itself with that function, willing to leave business details to the marketing firm. Wright agreed to submit designs and Bauer would supervise, criticize and make final decisions on the 20 pieces which would comprise the line. Bauer's ceramic engineers and Wright's ceramic consultant were to work out production details. Wright was to design, and help with sales literature, advertising, promotion and assist with Raymor marketing. He was to retain ownership of the rejected items but he agreed that he would not place another art pottery line on the market nor would he cause another such a line to go into production for a year. Even that was extended to restrict him from art pottery design so long as Bauer's sales held at $150,000.00 annually. Bauer was not to make shapes similar to his nor could they use his glazes on other parts of their line without his consent. Given that, he was to be paid 2% royalty on those items. The 20 production items which he was to design would pay royalty fees of 4% if first quality, 2% on "off selection" seconds which were to be sold at a discount. Wright was free to examine Bauer's books at any time and was to receive a monthly statement of his account. Monthly payments of $6,000.00 were to be paid from July 1, 1945 and these were to continue as long as the line was sold. This payment schedule gave him returns while the line was being designed. Approved designs were to revert to Wright if the Bauer Company ever became insolvent.

The Wright signature was to be molded or stamped on the bottom and this was to present a problem. Wright had designed bases with deep ridges purposely put there as built-in flower frogs, securing stems and branches. Marking was difficult because of this.

Troubled times began at once in spite of these detailed contractual agreements and glaze trials seemed to be the cause of many Bauer/Wright problems. Doris Coutant, the dependable expert ceramist was in Atlanta for a year and ran over 1,000 glaze trials. Mail flew between Wright, Bauer and ceramist and still the glazes did not please those most concerned. Irving Richards from Raymor made a personal trip to help but came back with the news that Wright was too exacting, in the opinion of the pottery. This surprised the designer and his reaction was to deny that he was difficult to work with. To the contrary, he was willing to compromise his opinions and from time to time almost washed his hands of the whole affair, telling Coutant and the Bauer ceramist to use their own best judgment. More often than not, this was post-scripted with specific requirements. Bauer warned him repeatedly that the handmade look he was attempting with these glazes could not result in the uniformity and consistency they both required. Color variations would be certain to result and the pottery felt that most pieces, if not glazed differently, would be "off." These silica glazes as specified were unusual and they often produced surprising results. The combination of two glazes on the same item led to unpredictable outcomes and repetitive results were impossible to achieve. Herb Brusche, president of Bauer at the time told me that this line would have ruined their kilns in six months if work on it had continued. Approved colors were: Jonquil Yellow, Dirty Yellow, Lemon Yellow, Atlanta Brick (terra cotta), Cinnamon, Bronze, Gun Metal, Green, Potlach Green, Raymor Turquoise, Aqua, True Blue, Georgia Brown (a rich earth brown), Black, Rust, Bubble White, Figured White and Glossy White.

With these colors in combinations, a very large line would have resulted and had quality been uniform all parties would have been pleased. This was not to be. Glazes ran, bubbles of glaze burst. Drips and all sorts of imperfections made for little uniformity. Most of the production was of second quality.

The designs were sent to New York for showing in January 1946. Predictably, they met with little enthusiasm from the trade. In an art pottery market dominated by Roseville, Weller, Rookwood and other giants of the art pottery world, these new designs, however modern, were not appealing. Not one of Bauer's 600 accounts placed an order and reasons given were that they were too much of a departure, too much of an oddity, too modern. A few orders were received later and aggressive sales methods were put to use in an effort to salvage the line. The trade was told that ceramic departments in universities had been consulted to achieve the INTENDED textured pieces. It was said that some of these glazes had been seen before only on ancient Chinese ceramics. Explaining that some of the items were made of heavy clay, releases to the press said that Wright believed that the feeling of the weight of an earthen material made a more natural settting for plants and flowers. His inspiration, it was said, was from rocks since that is the natural habitat for growing plants. Colors were purposely subdued to allow the plants to show to the best advantage and soft and flowing lines allowed the light and shadow to appear in the flowers and plants. Items were advertised as individual "gallery

pieces." The claim seems not so extravagant today, but it seemed not true to buyers then.

Much thought, attention, and care went into this project and all parties were disappointed when sales results continued to be poor. Orders taken for the last six months of 1946 were for $43,000.00. With production stopped, sales out of inventory for the first six months of 1947 were just over $5,000.00. These were sales with no credits or returns.

To an observer, so many years later, it seems possible that much of the trouble with the line resulted from Bauer's agreement to pay Wright while items were being designed. It appears that Bauer may have been too eager to recover costs in order to pay royalties. Had they not offered these imperfect pieces for sales, had they taken their losses and waited for better results, the ware might have been better received. Wright had put many hours into this line and if we consider the short time between contract and the New York showing, we sense that Bauer may have rushed production and sales.

Twenty items glazed in combinations of all the possible colors adds to an overwhelming amount of work and we are not certain that all were sampled or run in each proposed combination. With such extensive work, some may actually have been tried and rejected in these combinations. It would seem that, in the frenzy of trials, what "worked" would have been a victory. We are able to list the items as were approved:

Catalog Number	Description	Main Glaze	Inside Glaze
#1A	Pillow Vase	Figured White	Aqua
		Jonquil Yellow	Georgia Brown
		Atlanta Brick	Rust
		Aqua	Georgia Brown

Slender and graceful for a few cut flowers. Especially suited to a narrow shelf of a bookcase. Shaped for easy arranging. Simple opening long and extremely narrow.

#2A	8½" Vase	Figured White	Figured White
		Jonquil Yellow	Jonquil Yellow
		Aqua	Georgia Brown
		Gun Metal	Gun Metal

Slender elegant vase for average length stems. Top cut at a slight angle so there is no harsh straight horizontal line to intrude on the natural grace of flowers or leaves.

#3A	5" tall vase, narrow top	Gun Metal	Gun Metal
		Figured White	Figured White
		Jonquil Yellow	Jonquil Yellow
		Atlanta Brick	Rust

Said to have been made especially for holding corsages after wearing. 5" high with a small narrow opening at the top and wide full base.

Catalog Number	Description	Main Glaze	Inside Glaze
#4	9" tall vase 24" around	Bubble White Jonquil Yellow Bronze Aqua Atlanta Brick	Georgia Brown Georgia Brown Bronze Georgia Brown Gun Metal

Large heavy earthen jug of irregular lines, almost primitve in shape. Designed to lend emphasis to large clusters of flowers. Resembled large pitcher with no handle. Top opening is comparatively small, cut off at right angle.

#5A	22" tall vase	Figured White Jonquil Yellow Georgia Brown Atlanta Brick	Georgia Brown Georgia Brown Georgia Brown Rust

Large oval vase designed to hold a crop of long stems. Wide base, narrow top. This is the floor vase.

#6A	10½" vase	Bubble White Jonquil Yellow Georgia Brown Atlanta Brick Aqua	Georgia Brown Georgia Brown Georgia Brown Gun Metal Georgia Brown

Tall table vase oval at top and bottom.

#7A	17" long 9½" wide	Figured White Jonquil Yellow Aqua Atlanta Brick Gun Metal	Figured White Bronze Bronze Glossy White Bubble White

Centerpiece bowl for flowers or fruit. Massive, long and shallow. Ideal for short stems offering a rock-like setting.

#8A	6½" long Ashtray	Figured White Figured White Jonquil Yellow Georgia Brown Aqua	Raymor Turquoise Bronze Bronze Raymor Turquoise Bronze

Off-center low ash bowl squeezed almost shut at one end.

#9A	24" long 4" wide	Figured White Jonquil Yellow Gun Metal Georgia Brown Atlanta Brick	Figured White Bronze Bubble White Georgia Brown Atlanta Brick

Mantelpiece bowl offering a garden setting for foliage on a narrow area. Solid, rock-like in appearance. Side walls are thick and heavy.

#10A - No details available

Catalog Number	Description	Main Glaze	Inside Glaze
#11A	Irregular large 13" bowl for centerpiece	Figured White Jonquil Yellow Gun Metal Aqua	Gun Metal Bronze Bubble White Bronze

Free flowing form approaching ceramic sculpture. Heavy clay with sides that flow up and curve down with rhythmic abandon. Said to be a vase in a new guise, departing from time-honored shapes.

#12A	4½" square flower pot	Figured White Atlanta Brick Jonquil Yellow Georgia Brown	Georgia Brown Rust Georgia Brown Georgia Brown

Small square flower pot. Often grouped in threes or more. Part of home furnishings for which no decorative item had been made.

#12B	7½" square flower pot	Georgia Brown Figured White Atlanta Brick Jonquil Yellow Georgia Brown	Georgia Brown Georgia Brown Rust Georgia Brown Georgia Brown

Larger version of #12A

#13A	7" tall flower pot	Figured White Jonquil Yellow Atlanta Brick	Georgia Brown Dirty Yellow Rust

Flower pot appears to be a one-piece pot but combines the saucer in such a way that an effect of unity results. Dirt which seeped to saucer from watering would go into unseen cavity. Saucer is integral part of the shape separated by a groove from the upper portion which has the usual hole for drainage.

#14A	No details except that pairs were sold	Georgia Brown Atlanta Brick Aqua Jonquil Yellow Figured White Bubble White	

#15A	Long centerpiece bowl	Figured White Jonquil Yellow Atlanta Brick	Figured White Jonquil Yellow Atlanta Brick

Said to be a space saver. Centerpiece bowl with candleholder ends. A solid slab of clay with overlapping ends which form holders for candles. Centerpiece open for fruit or flowers and greens.

#16A	7½" tall vase	Bubble White Jonquil Yellow Atlanta Brick Aqua Bronze	Georgia Brown Jonquil Yellow Gun Metal Georgia Brown Bubble White

Large planter for growing plants. Soft curving of contour with full and wide proportions designed to hold spreading roots.

Catalog Number	Description	Main Glaze	Inside Glaze
#17A	11" long low bowl	Gun Metal	Bubble White
		Figured White	Bronze
		Jonquil Yellow	Bronze
		Aqua	Bronze
		Atlanta Brick	Gun Metal

Description is of a hard boiled egg cut in half with yolk lifted out. Designed to hold bulbs but with thick walls, makes a sturdy masculine ashtray.

#18A	12" tall oval vase	Bubble White	Aqua
		Jonquil Yellow	Jonquil Yellow
		Aqua	Bronze

Off center oval vase in style that would fit all purposes and all decorating schemes.

#19A	8½" long low bowl	Figured White	Bronze
		Jonquil Yellow	Bronze
		Aqua	Bronze
		Atlanta Brick	Gun Metal
		Georgia Brown	Raymor Turquoise

This bulb bowl is not oval but round and deep. Its usage would include that of an ashtray.

#20A	20" square vase	Bubble White	Georgia Brown
		Georgia Brown	Georgia Brown
		Jonquil Yellow	Jonquil Yellow
		Aqua	Georgia Brown
		Atlanta Brick	Gun Metal

A massive container for leaves, branches, evergreens or berries. Intended for heavy sprays. Note that Black, a known color is not listed as a base color.

Wright was not to return to the world of art pottery, having exhausted himself, his staff, Raymor and Bauer. Hastily assembled, these Bauer pieces discouraged all who were associated with them. Wright and Bauer had lost patience with each other and themselves, and the many experiments to achieve all of the above combinations had worn out any goodwill which the parties might have enjoyed. New collectors, looking at the above listing may believe that there is a good bit of this Bauer work to be found, but that is not the case. Each piece is a personal triumph for a collector. Those who search for Bauer, as a rule, consider the imperfect pieces to be acceptable. Production damage makes the item no less valuable since most pieces are "rough." Those which we find are considered to be the "gallery pieces" which Wright intended them to be.

On Pricing Bauer Art Pottery

Unusual colors add to Bauer values. White and bronze is the common color combination. Black is more difficult to find as is a coral which we believe to be Atlanta Brick. The Greens, Blues, Rust and Cinnamon have not been found and we do not have a clear distinction between Atlanta Brick and Georgia Brown. Chartreuse is a yellow variant. It is probable that not all of these combinations were actually run so any amount of them would be rare. What we have found has become scarce as they have become parts of art pottery collections, Bauer collections and Russel Wright collections. With three groups searching for Bauer, it is one of the most collectible of Wright's designs. This line never achieved permanency and we may expect variances in the combinations listed here.

The following four photographs are from the collection of B.J. Smith and Jack Brooks. Photographs by Robert Bozarth.

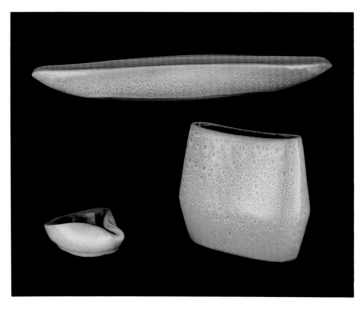

#9 bowl, #8 ashtray, #1 pillow vase.

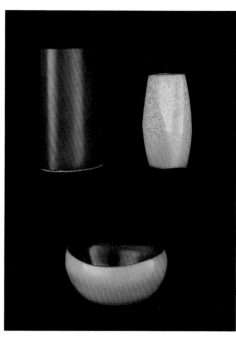

#6 vase, #2 vase, #19 bulb bowl.

#3 corsage vase, #18 oval vase, #12 flower pot.

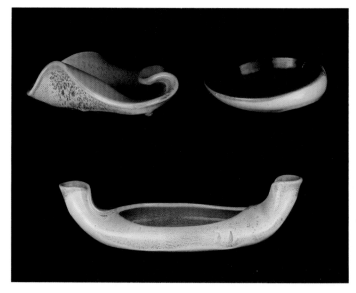

#11 centerpiece bowl, #17 bowl, #15 candleholder bowl.

The following six photographs are from the collections of Jose Machado, Alvin Schell and Ann Wright. Ann's photos include the two unidentified/unlisted items. The #12 flower pot is from the collection of William Strauss.

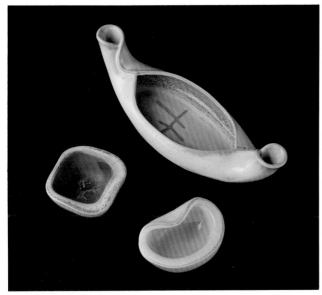

#15 Candleholder bowl, unidentified item, #8 ashtray.

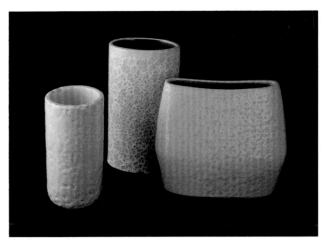

#6 oval vase, unidentified item, #1 pillow vase.

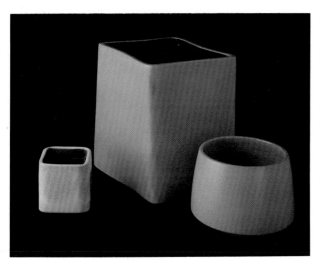

#13 flower pot, #12B flower pot, #12A flower pot.

#2 vases, #17 bowl, #8 ashtray.

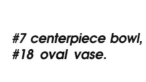

#4 jug vase, #2 vase, #3 corsage vase.

#7 centerpiece bowl, #18 oval vase.

More On Cutlery

Sorting out our information, our concepts and our misconceptions of Russel Wright cutlery may be difficult for we do have some new information, some new ways of considering old information and some new finds. All add substantially to what we have known about this popular segment of Russel Wright's work.

When we first studied Wright's Hull stainless steel, we were told that only one line of stainless was made and that was the line which was the Highlight line (also called American Modern Stainless by collectors.) We must be aware, however, that there is another name for it. Wright called it Pinch - at least in his files. No other set of stainless specifically designed to accompany American Modern exists. The Highlight line listing included: teaspoon, fork, salad fork, ice tea spoon, knife, berry spoon, sugar shell, soup spoon, oyster fork, butter spreader, table spoon, cold meat fork and gravy ladle. Not all items have been found but the listing should be accurate. It remains highly sought-after, highly prized.

New facts, however, have shown that Wright's Pinch was only one of several lines which collectors may find. In 1986 a different stainless pattern, made by Hull and signed by Wright was found. Shortly after, a third pattern surfaced and where we had one pattern, we suddenly had several. It was no surprise, then, to find these new lines documented in Wright's personal files. This proved identity that could not be explained by some of Wright's associates and questions remained. Certainly we now had proof of design, proof of sampling at least, and we had names. Details have come to us in some confused information in the files but it now seems certain that Lily and Threads, as they were called, involved both National Silver and Hull Cutlery.

The story of Wright's association with Hull now appears to have started earlier than we first supposed. As far back as 1951 correspondence tells us that Wright and Hull were having difficulty in their relationship, and at that early date it covered the Pinch set which would not be introduced for another two years. Hull, with a history of manufacturing and labor troubles, had at that time, a subcontractor who wanted a separate contract from the one Wright had made with Hull. Relations broke off over this, and designs reverted to Wright. In 1952

Wright again agreed to work with Hull on the design providing royalties were paid as defined and items produced in six months. Correspondence fired back said they could not find material for their work and later that year Wright again cancelled their exclusivity, undertaking the sale of the design to others, including National Silver. Hull remained anxious to resume and once more an agreement was formed but they remained slow with royalty payments. Back and forth correspondence always reflected Wright's displeasure over the lack of uniformity in their business dealings and the fact that they could not be depended upon to pay royalites when due. He wrote: "We have bent over backwards in a manner not at all in keeping with the standards of our profession and our status in the field of industrial design to an extent that we have never gone with another client and at fees too low in signing an agreement to help you. May we please hear from you?" Hull with their own labor troubles, had moved their operation to Japan and Wright went so far as to as to register his design with the Japanese Patent Office in an effort to avoid further problems. But once again, it was necessary to take back the designs. Policing the Hull account became increasingly difficult. The on-again off-again arrangements did not please Wright but he seemed to return to Hull for lack of another manufacturer. Often unable to do the work they were given, they asked for other designs - a wood handled or plastic handled design. Those requests never brought response and it would seem that their relationship was as complicated as Wright could endure. He believed it to be important to find another supplier as quickly as possible.

National Silver, was approached in 1954 and they were to do extensive work with Wright. The sterling silver set pictured here is the prototype set, recently made and sold in silverplate by the Metropolitan Museum in New York. This flatware is a wonderful set, carefully executed and more modern than any flatware made in this country at that time. National became as troubled as Hull, however, and no real work was done in spite of extensive planning. The records show that this line called for eight models of each piece to include: tea spoon, dinner fork, knife, soup spoon, salad fork, oyster fork, butter spreader, berry spoon, gravy ladle, pastry server, coffee spoon, ice tea spoon, table spoon, cold meat fork, sugar shell, butter knife, bouillon spoon, salad serving fork and spoon. Though not really produced, it seems important to list these items since the number of models is larger than we had known. The silver flatware made for and sold by The Metropolitan Museum in New York City is of 1980's production, but it may be considered authentic original since the Wright design was sampled in Sterling and never produced. Collectors who cannot find Highlight should consider this wonderful Metropolitan silverplate as an option.

A sterling silver tea set is known to have been sampled but we have seen only one of these.

Wright hoped that National Silver would produce Lily and Threads as well as Pinch in stainless steel. Unfortunately for all concerned, National was not able to go ahead with any of his work and with no other manufacturer at hand, he was forced to abandon his silverplate line and return Lily, Threads and Pinch to Hull. Other firms had not been interested. Our facts leave off there, but it is certain that not much production was done on any of the lines. Hull had never been able to make Pinch in the amounts Wright wanted and Lily and Threads stretched their troubled production to the point where these lines were sampled, not produced beyond amounts which allowed it to be presented to the trade.

This Highlight line, the Pinch line, is not a severe line, but is an example of contemporary design suited to accompany Wright's not severe Highlight dinnerware. It is softly contoured with a soft brushed satin finish. Tarnish proof, it offered a carefree alternative to silver. The knives show the pinch more than do the other items. Considering it a bit lightweight, users were told that it was tapered in thickness for better balance. Carrying a lifetime guarantee of service, it was sold as open stock. The flatware was accompanied by a storage chest with a reversible unit which became a cocktail tray.

It is not surprising that this stainless steel joined other Wright award winners and the Museum of Modern Art singled it out at once for its Good Design Award. Macy's in New York premiered the line and it won immediate approval by the public. A six-piece set sold for $6.95 and the chest was $7.95.

The backstamp on these pieces may be found with two different marks, neither of which should make you suspicious. That made in America has the Wright signature, the words "Hull Stainless" and a patent number. Those made in Japan after Hull moved its operation there are the same product exactly but the mark bears the word "Japan." Collectors make no distinction where desirability is concerned. They are used interchangeably as they are identical. Highlight knives are still the rare finds of this very rare line. It is explained that hollow handled knives were in fashion in the 1950's and stainless buyers did not like Highlight's solid handles. Finding the "open stock" option useful, they bought other knives.

Collectors today find these knife-less sets, often in combination with the knife alternative still in place. Wright would have, without a doubt, redesigned these knives if working with Hull had been easier. Redesign and market research were not done, for good reasons, and we have little of the original work today.

Wright's stainless steel came on the market when it was dominated by the Scandanavians and he found his work in direct competition with many of their lines. Similarities exist, but it was the "new look" of the day, another departure from the traditional. Seen as an example of design styles developing, it bears a resemblance, of course, but its softer statement sets it apart from the bulky Scandanavian influence.

There remains the possibility that some other work which would have included plastic handled stainless will be found to be part of the work done for and by The Englishtown Cutlery Company in the time frame of 1947-49. The firm was on shaky ground, having just survived a fire, but they agreed to do two sets of four- to seven-piece place settings in stainless or stainless with plastic handles. Wright was wary because of his Hull experiences and he stipulated that while they had exclusive services for these sets, they were bound to pay him $5,500.00 if they did not produce in 11 months. They could use his name but if they became insolvent, they could not sell the use of this name. In a short time the firm asked for a six month extension on the plastic handled items. That granted, they tried and rejected several patterns, finally agreeing to do two. They were not able to do so, the matter went to arbitration and Wright was given a cash settlement. Our loss, of course, but some findings may exist.

Some few early examples of pearl handled cutlery would include a place setting of a knife, fork, spoon, butter knife and a soup spoon. This was part of an early pearl line which included other accessory items as well. When this work was done, Wright's records were very unsophisticated and while we are aware of the line, we can be sure that not much was made, not much will be found. We would do well, though, to examine any interesting pearlized items which we find.

The nature of the Wright files makes reproduction less than desirable for printing purposes, therefore, we cannot picture Lily here for you.

The story of cutlery work done by Wright is plagued by manufacturers plagued with internal problems. Never sure of production, always in arrears with royalties, the firms Wright chose to do this work are at the heart of the little stainless steel produced with Wright's approval. Pieces of it represent some of the most difficult to find items which Wright designed. They are rare and finding them requires extreme patience for they have usually been found in boxes of stainless, not yet a collectible. Separating the Wright from the wrong calls for a good amount of patience and effort. Pieces will be expensive if you buy them from someone who recognizes the Russel Wright name. They may be almost free if you find them in a box at a sale down the block. I always look. A good example is the collector from Oklahoma who found the knives, recognized the signature and thought they might be "good." She put them aside but in a spurt of generosity, tossed them in a box of things to be sent to flood victims. There are not many such stories. There is not nearly enough to please collectors.

Threads - John Hull Cutlery.

Highlight/Pinch stainless steel - slotted spoon, cake lifter, serving spoon, dinner knife, butter knife, dinner fork, salad fork, soup spoon, teaspoon, ice tea spoon.

Pearl handled cutlery. Part of an early Pearl line done by Russel Wright Accessory Company.

National Silver Sterling Flatware. Recently produced in silverplate and sold at the Metropolitan Museum in New York City.

The World Of Plastics

Many collectors have grown up in a world which considered synthetics as disposable products. While having served a real and important function in our lives, their use has suggested "second best" and they are often considered to be inferior.

When these products first came to us, however, they were thought to be imitative miracles which science and industry had invented. We were certain that these new products would change our lives, adding ease and affordability in ways we could not know. Collectibility rests somewhere between these divergent poles. There are those who see no value in these plastic products and claim an allegiance to those things "natural." On the other hand, (not the other extreme), there are those who look at the short time these materials were used in home furnishings products, look at the small likelihood that they will be so used in the future and predict that plastics will take on a collectible life of their own, if, indeed, they have not done so already. Some collect avidly, some will "wait and see," but many of those who collect Russel Wright designs will find a place for a "picnic set," at least.

Wright was quick to see the possibilities which these new materials presented. Having already espoused the creed of economy in time and materials, he seemed to know intuitively that these new products would change our world in yet another way, leaving us with more leisure. Anxious to find his place on the bandwagon, he turned to the American Cyanide Company in New York which was testing a synthetic product they had patented and named Melamine.

This new material fascinated Wright who submitted an outline of a cost plus basis for design work to American Cyanide on a test group of institutional plastic dinnerware. The agreement stated that AC would pay costs and direct, criticize and instruct him in the use of their material on his designs but all the right, titles and possession of designs were to be his and would remain with him if they or any other firm became interested in producing it. Any purchaser would be bound to make arrangements with him in the use of it and he would be paid the price of each designed item ($800.00) plus a royalty of 2% of gross billings. The commissioned set which Wright engaged AC to produce from Melamine was named Meladur.

In the planning stages the manufacturer was to contribute their resources to aid in the search for a manufacturer to produce this pilot set. Off to a slow start, the potential of the new material was not realized immediately and four years later American Cyanide asked Wright to terminate their agreement and to agree to a lapse of options. He countered that the agreement stood and if they desired to have it produced, they were bound to buy the design and pay royalty on it. They disclaimed by refusing to buy the designs themselves and telling him that they did not intend to use the ware themselves, having only been interested in it as an experimental project. They felt they had a legal position in the matter since the patent and experimentation work was theirs but Wright was adamant in his claims to ownership of the set. The matter was turned over to arbitration and American Cyanide was required to relinquish all rights to the newly named Meladur.

Cross pollination had occurred in the dinnerware industry and it would never be quite the same. Stoneware, earthenware, china, porcelain, many types of materials had been used before but in the mid-century mark of the twentieth century, a new concept was added.

This prototype set, Meladur was the first step in the multi-million dollar development to which Wright's designs were to become so important. All that followed was based on this one step and the claims which Wright made on it and for it. His ownership of the designed set had been established by the courts and by 1951 he was in a position to deal with General American Transportation's Plastic Dinnerware Division in the production of a synthetic dinnerware. The firm was restricted to using his name only with his approval and he was to be allowed to review that use as he felt it was needed. He was to approve all of their advertising. With these restrictions, his standard contract applied. In return, they were to produce a "furnished set." The contract signed, General moved at once to produce and market Melmac dinnerware. It is difficult to understand that Wright, for reasons of his own, soon lost interest in the project. In those early days of synthetics, the dinnerware concept was confined to institutional use and it may be that Wright recognized imperfections in the application of this material and realized that the profit-oriented restaurant ware industry would not long be held captive to a material which would be flawed as Melmac was.

In 1953 Wright relinquished, granted and sold to General all rights and titles. They were to have complete ownership of the designs and modifications in return for a lump sum payment fof $15,000.00. General had the absolute right to produce, use and sell. They could add to the line or modify it in any way they chose but when the existing stock was sold, they could no longer use his name. Further specified was that if they sold the rights to this line that buyer was also prohibited from the use of Wright's name. As you find Meladur you will find some with the signature and some without. The signed pieces were made before Wright sold to General and the unsigned items reflect the change of ownership. Additions which General made before Wright sold to General and the unsigned items reflect the change of ownership. Additions which General made to the set were not signed. Bound by this agreement, Meladur was made in pink, mint green, yellow and blue. It was said to be one-third lighter in weight than ordinary restaurant ware and that it had been engineered with qualities which would not allow it to slide even when the saucer was tilted at a 70 degree angle. It could be used for warming and would outlast traditional dinnerware four to one. Our list of items made in the Meladur line remains, for the most part, as we found it in the dinnerware book, but we must be aware that many more items were considered at all stages of its developement. There may be some few examples of those which were prototyped or sampled. Small items, said to have been considered but not produced would have included a coffee cup cover, 7 oz. mug, egg cup, small platter and footed drinking glasses. All things are possible and rejected samples may be waiting to be discovered.

In just two years, then, America had learned that it could not function without this new material and mold makers were rushing to use Melmac in their own lines. Wright, predictably, had a new line waiting in the wings. Residential, produced by Northern Industrial Chemical Company was Wright's most important contribution to this new industry, a full dinnerware line intended for home use. By 1957, it was the best house-to-house selling dinnerware in the country with sales of $4,000,000.00. Consumer's Union had tested it and while they did not like the cups, they gave it a high rating because of its 10 year guarantee against breakage. Pasteboard boxes

holding one place setting suggested open-stock and gift-giving. In both 1953 and 1954 The Museum of Modern Art had given Residential its Good Design Award. With so much success, it is difficult to believe that Wright was not happy, but the fact remains. His royalties, in spite of the sales volume, were not enough, he complained. He felt Residential had not been promoted aggressively and that Northern's sales efforts had been lax. Northern responded by saying that if these complaints were to continue, they would discontinue the Residential line and replace it with another Melmac line done by a different designer. Wright responded that if they dared that action, he would bring suit and claim royalties on any line they produced. They felt the line to be imitative of his Sterling line and that their restaurant sales were hurting because of that. They claimed that it was not their intent that he should design pieces for them which would meet his artistic standards irrespective of the consequences.

Residential performed so well in the marketplace it brought harmony to the situation and it seemed best for both parties to continue with what was working. A spirit of cooperation was restored, but Wright, still in pursuit of better royalties obtained the services of Home Decorating Service to distribute a variant of Residential and added a new line, Flair, in 1959. The wonder material had a life of its own. The files indicate that Northern approached Wright as late as 1963 but no new line of dinnerware resulted.

Residential remains a different product than other synthetic lines popular in the 1950's largely because the designer was never satisfied with the obvious. He aspired to difference and variance. To design an amorphous dinnerware from this new material was a challenge Wright could not resist in spite of the negative qualities becoming more and more obvious. It did loose sheen with use, knife marks did mar surfaces, coffee did stain and with scratched surfaces, sanitary considerations were questionable. None of these were considered obstacles, though, when the country first embraced these new dishes. Those objections would come later.

Residential, with a great deal of experimentation, achieved a body with a cloud-like speckled effect. Two colors overlapped, leaving the base coat showing through unclouded in some areas. No other Melmac of which we are aware was imitative of this process. Items in the line were redesigned as needs indicated. Tumblers, not an original item, were soon added as buyers used sugar bowls for drinking. Items were added as customers asked for them. Many items did double duty as would be expected in a casual line with different versions of the same item becoming standard.

Original colors were Sea Mist, Grey and Lemon Ice, Black Velvet (black with a scattering of aluminum dust) and Copper Penny (brown treated with copper dust). White, Light Blue and Salmon (an orange red) followed. The colors added to a good selection but we must again remind ourselves that not all retailers were bound to sell all colors and regional distribution may be the reason for shortages now. Certainly the designer gave the line his whole attention, never relegating it to a second quality status. In spite of his dissatisfaction with the business matters attendant upon it, he was aware that synthetic dinnerware was here to stay - at least for a time, and he knew that he must work with this new material. It appears that he hoped to improve the industry by improving the product.

Widely advertised, widely distributed, Residential is found more easily than other of Wright's plastic lines. It found itself however, in direct competition with other plastic lines done by some of the most popular designers of the day. Belle Kogan and George Nelson both worked with the new material as did others. None, however, accomplished the amorphous shapes which Wright achieved.

Made on the residential shape and in the same items, the Home Decorators version differed in that it was not clouded but opaque. It was available in White, Blue (turquoise), Salmon and Pink. Patterned Melmac had been problematic from the first but Home Decorator's patterns used a color overlay process with naturalistic themes treated differently on each piece, adding to its informality and interest. It dates from 1954.

The Flair line, also patterned, appeared in 1959. It was made on a different shape and with qualities that made it distinctly different. It possessed a light, fragile body, almost translucent with several design treatments. Golden Bouquet featured puffs of white on golden stems. Spring Garden was blossoms of pink and blue on green stems. Ming Lace was made of actual leaves of the Jade Orchid Tree imported from China, cleaned, tinted and permanently molded into the body. Woodland Rose suggested a more formal design, with pink roses and green leaves on eggshell background. Golden Bouquet was white puffs on golden stems, an eggshell floral pattern. Arabesque was a lively swirl pattern, formal in concept, in two tones of gold or gold and turquoise on eggshell. Each piece of these patterns borrowed a slightly different aspect of the design, a leaf on a saucer, a bud on a cup, a plate with a full design. All added interest to Flair and it deserves the praise which collectors have for it. It is an example of what Melmac could have been and wasn't.

Fortiflex, an altogether different synthetic material, was used in a dinnerware group designed for the Ideal Toy Company. Fortiflex was not waxy, but soft, not imitative of pottery but less rigid and firm than his other synthetic lines. Again Wright had rushed ahead of others with this different product made in 1957. He hoped buyers would find it competive with ceramic for he proposed that this go from the refrigerator to table with no stop to transfer contents into a ceramic piece. Bowls were designed to fit frozen food packaging and thawing in the serving bowl was a new feature. The concept of a refrigerator to table product was one already promoted by other manufacturers but Ideal and Wright hoped the special design and the prestige value of Wright's name would influence buyers to "trade up."

Both the designer and the manufacturer were quick to point out how Fortiflex differed from all that had come before. It possessed a quality of design, a newness of material. It stacked neatly and it was easy to care for but, in addition, this new ware was "freezer proof" with snap covers and ridges to avoid spillage. Official names which pleased the designer and delighted the collector were Mint, Carnation, Snow, Blue Mist, Shrimp and Citron. Little has come to us as collectors probably because its claims did not meet the designer's expectations. Flimsy, pieces were hard to handle and not really attractive. It faced stiff competition and found no real place for itself on the market. It was not as elegant as had been intended. It won no awards and was soon discontinued. It appeared that finally buyers had found flaws in this once-promising material. Though few of these Ideal items are found, we do have a new piece listing which indicates that a wider variety should exist. Predictably, they will be hard to find. Yesterday's marketing failures are today's rarities.

An altogether different story is the Ideal Toy Company's plastic line of toy doll dishes which were exact copies of the American Modern dinnerware line. Made from a harder material than Fortiflex, this toy line was an instant winner with junior cooks. First offered in the Sears 1959 Christmas catalog "Just like the Russel Wright set Mommy has," these sets could be bought in service for four for $3.76. Silver and crystal (clear plastic) were not Wright designs but the dishes themselves were accurately scaled, exact miniatures of the Steubenville pieces. Two years later one could choose from a serving for four or for six but the colors were "off" from those they replaced and from the Steubenville colors. They appear again in 1961 and in 1964 but no others followed. Collectors of all ages are interested in these wonderful tiny dishes but most prefer the original colored ones.

We should add Mallory and Randall to our list of manufacturers of plastic materials. With no examples but with interesting detail, the files mention Thermo cups and tumblers with metallic accents - gold spangles, diamond dust, gold threads and Chinese characters. Some of these should be among the 1950's things which are just now being rediscovered. Probably no signature will be found, however.

Wright added interest and integrity to the field of synthetics and the fact that his designs have become the first which collectors have sought out may be a temporary situation. Bakelite and celluloid may have to move over to make room for Melmac.

On Pricing Russel Wright Plastics

Our 1985 truism still holds. Fewer people want these plastic dinnerware lines, but those who do are are willing to pay the prices listed here. Their numbers, however, are increasing. Plastic dinnerware is still a new collectible and of all that is sought, this Wright plastic is the most desirable.

Condition is very important with these dishes. They do scratch, they do stain and they could even be unsanitary. To attract the high prices listed in the price guide, they should be in almost unused condition. If abused, they are worth little as a set, only a bit more if a collector wants a color example. Meladur remains much as we left it in 1985. Residential, Home Decorator and Flair are more popular. In the Residential line you should think of Copper Penny and Black Velvet as higher than prices listed. All Flair should also be at the high end of the scale. Home decorator and the original Residential colors should reflect a lower value. Ideal Adult Kitchen Ware is the surprise of the plastic line. Its price increases are difficult to explain but all of those who helped with pricing reported the same advances.

The children's toy American Modern dishes remain popular. For many reasons, these add interest to a collection of American Modern and many of those dinnerware collectors want the toy dishes. Often they come to us as pieces, not as sets, but collectors buy them one piece at a time and seem to care little for the increase in pricing. Boxed sets, any of them, are to be prized.

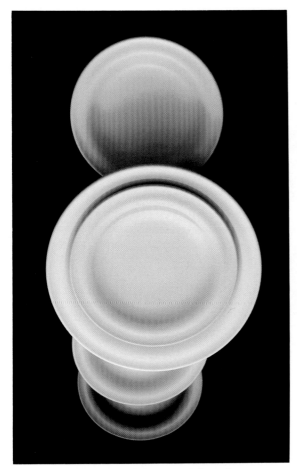

Meladur plates and bowls.

Meladur dinner plate, salad plate, soup bowl, and cup and saucer.

Residential platters, dinner plate, salad plate, bread and butter plate.

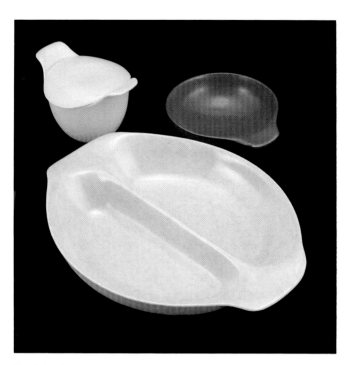

Residential sugar, soup and divided vegetable bowl.

Residential cream, covered vegetable bowl and covered onion soup.

Residential tumbler shapes.

Residential Black Velvet cup and saucer, vegetable bowl, soup, soup on saucer, divided vegetable and dinner plate.

Late Residential items made after Wright's contract had expired. Cup and saucer, sugar/tumbler, tumbler, redesigned sugar.

Set of Residential in original packaging.

Advertisement for Residential.

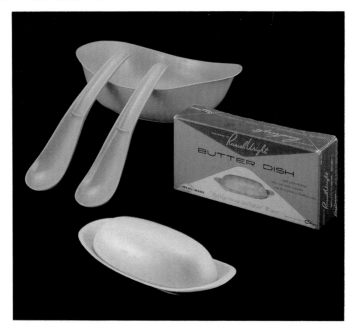

Ideal salad bowl and servers and butter dish with original box.

Ideal Fortiflex.

Flair solid color. Covered sugar, platter, dinner plate and cream.

Flair solid color. Fruit, oval vegetable bowl and cup/ saucer.

Flair Ming Lace.

Flair Golden Bouquet.

Flair Arabesque.

The following are original brochures showing the Flair patterns of Ming Lace, Golden Bouquet, Arabesque, Woodland Rose, and Spring Garden. The last photo shows an open brochure illustrating the Flair shapes.

The next three photographs are Home Decorator's patterns.

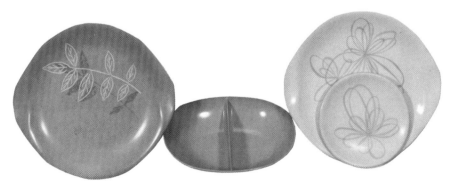

Home Decorator's plate, children's Ideal Toy American Modern plastic dinnerware.

Ideal Toy Children's American Modern plastic dishes. "Off color" set.

Glass To Match

The Sherry pitcher pictured below is representative of the small amount of glass made under the early Russel Wright Associates label. Unmarked, these early glass pieces are not easy to identify but they are typical of Wright's clear preference for combining two or more different materials in the same object, and by so doing, achieving surface ornamentation.

Our real study of the glass done by Wright begins in 1945. Century Metalcraft, in that year asked for a group of glass accessory items. Reasons are still unclear as to why they did not produce, but by 1947 the contract had been sold to American Crystal who was to take over all the production of this line. It was to have been the companion line to American Modern dinnerware. With stickers gone, we are left wondering if either of these glass houses ever produced a Russel Wright line. We can be sure that some was prototyped, however, since we have a proposed listing from American Crystal as well as a publicity picture and a finding on the salad fork and spoon, it is safe to assume that some production resulted. Listed items were a punch set, tumblers in three sizes (juice, water, zombie), centerpiece bowl, salad plate, cup and saucer, cheese board, salad servers, tray and coasters.

During the same time span Raymor approved a smaller accessory line to be made by the Appleman Bent Glass Company. This line also was to complement American Modern. The nature of bent glass limits the number of items which could have been made but even with those limitations, a generous proposed list was made. It was found to be expensive to produce and, in spite of many trials, it is believed little resulted. A textured glass, seeded, it has properties similar to the Paden City Glassware. The process used was complicated one using a powdered colored glass and applying it to a clear or "flesh" colored body. This was approved, but a swirled pattern as well as a silver mirror pattern were rejected. Various colors, unlike those which Wright usually worked were tried and you may find some in Apricot, Amethyst or Green as well as the "flesh" color. Frostings to the point of milk glass would have resulted from suspending particles of powered glass in the clear body. Possible items: relish rosette, 6" plate, chop plate, highball tray, dinner plate, cocktail tray, ashtray, bread tray, 18" boat shaped bowl, double jelly dish, olive relish dish, candleholders and salad plates. A bent glass warming tray, pictured later in this chapter was made by Appleman and is signed by them. It was identified by a collector who felt it might be Wright's work because of the blonde wood handles. That it was bent glass meant that if it were a Wright design, it should have been made by Appleman. Finding that it was marked with their mark, he had located what would have been lost without the sleuthing necessary on many of these unmarked Wright designs. This is an electrical piece and may have been stickered. That it was part of a larger group means that more may be found. Look for wood, rattan, reed, cork or other natural materials in combination with the bent glass.

Our understanding of the work to have been done by Fostoria is explained by the "empty contract" concept. David Dalzell, president of Fostoria told me in 1980 that their work with Wright would have been of a textured glass type, but Fostoria was unsatisfied with the results, considered it to be unsanitary and produced none. I, at the time, let the matter rest there, telling myself that Wright had gone down the road to Paden City Glass for the textured glass that was to combine with pottery to form the Highlight line. That was where we left this sad story when we spoke of it last. Since then, my mail has brought me word that at least one collector, seriously researching, found his way into Fostoria's morgue and found there samples, perhaps prototypes of work which Fostoria would have done. With good fortune, they are in the collection of the Huntington Museum in Huntington, West Virginia where we all may see it. More examples of this seeded glass may exist for in his search for that sort of glass production, Wright contacted various glass houses. A few pieces, experimental, we believe, are in Ann Wright's personal collection and I can report that while it is textured, it is less granular than Paden City Snow Glass and the surface is less even. Having seen Snow Glass, we are not likely to confuse the two. A proposed listing would have included: small dessert plates, a cup and saucer, small bowl, low bowls of various sizes and tumblers - 12 oz., 9 oz., and 5 oz., as well as a 4 oz. cocktail and a 6½ oz. Old Fashioned. All were to have had sham bottoms in much the same styles as Wright turned to later with the unproduced Theme Flormal line. The cup had the handle we have come to describe as the pony tail handle. Rutgers University did the glass experiments for this line and the result was a dense, irregular glass to have been made in colors as well as white. None was made commercially. They also tested a bowl described as opaline by them, "alabaster" by others. At least one of these exists. From first to what now appears to be the last, this Fostoria story had taught us much about experimental pieces, prototypes and contracts.

Our information on the Old Morgantown glass made to complement American Modern remains, for the most part, as we knew it in 1985. Made in 1951, this handmade glass included tumblers in three sizes - a 5" ice tea, 13 oz.; 4½" water, 10 oz.; and 4" juice, 7 oz. Five stemmed items included a 4" goblet, 10 oz.; 2½" sherbel, 5 oz.; 2½" cocktail, 3 oz; 3" wine, 4 oz.; and 2" cordial, 2 oz. The dessert dish is a 2" bowl. Shortly after production began, additions were made to include a 7" Pilsner, a chilling bowl 3" tall, 5½" wide, 12 oz. (pictured later in this chapter), and a Double Old Fashioned shown in the sales brochure reprint. Confusion still surrounds the separation of the wine and the cocktail for there is very little difference in their sizes. Seen together, the wine is slightly larger, seen apart, it is hard to tell the difference. Measurements here are approximate since handmade glassware is subject to minor differences. You will find more uniformity with this line, however, in this line than in Wright's Imperial line.

Made in colors suited to the American Modern palette, Coral, Seafoam, Chartreuse, Smoke and Clear Crystal, these lightly colored, delicately shaped glass items are very wonderful. Often they come our way as surprises for most have lost their identifying stickers. Too often they are not recognized. Color is our best guide as shapes are not distinctive. Be cautious with this line, especially with the tumblers. They are not easily separated from look-alikes and are found less often than the stems. In 1950 Wright wrote to Morgantown suggesting that he design new pieces to accessorize American Modern. He proposed salad plates, candy dish, fruit bowls, ashtrays and a tray with relish compartments. With no reply in the files and none reported, we may assume that the American Modern line remains as we have known it, but we must remember prototypes could exist.

Easier to identify is the Pinch line done by Imperial to accompany Iroquois Casual. It had been added when Casual was redesigned in 1951. There are three sizes of tumlers - 14 oz., 11 oz., and 6 oz. appropriately named "Pinch" because of the bottom depression. Made in Verde, Seafoam, Smoke (a warm brown), and Canteloupe (a light amber), Chartreuse, Ruby, Pink and Crystal. Ruby and Canteloupe are still the missing links in this glass chain. I found a very few examples of these when Imperial was emptying its morgue at the time when they were closing their Research and Developement department. Those were final close-out days for Imperial and there was no one to tell me the story behind these colors. They may have told it, however, by the manner in which they were sold. Ruby and Canteloupe were priced higher than other Pinch items shown side by side. These may be only samples since we have had no reports of other findings since that day in 1982.

Variation in thickness in the tumblers indicates a mold change, and finding that difference as well as a slight color difference is to be expected. Some Imperial tumblers have ground glass bottoms and some do not. These differences are not explainable and they are troublesome. Quality control is questionable. With these differences, it is difficult for new collectors to sort Pinch from similar glasses in other fine handmade glass lines. Both Heisey and Fostoria did lovely tumblers with a Pinch depression. Our Pinch line has softer edges, not so sharp as similar styles. I am told that Imperial tumblers are more difficult to find than Morgantown's American Modern tumblers.

Everyone who writes must assume the responsibility for errors in their work and I must do so here. In the early days of our study, I wrote to Imperial about their work with Wright and the reply which I had from them outlined their production much as we have come to know it. I had questioned them as to stem-work which they might have done for Wright and they assured me that they had made no stems to include in his lines. From that day to this, I have had letters asking the same questions I had asked and, almost always, I was able to answer those by quoting from the Imperial letter or by turning to old Imperial catalogs. A #69 catalog shows a stem line in just the right colors but identifies it as "Dawn." This Dawn, with a pinched bowl on a slender stem, has confused many collectors. Sure of my position, I was surprised to hear from a collector who had found some Imperial stems with a Russel Wright sticker on them. My confidence in the matter was gone.

Shortly after that Ann Wright loaned me her father's photograph files and I found a picture of these same "stems" called "Twist." The evidence was in. A look at the twisted part of these "stems" does leave some room for doubt and Imperial may have had good reason to say they were not stems. In the lexicon of glass houses, the words "stemmed" and "footed" are not synonymous. These should properly be called "footed tumblers." I know now that Imperial called them so. This Twist group dates from 1949 and would include at least, ice teas, water tumblers, juice and Old Fashioned glasses. They were found in Smoke, Seafoam, Coral and Crystal. Let me know if you can add to these findings.

Flair glassware was made by Imperial for inclusion in Wright's American Way program. Believed now to have been produced for about five years, it had a smooth inside, a granular outside. Textured to the touch, it was appropriately called "Seed" glass. Our information on Flair is contradictory in several ways, not the least of which is the fact that the new files show this glass to be spelled FLARE. The sizes as they have been found are the 14 oz., 11 oz., and 6 oz., and these are as we have expected. The new files, however, tells us that we should expect 12 oz., 10 oz., 6½ oz., and 3 oz. We have consistently found these in crystal and pink but the new information tells us that they were to be made in Yellow, Blue, Smoke, Turquoise, Amber Brown and Crystal. Strangely, our pink is not a listed color. We have heard of, but not seen, an ice bucket. That is not listed in the files. Advertisements of the day show finger bowls and underplates but we find them not listed in the files. There surely DOES seem to be something new under the sun. The Flair (Flare) appears to be the "sleeper" in Wright glass lines and is highly prized. Please share your findings.

Before we leave this Imperial work, I must antici-

pate a problem. You will find here some information on work done for Wright's not produced Theme Formal group. This is rare, beautiful opaline glass done in footed shapes and sham bottoms. Do not confuse this with an almost identical Imperial tumbler. Imperial's similar shapes are from the same time as Theme Formal but they came in several colors, none of which have any connection with Wright and should not be confused as part of his work.

A Duncan Miller glass line was made as part of the American Way project, but it was not a Wright design.

This brings us to the incomplete story of the Bartlett Collins novelty glass tumblers. In 1957 Wright agreed to do a line of tumblers for this glass house and he further agreed to do the decorations for these tumblers. It is difficult to reconcile this Bartlett Collins glass work and even harder to present it in a favorable light. This is a low point in Wright designs. He would not allow his name to be used on the glassware (no stickers), nor were they allowed to use his name in advertising in any way. The glasses were to be placed in chain stores (yesterday's equivalent of today's discount houses) and were to sell at a low price. Wright was aware that these customers paid so little that breakage did not mean the loss of any large sum and that a broken set called not for replacement of a glass, but rather a "set" of another decoration. He was told to keep the decorations coming and to "Pile on the gold - our customers love gold." The designs started, one worse than the other, with Gay Nineties scenes, cowboy motifs, bottoms-up graphics - all the sort of glassware so familiar and so out of character for Wright. With the full knowledge of the limitations a line with Bartlett Collins would have, he had faith in good design and had hoped to achieve his share of the market which, at that time, favored over-done, over-decorated treatment. He felt that he could enter this market and "manage" it to accomplish a better but equivalent result. He was wrong. It didn't happen often.

Some good was to come form the frenzy, however. A polka dot motif with overlapping solid circles was designed. Named "Eclipse," the overlapping "moons" distinguish it from other patterns of the day. Remembering the description of an eclipse may help you identify this pattern but you should be aware of a look-alike with moons which do not overlap and which is not Wright's work.

Finding Eclipse may take patience. It is one of the items that was everywhere a few years ago and is nowhere today. Sunburst, a geometric pattern with rays of color in vertical shoots represents restraint also. Both of these patterns were made in Yellow, Turquoise, Green and Flamingo Pink, all combined with gold. Other colors may exist and we know now that ice buckets and other bar-related glass items were made to match. These would be on the flaired Oklahoma shape and would include a 3" cocktail, a 3½" Old Fashioned glass, a 3¾" slightly large Double Old Fashioned, a 5" highball, a 7" zombie and a 2" shot glass. An ice bowl is 5" tall. Some variation in sizes may be expected for this glass house was prolific and molds were replaced frequently, leaving a measurement less accurate than we would wish. Bartlett Collins had exhausted Wright, leaving him only a little richer. The designer was glad to be severed from these designs and since they were so different from the great body of his work, it seems best to close our eyes to most of it.

In addition to the glass work listed here, we should be aware of Wright's work done by The New Martinsville Glass Company. American Way records show that this work involved several tumblers, but our information stops there. Probably stickered only, and perhaps only with the American Way sticker, these would be difficult but not impossible to identify. Those who bought American Way items were made aware of the importance of this work and their recall, combined with American Way verification will help us with future identification. That this New Martinsville glass work is in a grey area, not yet found, may be temporary. The possibility of another glass line, another product for collectors to search out is exciting and your findings, even if not complete, will add to our understanding on this.

Look for information on the Paden City Highlight glassware in the Paden City chapter. The Yamato Theme Formal glassware is discussed in the Theme Formal/Informal chapter.

American Modern Old Morgantown sherbet, goblet, cocktail, wine and cordial.

Old Morgantown
American Modern
Old Fashioned glass. Very rare. 3⅛" tall, 3⅞" diameter.

American Modern chilling bowl with liner.

Old Morgantown American Modern chilling bowl. Very rare. 3" tall, 5¼" diameter.

Old Morgantown American Modern dessert dish. Difficult to find. 1⅞" tall, 4" diameter.

Old Morgantown American Modern ice tea, water, juice and dessert dish.

Bartlett Collins Eclipse ice bowl, ice tea, water, Double Old Fashioned, juice and shot glass.

Bartlett Collins Sunburst.

Imperial Pinch tumblers, 14 oz. ice tea, 11 oz. water, 6 oz. juice.

Imperial Flair tumblers.

These two photos are samples of unproduced Fostoria Glass. Courtesy of Huntington Museum of Art.

Imperial Twist footed tumblers. Stickers attached - measurements not determined. Old Fashioned, ice tea, water and juice.

Appleman electric warming tray.

Table service in Residential Black Velvet, shows American Modern pilsners.

Advertising brochure for American Modern glassware.

The Fabrics

The story of Russel Wright's work with linens is a much larger account than we had believed it to be. It is a complicated story with lines very similar and times of work so close that rejected lines by one client were often presented to another. While names, pictures and desciptions in the files do not give us the detail we would like, we are still able to examine a very large production and with the guides which we have used with other of Wright's work, we are able to identify many of his linens.

Solid colored table linens were made by Ellison and Spring for the American Way in 1940. This production is earlier than we had supposed. These solid colored fabrics can be listed as scarves, runners, table cloths, napkins and were made in Quaker Blue, Coral, Turquoise, Rust, Yellow and Spring Rose. Monotoned, they were to be ensembled with American Modern dinnerware and were advertised as more sophisticated than printed linens. The listing would include:

    12" x 18" mat
    12" x 24" scarf
    12" x 36" runner
    16" x 36" runner
    16" x 45" runner
    52" x 52" tablecloth
    52" x 70" tablecloth
    12" x 12" napkins
    15" x 15" napkins

One of Wright's largest linen contracts was with the New York firm of Leacock and this association began in 1948. It is the Leacock cloths that have caused collectors to draw breath for the colors are Wright muted colors, restrained. Abstract geometric designs typify these cloths and they were like nothing on the market at the time. The colors were the American Modern colors - distinctly HIS colors. Brushstrokes, Crosshatch and Abstracts, all names given to these colored cloths are, we hope, descriptive enough to help collectors.

Cloths may be found in 54" x 54", 54" x 72", and 63" x 80". Solid colored napkins were available as were plaid ones. We can expect to find cocktail napkins also. These plaid cloths were to be made in durable sailcloth and, when found today are usually in good condition unless faded. With no reason, these same cloths are found with rayon content and these cloths are not as nice as the sailcloth ones. The rayon and cotton combination tended to pucker at the selvedge edge, and are not as neat on a table as the sailcloth ones.

At least three other cloth sets were included in the Leacock line and these were Silver Lace, an Ivy pattern on lattice with background colors of pink, grey, aqua, clay taupe and raspberry ice. A scroll pattern, called Symbol had interesting color names. Mary may have had a hand in naming them. Look for Root Green, Endive, Earth Green and Pink Copper as well as Brown, Aqua, Turquoise, Chartreuse and Grey. The third Leacock pattern was Bandana, a red and white print. All these were made in 52" x 52" and 52" x 78". Leacock also made solid colored cloths and these seem not to be the Ellison and Spring cloths reworked. This line, also compatible with American Modern incorporated more colors and it would seem that he may have intended this design to accompany Iroquois Casual as well.

The Simtex Modern linen line, done in 1950, is recognized by the bold geometric patterns which had worked so well for Leacock. Colors were so similar and the lines so much alike that customers were said not to have lost a step in the change of manufacturers. It seems likely that designs done for Leacock, rejected by them, or unused as their contract expired, were presented to Simtex.

The Simtex product was of excellent quality. Spice, one of the most popular of the plaids which Simtex made, was a winner and captured the Museum of Modern Art's award for the best design of the season. Sizes remain as they were with the Leacock cloths but purchasers were told that the napkins, doing the Wright double-duty function, were "Matkins," a new name for place mats. All the Simtex cloths were to use the same American Modern colors in their early production. Later Simtex lines centered around a "Harvest" theme. Cloths in that line were Harvest Moon, Square Dance, Thanksgiving Dinner, Harvest Hayride and Halloween Party. Square Dance is a woven shepherd's check pattern in two tones of Seafoam. Harvest Hayride, a "Horse Blanket" plaid was rayon and cotton which was said to combine the sheen of damask with the earthiness of homespun. It combined "apple orchard colors" ranging from deep green and brown to soft yellows and greys. Thanksgiving Dinner was an overall pattern of huge squares defined in greens, grays and browns. It could also be found in a blending of currys and greys. Harvest Moon Dinner, another lattice pattern in the harvest colors of gold, curry and grey was woven into huge squares. Luster in all these patterned cloths was achieved by combining rayon with the cotton. Look for the manufacturer's fabric label to be used on these cloths. It should be sewn into the hemmed edge of the cloths and would give the Simtex name, probably not the Wright name.

In 1955 Simtex sold their plaid patterns to a company named Edson who used them in slipcovers and bedspreads. Wright went on to design chintz drapery fabric for Edson and his royalties continued through this transition, figured on yardage produced. These fabrics date from approximately 1955 and were sold through Spiegel catalogs. They were considered "jumbo sellers." Other chintz drapery fabrics were done for Everlast and were featured in "McCalls" magazine.

We know that Wright worked with Patchogue Mills, designing two woven tablecloths for them in the 1949-51 time span but he would not allow them to use his name in advertising. Described as geometric in pattern, they were said to have been woven on Nottingham looms. Other work done for Patchogue Mills included a line of "summer rugs" which they displayed in their New York showroom. These rugs were of sisal and fiber, made in throw rug sizes of 27" x 50" in colors of blue, green or turquoise. It is interesting that rugs of this sort were also made in the room sizes of 9' x 6', 9' x 12', and 9' x 15'. Pattern in these rugs was achieved by weaving various colored yarns in random sequences. Inexpensive in their time, none have been identified.

Other fiber rugs, also called "summer rugs," were made by the Waite Carpet Company. A limited amount of production would have included 27" x 54" rugs in green, rattan, red and blue. Room sized rugs were made in 9' x 6', 10' x 12', and 9' x 15'.

These rugs are important to our understanding of the scale of Wright's work. The inexpensive fiber rugs entered the market at a time when it consisted mostly of huge oil painted, stenciled patterned rugs. Wright believed that pattern, achieved through the weaving of various colored yarns could be more attractive and interesting. He reshaped old Jacquard looms to obtain this effect and plaids, basket weaves and tweeds soon found their way into the rug industry. Neutral, tailored and smart, their low price made them popular in their day and they have been so since. Again, the Wright influence made a drastic change in home furnishings.

In 1950, promoting a "Designs by Russel Wright for Easier Living" program, Wright worked with Comprehensive Fabrics Company. The arrangement was that they would make the fabrics he required and that if they wished to carry these in their regular line, he would submit new colors and supervise production. They could use his name in their advertising and would pay him royalty on any part of their line which he designed. The arrangement was a temporary one but one which drew attention to his work since the draperies used in a "McCalls" feature advertisement were mentioned as his design.

A less satisfactory relationship grew out of a contract with The Tilbury Fabric Company for whom Wright was to design cotton and slipcover fabrics in printed patterns. He submitted nine designs, all of which they rejected. Ten more were sent and of that amount, only one was found satisfactory. He later sent two more and, again, only one was found to be acceptable. These rejections were costly to Wright who felt they did not examine the designs and their possibilities and that Tilbury tried to influence his talents beyond his acceptability. The matter went to arbitration and he was paid. Wright had cautioned them not to "show these (rejected) patterns around" for he had not yet decided whether or not to submit them to others. This working arrangement, in spite of legalities, lasted from 1952-1957 and serves to point out once more that no design which Wright submitted was ever rejected by the designer himself. Having put so much work into it, he was certain to try to use it another time and with another customer.

Of course, vinyl fabrics interested Wright and he was quick to put them to use in table settings. Cohen, Hall and Marx were early producers in this market and their cloths and mats date from 1946. They were to have exclusive use of his work in that field and could use his name. No copies or imitations were to be developed. He submitted 10 designs but for internal reasons, they did not produce during the two years he worked with them. Turning to arbitration again, Wright claimed he was owed $4,000.00 and needed these patterns released so he could submit them to others. The case was settled in his favor. These facts are updated by the new records.

The Aristocrat Leather Company in 1951 contracted to do a line of vinyl table mats which could use Wright's signature. He stipulated, however, that these mats would be recalled and the use of his name rescinded if the quality of the mats fell below his standards.

Wright had a working arrangement with DuPont which allowed DuPont to sell their product, designed by Wright, to many manufacturers. These synthetic fabrics included leather effects of all sorts, reptile and pony skin as well as the popular saddle type. "Color conditioning" was said to combine correct colors for different usages of which there were many in DuPont's production. Imitation cowhide used as automobile seat covering was the most popular of the products made by DuPont.

The Hedwin Corporation, manufacturers of vinyl table mats and cloths met head-on with Wright. He agreed to design eight mats of thermo plastic material which would not be imitative of natural fabrics. They gave him a minimum guarantee of $3,000.00 which he considered to be too little. Hedwin complained that he was slow in submitting designs and Wright believed them to have resorted to "fast sale" techniques. He further believed they took parts of his designs and used them on other patterns of their own on which he did not draw royalties - a not uncommon practice. Neither did they use a national distributor and Wright had little respect for their sales organization. To all this add that he claimed their price was too high. He said he had enough experience to know that excellent quality ware, priced too expensively, "sat" on retailer's shelves. His serious objections were fundamental to his own business practices and Hedwin was forced to withdraw all of the objectionable merchandise (that which had pirated a portion of his designs), and replace it with the correct designs. From that time on he drew royalties on any mat which incorporated any portion of his design and became Hedwin's color consultant. Slow sales forced the line to be dropped in 1954. Known to have been made were three lines, Spencerian, Venetian and Loop Dot. No pictures or descriptions are available but the line was to have been extensive.

Our 1985 notation that work done for Frank and Saden is the only reference to that work which we have found.

It is important to understand that these vinyl lines were no less significant to Wright than had been his fabric lines. Vinyls had not been around long enough to get the bad name they later acquired and Wright considered them to be the table linens of the future.

Russel Wright linens, in good condition, are rare. Our pictures here show Wright dinnerware pieces on some of these cloths. A quick look at these gives us a better understanding of the effects which Wright knew could be achieved by blending the colors of cloths to use with his dinnerware.

Original paper tags from linens.

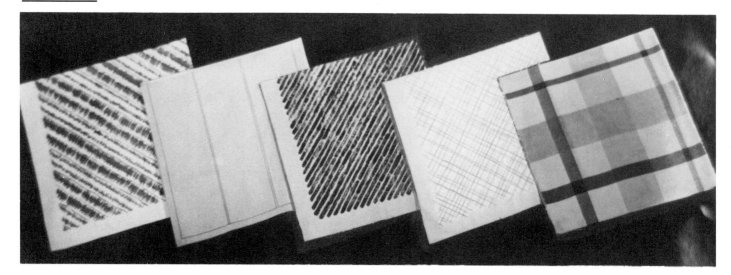

Various Leacock patterns.

Leacock Brush Strokes cloths in Cedar Green and Seafoam Grey. Shown with American Modern Canteloupe vegetable bowl.

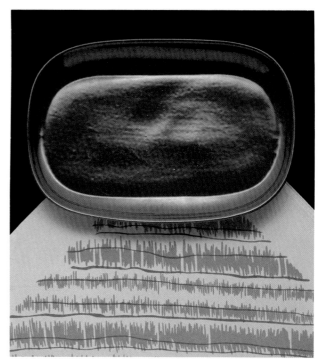

Leacock Abstracts cloth shown with American Modern platter.

Russel Wright wooden bowl on Leacock Crosshatch.

Leacock Crosshatch. Came in combinations of dusty red/chartreuse/brown, aqua or coral with chocolate, taupe/blue/green, and red/blue.

Leacock Silver Lace shown with American Modern Dinnerware.

Leacock Bandana shown with Residential dinnerware and Flair glass tumblers.

Leacock Symbols shown with Iroquois dinnerware.

One of the Harvest themes from Simtex.

Simtex Harvest cloth shown with American Modern celery.

Simtex Harvest variation.

Simtex Harvest variation.

Unknown cloth. Represents the naturalistic theme which Wright used in many of his works.

The American Way
The Great Experiment

In other accounts of the Wright story, we have been able to overview the extensive work done by Wright and others in the program he named American Way Inc. It seems important to do so again, for we have a great deal more information than we have had before and some of that information is exciting to those who are under the "Modern umbrella." This information is difficult to document for several reasons. Much of the product work which Wright contributed to this marketing group rightfully belongs in other chapters and we have placed it there. At the same time, all of the work sold and distributed by the Way was approved by him, some even conceived and supervised by him. In addition, the large body of the work comes to us in extensive listings, not pictured. That much of it may never have reached production makes those listings questionable - but very interesting since they would represent prototypes, experimental items, short runs. In some instances, the products WERE made and went into manufacturer's lines after the Way collapsed.

Our Way information does not end with product information, however. In overviewing the Way, we come to a new understanding of Wright's social philosophy. We had come to question and to ask ourselves how to reconcile this social reformer with the artistic-minded businessman. Product and philosophy co-existed but our understanding is incomplete until we look at this Way information, its purposes, Wright's purposes, and the background of world events against which they all played. His constant messages to Americans to throw off the yoke of European influences and take pride in our own artistic instincts were rooted in pragmatism. All falls together when we understand that the philosophy, put into practice made possible the product which would result. In a round-robin effect, all were interdependent. Wright knew this and in advocating his cause, he advanced his work.

The Way concept was rooted in the events of World War II which played into Wright's hand, causing a need for American products. He gave reason and voice to that need. He believed that the war would leave Europe disabled creatively and crippled economically. He saw that American manufacturers would be able to step into the gap and, in so doing, would need help from American designers. A demand for new products must be created. If that demand were for an American product, styled in a contemporary fashion, there would be little chance that Americans would again turn to outdated European styles. Educating the American homemaker and changing her ideas of "good design" was the first step necessary to secure the position of American manufacturers and American designers. He set out, almost single handed, to change the face of the home furnishings industry throughout the Western world - and he made important changes.

The Way had its beginning in 1941 and was similar in concept to the honesty of style expressed in the Arts and Crafts movements. It was a merchandising group, formed to facilitate changes as they are expressed here, to incorporate, coordinate and to accelerate art-in-industry in the home furnishings field. It would offer the best of American design in a concerted presentation, lending conscious direction to the contemporary design movement. It would develop a more inherently American expression and relate that to every day furnishings.

The Way was divided into two groups. Established artists/designers would sell their work directly to the American Way. Those who were new to the design world, but known to be good craftsmen were to be given designs which had been approved by Wright. They would do the work under his direction. These two groups were chosen after extensive scrutiny. Their work was carefully monitored and assembled in New York around 39th Street and 5th Avenue and here they were to promote and display their work in allocated space often actually producing their handwork there. Both the handcraft group and the established designer group would add to and refresh their lines twice a year following a seasonal change. The contributors were to be responsible for stimulating consumer interest and sales by a planned publicity program. Distribution was to be on a national scale. Advertisements in the trade papers as well as in home furnishings magazines were all components of a well-considered merchandising program. In an effort to achieve exclusivity, the plan called for a one-store-at-a-time plan which would, for a time, make the goods available only in one outlet in a city. Wright felt that with close cooperation with consumer groups, museums, personal appearance tours, radio and newspaper publicity, demand for the products would soon multiply. Stores who were to feature these products would allocate space for entire rooms, sometimes many rooms, with all items representing the work of the program. Invitations were sent out from Macy's in New York inviting customers to the formal opening by Eleanor Roosevelt on December 21, 1940.

Almost one hundred designers and craftsmen formed the body of those who would design for American Way and a listing of those represents work sought after by collectors in various fields: John James Audobon, Raymond Loewy, Glen Lukens, Dorothy Warren Ohara, Dorothy Thorpe, Grant Wood, Norman Bel Geddes, Henry Dryfus, Donald Deskey, Eliel Sarranen, Mary Wright and more. Breaking down the country geographically allowed a broad sweep of manufacturers who would produce. Under headings of: California, Middle Coast, New England, New York, North West, South and Southwest more than 200 leaders in the fields for which they were chosen were represented by: Cabin Crafts, Everlast Metals, Fulper Pottery, Imperial Glassware, Klise Woodworking Company, Herman Miller Furniture Company, Duncan Miller Glass Company, Jugtown Pottery Company, LePere Pottery Company, Weller Pottery and Zanesville Pottery.

With such prestigious involvement, such an impressive beginning and such elaborate planning, it seemed an important loss when it failed. After a year, the project as a whole was abandoned with some work ideas only, never making production.

The cause of failure rested not with the concept or the quality of the product, but with the complexity of administering the plan at the onset of World War II and the demands on production which that made. The times were different in all ways and our small world now was much larger then. With a widely divergent group of people, quality control was difficult to achieve and uniformity was difficult to maintain. Communication as we know it did not exist then and work done in so many locations made sales and distribution a problem. Supply was not always where it should be. Demand, equally confusing, called for different products in different sites and the entire scheme fell into confusion for lack of better management than Wright had time to give it. It took him ten years to pay costs incurred by American Way, but failure brought him closer to

his developing philosophy and his expanding interest in emerging arts and craftsmanship. He was not a "bitter ender" and lesson learned, the qualities of other's work observed, trends recognized, all enriched his own work. The costly experiment was not completely wasted.

Wright's own product work with the Way was extensive, and in some ways surprising. Through work distributed by Raymor, he included Spun Aluminum and buffet accessories. Wooden ware done for Klise is listed as is his American Modern dinnerware. An unexpected listing, however, is that he contracted to do glass work done by The New Martinsville Glass Company. We have no further information on these, but it seems likely that an example, with a Way sticker to confirm it as authentic, will come our way, opening up a new area of glass for collectors.

Wright contributed a listing of seven pieces of marble decorated accessories done by the Vermont Marble Company in Proctor, Vermont. The listing is complete but there are no pictures to present. A console dish, candlesticks, a vase and bookends were made in Travertine and Rose (a rose-beige). A vase, ashtrays in three sizes, a covered urn and bookends were offered in Olive and Grey (a grey-green marbled effect). It is interesting to speculate on this material used in a modern treatment.

Gold Aluminite serving pieces were part of Wright's product work for the Way. Made by Everlast Aluminum, these pieces were important to Wright. He painstakingly carved the original models for the pieces out of alabaster in an effort to insure a truly beautiful form. Aluminite was a heavy gauge aluminum and had been used previously for airplane and automobile parts. Finished in a pale gold, it did not require polish and did not peel, chip or corrode, making it safe for all food and drink. The finish is much like what we later called annodized aluminum. Made in such limited amounts, we still may find: three sizes of bowls, a dinner plate, a pticher with a blonde maple handle, and a tumbler. With colored aluminum just becoming collectible, we may expect to see examples of alumnite soon. We have no information on marks on this, but they should have been marked with the Way sticker, at least.

Other of Wright's Way work is discussed in other chapters and Mary's contribution is presented in the chapter devoted to her work. These listings are the total of Wright's work done in his own name but it is only a small part of the work which he suggested/directed/approved. We must be cautious if our collections are to be confined to Wright designs. Fifty-year-old recall may be exactly correct that an item was purchased as part of a Russel

Wright Exhibit, but the notion that all of that work was his is not correct.

The Way program added a substantial amount to Wright's work, but the great body of work done by others and approved by Wright cannot be listed here. There is simply too much of it. Pictures are lacking in the files, but descriptive information included there tells of another world of good design in the first half of this century. This work is listed under the artist/designer's name or the manufacturer's name. I have cross-referenced this work and if you will allow me some patience, time, a stamp and a specific question, I will be glad to help you with any study you may be making. Any findings which you can offer will add to that which I have in my records and will pass along as part of the record of Wright's work.

This work brings collectors/students/researchers to a natural divide. Some, able to confine their collections and interests to Wright designs will stop here, develop their collections and become "advanced Russel Wright collectors." Others of us, more addicted to Modernism, will continue to study and collect the work of others as well as Wright's. The listings of the American Way projects are a good point of departure.

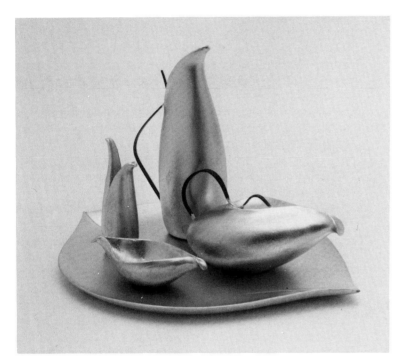

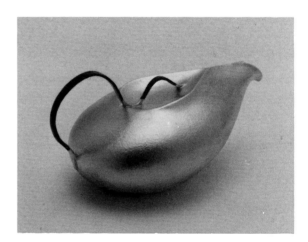

Everlast Aluminite.

In Her Own Way
Mary Wright

Much of the information on Mary Wright's work comes from the American Way files since she was an active participant in that project with many contributions to it. That this program was short-lived and that her own dinnerware project, Country Gardens, was not accepted in the pottery industry combine to suggest that her work was minimal. That myth was given credence in the American Way files where a biographical sketch said that "Mary Wright's claim to fame is that she is married to Russel Wright." With that red flag in mind, we will try to add as much information as possible on the numerous design works done by Mary. Her contributions to her husband's work were too important to ignore, and her own talents deserve better treatment than has been given until now.

Certainly we cannot believe that Wright's way would have been the same without her. She calmed the waters, opened doors, paved the way and often paid the way which he was to follow. Hers was a minor role to his when they shared his work. When involved with her own work, she was found to be of considerable talent with an intuitive sense of good design. That she had a way with words is evident. Her names often described Wright's designs. She was tireless in her efforts to promote her husband's work and often sublimated her own activities to advance his.

Mary was born Mary Small Einstein, related to the famous scientist, but from a branch which had chosen the marketplace in which they amassed a very large fortune in the ribbon and lace industry. Theirs was a family which was not to be influenced by the Great Depression and theirs was a world of many social and business contacts. They objected to her marriage to Wright and the couple eloped in the face of open hostility to her new husband. The year was 1927, not especially important to the stable Einstein family, but catastrophic to the business community at large. The Depression was to influence the newly married couple.

The Wrights were not short on good ideas and energy and Mary, in a role she was to play for the rest of her life, threw herself into every position that needed a hand, promoting her husband as she went. In the beginning, it helped that she knew owners of boutiques, small shops with good names in accessory sales and she knew, or came to know, those who were in favored positions in the design world in which her husband hoped to excel. With his animals and decorative items in hand, she made a persuading salesperson and her efforts to put Wright's work in the right hands was very important to his early career.

Soon their horizons expanded to include Spun Aluminum. Mary took charge of organizing the downstairs of the coach house home in which they lived, turning it into a small metal factory with the new metal the most important product. She set up a model sales program, complete with hand drawn advertisements and copy. All this was to free her creative husband of the business details which he claimed to be a burden. We are told that from these early days Mary kept two sets of books. One set showed a profit which encouraged Wright, the other, more accurate, reflected the true situation and the support she gave from her own funds. By 1936, however, with the worst of the Depression behind them, the Wrights joined with Irving Richards, by then an "old partner" for he, too, had promoted Wright's early work. Together they formed the Raymor Company. As part owner, Mary was an important contributor to the firm and she and Richards wrote textbook principles of marketing to which Wright would return again and again in his work.

Those days, for a time, were good days. Mary went to department stores making speeches, giving demonstrations, developing advertising plans. She actively promoted the American Way and fit herself into other of Wright's work where she was needed. In collaborating with him in writing "Guide To Easier Living", their book on home management, she affirmed her approval of his philosophy as well as his products. Mary sold Wright with style, we must repeat, but she brought to that work a clear concept of value and worth of excellence.

Collectors know Mary's own work best as Country Gardens, the dinnerware line which was to have been made by the Bauer Company in Atlanta. She was working with the Atlanta people and with that branch of the Bauer operation in Los Angeles during 1946, at a time when Wright's work with Bauer was in trouble and both Wrights were at odds with glaze treatments by Bauer. Wright's own problems are discussed in the Bauer chapter, but we should note here that Mary and Doris Coutant, Wright's ceramist were working with difficulty to establish glazes which could be machine made at a margin of profit which Bauer had established. With no doubt, Wright had his hand in these problems, for correspondence showed "cover letters" from Coutant outlining problems with his art pottery line as well as those connected with Country Gardens. Wright would fire back a reply that he should not be bothered by these questions, that this was his wife's affair and he should not be distracted by it. Then would follow a list of his comments on each glaze, with glaze formulas as well as general advice on Country Gardens. Protecting himself he would add that he was "sending a copy of this letter to Mrs. Wright so you will both know my suggestions." Mary's less frequent correspondence shows her more tractable and while giving specific opinions, she suggests that she will conform to the best efforts Coutant and Bauer can achieve. Country Garden, in some experimental glazes, was introduced at the Atlanta Housewares show on May 12, 1946. The buyers were not pleased and Bauer, discouraged by lack of interest as well as high production costs, refused to go into full production. No amount of persuasion moved them from that position.

Country Gardens, as planned, would have been made in green, pink and beige. The original pieces were to be a plate, bread and butter plate, cup and saucer, fruit, cream and sugar but also sampled were a large number of pieces, whimsical and abstract, which added to a line of uncertain numbers and names. We know that there were 2-cup and 5-cup pitchers, but it is difficult to ascribe names to some of the amorphous pieces which collectors are finding. New-to-collectors items, pictured here, may be samples or prototypes. Mary's intent to design a line for table use only, not to be used for decorative disguises may have been circumvented by her own lively imagination. While claiming to conform to "form follows function" she seems to have missed that mark. These light-hearted shapes, appearing to be handmade, are not easily identified. Pushing the boundaries of conformity,

they also seemed to crowd the capacity of Bauer to produce. The pottery claimed that they were not able to achieve these glazes on these shapes at a price competitive on the eastern market at that time. Mary's efforts to compromise designs, to find other producers, or otherwise to achieve production of Country Gardens met with no success.

Country Gardens was sampled at the Atlanta show, as stated, but it may also have been shown at other markets. Some made its way across the country, we are sure, and we know that some of it was sold in leading department stores. The likely explanation is that there were remains from sampling, remains from showrooms and that those remains were sold as lots to the stores. Some small amount is found by collectors today who prize it very highly. All Mary Wright Country Gardens must be considered as rare.

We are not more fortunate when we consider other of Mary's work, some, but not all of which, centered on the American Way project. She collaborated with Raymond Loewy to produce a group of buffet serving pieces made by Everlast Aluminum. Heavy gauge aluminum to ensemble with either modern or traditional settings used motifs of waxy spring flowers, hyacinths, lilies of the valley, crocus, dogtooth violets - all these in a group called "Spring Flowers." Items in this floral group were:

> Large rectangular tray
> Small rectangular tray
> Square basket with handle
> Deep round basket with handle
> Flat round basket with handle
> Flat round tray with two side handles
> Deep round bowl, no handles
> Shallow platter, narrow edge with two handles
> Coaster

An alternative pattern to Spring Flowers was "Fallen Leaves" with native American leaves as the motif. It was made in the same shapes listed above.

In addition to these two themes, some additional pieces are listed for us. These include:

> Ice bucket with ladle and strainer
> Oak Leaf relish
> Single Ivy Leaf bowl
> Double Ivy Leaf bowl
> Candlestick

We are left with few pictures, measured sizes or any information except those provided in listings in the American Way files but it is safe to assume that production of this line would not have been abandoned when the Way was discontinued. We can be certain that it would have been stickered with the Way sticker, but it is doubtful that it would have carried Mary's signature because of the complexity of the material. None of this has been reported but we are on the cutting edge of this metal as collectible and as we become more aware of Mary's work, examples may be found. Look for these motifs and the Everlast mark.

Also done for American Way was some lovely delicate basketry. Ann Wright tells us that her father wanted a firm in the Carolinas to do work from sketches Mary had made. That seems not to have been done but we do know from Way files that Mary was to have produced some basketry done by the Penobscot Indian Arts and Crafts Group in Maine. She was joined by Peter Cabot and Princess Goldenrod as designers for this small line. Using what was said to be a secret Penobscot Indian style passed on from one generation to another, these could have been used as incidental containers in the home. Sizes went from small to huge. To have been offered were Red strawberry, White strawberry, Black blackberry and a Maroon cherry. Sweet grass handles were said to lend an enduring perfume. A knitting basket, made in the form of a red cross, served as a symbolic reminder of work being done by the Red Cross in World War II. A full cylindrical knitting basket completed the group. It was done in natural color string and cane and was said to hold the longest knitting needles. While this completes the Penobscot group, it does not eliminate any sample work which may have been proposed by the Carolina source, or any such work which may have resulted from other contacts made by the Wrights. As has been stated, no design work was ever wasted because of unfavorable immediate circumstances.

Perhaps collectors will take a longer look at work signed by The Maddox Company in Los Angeles, for Mary did an accessory line for Maddox in conjunction with American Way. These were pottery flower servers with suggested usage for jams, jelly, candy or ashtray. They were made in white or yellow Daisy and yellow, blue or Brown Pansy. If found, these have not been attributed to Mary's work.

Mary's linens were made before the time of American Way. So wonderfully described in the files it seems sure that some collector will identify a Mary Wright cloth soon. These early cloths used a garden motif and there were three versions. Kitchen Garden was 54" x 54" in red, yellow and two tones of green. The design featured radishes, onions, carrots, string beans, peas, squash, tomatoes in rows with a large head of lettuce in one corner and a cauliflower in the other. It is not difficult to see her husband's hand in this work, for he used a similar treatment in the work he did for Campbell Soup in the World's Fair exhibit.

Fruit Orchard was made in the same size, and came in Sky Blue (noted to be the best color), lavender and turquoise. The design was of branches of fruit-bearing trees against clouds blowing across the sky. Sea Garden completed this group. With the same sizing and the notation that turquoise was the best color, it also was made in dusty pink, yellow and purple. Shells of all descriptions, sea horses, shark eggs, urchins, coral and seaweed were scattered in no definite pattern. All cloths in this group were made on Belgian linen. A later cloth, this part of a group of cloths done for American Way by several designers and manufactured by Leacock & Co., was Marine Garden. It was a 52" cloth and while we have no description beyond the name, we are told that it was made of a Spun-Glo fabric and came in red, coral, turquoise and yellow. As with her husband's designs, napkins were made in white with colored borders to match cloths. These were generous 17" squares.

Three Mountaineers Wooden Ware of Ashville, N.C. was represented in the Way by wooden accessory items done by Mary and two other designers, Miles Aborn and Douglas Maier. We have a listing of this wooden accessory line but it is not certain who did the design for each item on the list. The Acorn salt and pepper shakers which I own are in the original box but it bears Wright's name, not Mary's or other Mountaineer designers.

Mary's known work in this production is starred in our listing:

Peanut dish
Tobacco Leaf tray
Cheese board and spreader
Individual nut dish
Acorn salt and pepper
Apple bucket*
Footed 17" maple bowl
Ashtray and snuffer, cherry, lead lined
Cigarette box, acorn knob, cherry
Cigarette box, acorn knob, cherry, 3 compartment
Cigarette case*
Hurricane lamp, wood base*
Hurricane lamp, tin reflector, base 6¾"*
Hurricane lamp, tin reflector, base 8⅝"*
Hurricane lamp, tin reflector, base 10"*
Fruit bowl, cherry
Cheese cutter, stainless steel, banjo wire cutter, cherry handle

Mary's Apple Bucket was made in pine with a painted wood apple knob on the top. It appears to be an all-purpose container. The hurricanes and the cigarette boxes are said to have been new concepts. None of this material has been found and identified by collectors.

Our look at Mary's involvement with American

Way ends with that work done for Klise Manufacturing, which made Wright's Oceana. The listings for Mary's Klise work is taken from the files of the *Way* program and may not be complete since correspondence refers to items not listed. For now, however, these were made in Frosted Oak by Klise and enough of it has been found to know that Mary signed it with a burnt signature. These items include:

> Square cheese board, round center
> Rectangular cheese board
> Large square salad bowl
> Individual square salad bowl
> Rectangular salad bowl with plastic handles
> Rectangular salad bowl, no handles
> Serving tray with plastic handles
> Cigarette box
> Individual square plate
> Bread tray
> Salad fork and spoon
> Pine cone shakers
> Relish bowl with three glass inserts

We have no measurements or pictures except the one shown here, but we are told that any glass linings, as part of these items, were made by Imperial Glass.

Mention should be made here of the line of leather accessory items which Mary designed and which were included in early offerings. Her name did not appear as the designer but there was a notation that these were done "By a designer of whom Russel Wright approved." This leather line stands out as imaginative and altogether different from Wright's work. Treated casually, it incorporated the use of expensive exotic leathers and the pieces made were quite different from other work on the market in the mid 1930's. These would include cigarette boxes, cigarette cases, lighters, match box holders and a pair of bookends. Only one example has been identified as part of this line, but more pieces are certain to find their way into collections and we will hope these descriptions will point to it in a crowd.

The cigarette boxes were thematically fruit and vegetable shaped. Pear, Pineapple, Apple, Egg Plant, Onion and Tomato, all were done in leather in such elaborate treatments that once alerted, we are certain not to mistake them. All were of Philippine mahogany with leather coverings.

The Pear was 5½" overall. Box and cover were of tan pigskin, with a dark green calfskin leaf and fur stem. The Pineapple also held 34 cigarettes, was 7½" high, covered with mustard colored gold tooled pigskin with olive green calfskin leaves. The Apple was 5" high, covered with crimson morocco leather, apple-green veal skin leaves and brown suede stem. The Egg Plant was 5½" overall, and covered with egg plant colored kid skin, tan ostrich stem, and chartreuse green suede leaf. The Onion was 7½" covered with white, gold tooled kid skin with pale green suede shoot. The Tomato, 5", was covered with tomato red kid skin with dark green rosette. Ashtrays covered with matching leathers were fitted with a chrome grill top which removed for cleaning. They were available to match Pear, Apple or Tomato.

Match box holders were made to match all boxes. A lighter made by Evans, an important manufacturer of smoking accessory items was offered in chrome and matched Pear, Pineapple, Apple and Tomato.

Cigarette cases, larger than those just described were equally elegant. These cases were 6" x 4" x 1½".

The African frog skin case was described as having a top of that skin, slightly padded to give an upholstered look. The sides and bottom of the box were of matching kid skin. This leather was rare, reserved up until then for watch straps and other jewelry items. Choices were of beige or brown.

A water snake cigarette case of the same size was shaded subtly from brown to black and a wide band of the snake skin circled the curved width of the case. The remaining surfaces were covered with brown cowhide.

The largest of the cases, made of pony fur, was 9½" x 5½" x 1½". The top was completely covered with white and brown pony fur, the sides and bottom with brown cowhide.

Small cylindrical cigarette boxes were 3½", covered with assorted leathers in assorted pastel colors with flame-shaped striking knob. Completing this line was a pair of Snail bookends. 4" high and weighing 5 pounds, these were of gold tooled morocco, laminated to heavy marble dust composition. That description is as given in the files and leaves us unsure of the actual appearance. These were snail shaped, however, and identity should not be difficult.

It is doubtful that any of this line was signed for it came at the time before the Wrights had learned to sell their name as well as the product. In spite of that fact, these items are distinctive, so unusual as to shout as important to a collector. Again, we'll hope your sightings will add to these descriptions.

Mary's story remains a sad one. So talented, she was not to achieve the personal recognition her work deserved. In spite of her own talents, her work most often was in Wright's behalf.

That she had a way with words is sure. Her term "Blonde Maple" became the furniture industry term. She described the dark imitative furnishings which Wright pioneered against as being of "brothel style." She wrote narrative accounts of her life and the pleasures in it. "Guide To Easier Living," the book which she and Wright wrote drew upon her skills with the language. When you come upon a Wright descriptive term that is unusual, think of Mary. The bad news that Bauer would not produce Country Garden came just as they had learned of her illness and that there might not be time for another try. She used much of her last energy trying to persuade Bauer to change its mind on her pottery line but they remained firm. After her death, Wright carried on her efforts. He wrote to several potteries, and went so far as to send a price list, photographs and five cases of the various items which he had on hand and which could be shipped to them. Where molds had been destroyed, he offered to change or develop new ones as he would have done with his own lines. He asked for no guarantees against royalties and even agreed to turn over Mary's patents and supply a pottery with her glaze formulas. All refused production. With no American pottery willing to go ahead with Country Garden, he turned to Sovereign Pottery in Hamilton, Ontario, Canada. This firm had connections with Wright's sister and in turning to them, he hoped to achieve not only production, but financial help for his family. He specified that the line be marked "Mary and Russel Wright, Sovereign Potteries." What has been found so marked is very different from Country Garden as we know it. It is in the original Knowles "Wright shape" and bears no resemblance to Mary's Country Garden.

The Sovereign work which has been found is a speckled pastel pink or blue. Wright's associates feel that Sovereign used some pieces of the Country Garden shape, some of the Knowles "Wright shape" and applied their own glazes. If so, it would have put a better face on two lines which had not done well in this country. Spotted first by a collector in Canada, it has now been seen in the United States. Any amount of this would probably be small.

Mary's death in 1952 came at a time when Wright had much more to accomplish and his way was harder because she was not there in her supporting role. Over and over, I'm told, "Mary adored Russel" and those who knew them best add, "and he loved her."

Mary and Russel Wright.

Country Gardens. Skillet/server, 12" x 16", hinged lid casserole, oil or vinegar decanter, sugar spoon/sugar bowl, dinner plate, bread and butter plates, cup and saucer, 1½" individual butter plateau, 6" butter plateau. All very rare.

Country Garden patterned chop plate, dinner plate, sauce boat, sauce plate, patterned 6" plate, cream, sugar with spoon cover, cup and saucer and divided relish.

Country Gardens sauce boat.

Everlast aluminum made in collaboration with Raymond Loewy for the American Way. Ice bucket, Oak Leaf relish, Ivy Leaf bowl and Double Ivy Leaf bowl.

Three Mountaineers wood line designed for American Way.

Leather group designed for Russsel Wright Accessory Company.

Klise Frosted Oak. King size cigarette holder with rawhide handle, bread tray, Pine Cone shakers, serving tray with Lucite handles.

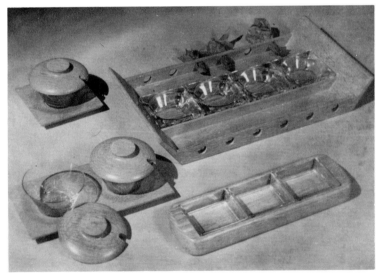

Klise Frosted Oak. Covered jelly on tray, wood tray with glass inserts held glasses, napkins, ashtrays and bottles. Side holes for napkins. Double covered jelly on tray, and relish tray with glass inserts.

Klise Frosted Oak. Relish boat with glass inserts, square cheese board, rectangular cheese board, rectangular salad bowl with Lucite handles, salad fork and spoon with Lucite handles.

A Return To Elegance
Theme Formal And Theme Informal

By 1963 Russel Wright, no longer meeting the marketplace on a daily basis, still felt himself to be "in touch." His Asian Handicrafts work had kept his finger in the pie as he helped third-world countries to develop small industries of their own. That work put Wright and his creed to work in an international scene and he now championed the needy of the world as he had worked for the average man in America. Using talents, instincts and skills honed early, he attempted to bring a good life experience to a larger group.

Never far from old habits, however, he was to test American waters again, this time in a major way. Some designs, worked on and put aside twenty years before, were brought out, reworked and polished to become a new ensemble of dining components. The entire work was divided into two separate themes and were to be called Theme Formal and Theme Informal. Wright contracted with Schmid International, an importer to market these new items which were to be made by Yamato in Japan. Raymor, still the giant of the American distributing community would be responsible for domestic sales. Hemisphere Agencies in Japan would distribute the lines internationally. This was to be design on a grand scale.

Both Formal and Informal would stand on its own as a complete group but serving different functions. When one owned both, it was said, you would never need other dinnerware. Wright coordinated texture, color and design to complement each other or to work well with already owned things in the home.

A sophisticated approach to dining, Theme Formal, in a complete ensemble of porcelain, glass and lacquered Bakelite made a strong statement for elegance. The core of this Formal group was the porcelain which was made in a translucent snow white or a spaced white on a grey double dot pattern. This fine quality porcelain has a soft sheen, elongated curves and looped finials which become knobs. More formal, of course, than his other dinnerware, it also has more than a touch of Oriental grace. The companion glassware is among the loveliest opaline glass, with sham bottoms and an intenseness of self-tint shading from white to a clear rim. It is elegant, unlike any other glass on the market when it was made, and it declares itself as important when found in a crowd of glass. The elongated hour glass shape is not unlike a shape which the Imperial Glass Company used later, but this glass is made in Japan and its opalescence sets it apart. Look for it in this one color only.

The lacquered Bakelite with an iridescent lining will be identified as something "special." It has been found in Shrimp with a Copper lining, Green with a Bronze lining and Black with a Blue lining. The linings are iridized and the pieces are marked with the Wright signature and signed "Shinko Shikki." This Bakelite is very special and lends a completely new dimension to dinnerware. Listings which follow may not be complete. They are from Wright's personal files and may indicate what was intended as opposed to what was actually made for showroom samples. Any piece of this Theme Formal is a treasure to those who collect Wright's designs. Theme Formal porcelain included:

> 10½" dinner plate
> 8" salad plate
> 6½" bread and butter plate
> Cup/saucer
> 8½" soup plate
> After dinner cup/saucer
> 5½" consomme/cream soup
> 4⅝" fruit
> 15⅞" oval platter
> 11" baker
> 1½ qt. covered casserole, 8½", ladle slot
> Gravy
> Teapot, 8"
> Coffee pot, 10"
> Creamer
> Covered sugar
> 12" oval platter

Those who look for this line today will be surprised that in 1965 a five-piece place setting was to be $3.75!

The Theme Formal Opaline glass ware included:

8 oz. goblet, 5"
12 oz. highball, 7"
5 oz. wine, 4"
3 oz. liquer, 3¼"

The trade was advised that the price of these glasses was a real achievement at no more than $1.50 for each glass.

Theme Formal lacquered Bakelite included:

Place plate
Salad/Dessert plate
Soup/salad bowl
Covered rice bowl
Salad serving bowl
Salad fork and spoon

Theme Informal concept was a casual country style, sturdy and solid, as completely detailed as was the Formal. It was designed to serve a different use and to achieve a complete entertaining group when owned with Formal. It was made in Dune, a mottled sand tone with heavy white speckles or Ember, a black/brown with orange flecks. I am told that the process is called the "Bristol Effect" and is an Oriental oil spot glazing which releases the iron in the glaze and allows it to come to the surface. It is quite unlike other ceramic dinnerware with an uneven texture which lends self detail and pattern. It was high fired and that resulted in a richly glazed stoneware, a medium which Wright had not approached commercially.

The handblown optic glassware which complemented Informal was made in warm amber and a subtle soft smoky green. Generously scaled, this Informal glassware is certain to have lost its stickers and may be difficult to identify.

The counterpart of Formal's lacquer was Informal's wood. It was American Elm with a natural finish that emphasized the exotic grain. The bowls, undecorated, were interesting because of it. We offer the listing of Informal with the same reservations that accompanied Formal.

Theme Informal stoneware included (measurements not available):

Dinner plates
Salad/dessert plates
Bread and butter plates
Mugs
Cream
Sugar
Stacking vegetable bowls
Oval platter
Rice bowl/individual casserole
Soup/salad bowl

Theme Informal glassware:

Tumblers in three sizes (ounces unknown but sizes were said to be generous)
Salad/Desert plate
Individual salad/dessert bowl

Theme Informal wood:

Salad serving bowl
Individual salad bowls

Backstamps on these lines are as shown in the marks section of the book. The Shinko Shikki mark is the backstamp for the Bakelite. Wood stickers are not available to us. Records indicate that glass was to have been stickered and that these would be metallic type, round to carry out the round style set by the other marks.

Theme Formal has been found only in plain white. Theme Informal has now been found in both colors. All of this work is very rare, costly and fine. Examples of Informal have been fewer than Formal.

With a small amount produced in anticipation of large orders, Theme Formal and Theme Informal were sampled at the New York showing in 1965 and dinnerware buyers, a group who had sung Wright's praises for many years, were silent. Too few orders were taken to make production practical and no sales were made of that small amount Yamato had made as showroom samples. The entire project was abandoned but the samples found their way into the side streams if not the mainstream of America. It is not possible to know what amount was made but it was very little, probably not more than a run. Whatever the numbers, Wright considered it an "empty contract" and an unproduced line. A small amount, enough to tempt collectors with examples has been found. Even that amount surprises those who were associated with it in 1965.

Wright had walked on the sunny side of the American market for many years and his ability to anticipate needs and desires of Americans can be largely attributed to his social concerns. He KNEW the average American. He had understood our ways and the ways in which we needed to change them. He did not know our children, though, and he did not know the great social changes that the 1960's brought to this country and its young. He had expected that there would be a return to elegance and had come face to face with the generation gap that troubled those years. Slow dinnerware sales had buyers cautious and, for the first time, those who had championed him in the past saw no room for him in the present. It was a sad circumstance.

The Midas touch seemed to have been lost and that was a personal sorrow that was difficult to accept. Having worked all of his life ahead of his time, he was now to face a market which he did not understand. He had mis-read the times. Young Americans were collecting causes, not home furnishings and their social concerns were as deeply rooted as his own causes had been earlier.

Had he lived, he would have taken pleasure that the collecting world has embraced his work. It would have pleased him that so many of us have chased his dreams and caught so many of them.

On Pricing Theme Formal and Theme Informal

This is a line with production limited to sampling for the showroom in New York. All items are rare, but a small amount of Theme Formal was made in advance of the showing. This accounts for the larger amount which has been found. Both Themes are extremely rare, and what is found is priced expensively.

We would do well to remember, however, that there are not the number of collectors which we find with the other lines. These pieces are very desirable - to those who are collecting examples, not so much to others whose collection has a different direction.

Having told you that there is little to none of this for us to collect, I also need to tell you that hope springs eternal still, that all things come to he who waits and that patience remains a virtue. A collector wrote to ask about markings on some dishes he had scouted out of an old jewelry store. They were in old inventory, bought from a salesman in the mid-1960's. Unsure that this was really Theme Formal, he wrote me and I was glad to give him the good news. Buoyed by that, the collector bought the "set" and asked the shopkeeper if they had other items with a different look, but a similar backstamp. A search located a set of Informal. Those are the only "sets" reported. All other sightings amount to not more than a hundred total. One who helped with pricing said "Name your own price."

Theme Formal glassware, 7", 6" and 4". Courtesy of Metropolitan Museum of Art. Gift of Russel Wright.

Theme Formal Shinko Shikki lacquered Bakelite. Covered rice bowls and salad plate.

Yamato Theme Informal Amber glass. Courtesy of The Brooklyn Museum, gift of Russel Wright.

Theme Informal Ember glaze treatment.

Photo from 1965 China Glass & Tablewares showing Theme Formal group. White porcelain teapot, coffee pot, creamer, covered sugar, cup and saucer, Bakelite cover and rice bowl on porcelain soup plate, Bakelite place plate, glass, wine and liquer.

Theme Informal rice bowl, Formal goblet, Formal rice bowl, Formal cup/saucer and Informal fruit and saucer.

Yamato Theme Formal cordial. Very rare. 3¼" tall, 2" diameter.

And More

Was there more? You know there was! Consider that Wright not only designed the products discussed here but did custom work for use in his own home as well as for others. His custom work extended to showrooms for clients and items designed could reasonably include dinnerware, stainless, crystal, fabrics, vending machines, disposable products, logos, counters, furniture and more. At one time he had eleven accounts for store displays and showrooms running on a continuing basis. Some of these involved the approval and use of the work of others but the amount of his own work seems overwhelming. It is not surprising that the full extent of it will take years to surface and collectors to document.

Wright did not only espouse economy of time and effort, he had to put those qualities into his work day in order to accomplish so much. His files are full of drawings, most done very professionally, but much was done on scrap paper with no reference information as to where it applied. Much of this casual drawing was saved against the day when it might fit into a project. This raw information adds to our understanding of Wright's work, but often specifics which we wish for are not available. We are fortunate that written correspondence was the usual means of communication during these times. Had phones been used more, much of the detail which we search out would be missing. It is safe to say that more specifics would be available had there been any indication that a collecting world would study these papers for the precise information which interests it.

In 1954 Wright had no original pieces of his Oceana and wanted to obtain pieces from which he could have casts made. His plans were to re-issue these in Lucite, and these would have been called Celomat. Some work may have been done.

In 1960 a plastic ring box was designed for the Arden Jewelry Case Company.

From 1950-52 Wright worked with the Sloan Babcock Company using vinyl in hard surface flooring He did wallpapers with deep intense colors, some with tropical designs and some which are similar to the Memphis styles of today.

In 1957 American Olean vinyl floor covering may not have been made but is mentioned in his files as a client.

Wright designed two products, a coffee pot and stove to be used together for The Silex Company in 1942.

Raymor in 1945 contacted the Buffalo Pottery for a hotel line to be made by Wright. Prototypes were made but no work was done. They were asked to return the examples and not to pursue a stove to table line. The correspondence indicated that it seemed important to "scare" them to protect Wright's interest.

Wright reached an agreement with Shenango Pottery Company and we can assume that restaurant samples were made. His contract was for one year but we have no information to add to the 1944 date.

A contract was signed with the Amplex Corporation in 1949. Wright would redesign their "Swivelite" lighting fixture line. His contract was standard and they were allowed to use his name.

A paper table service was proposed for Bowes Industry in 1950-51. They were to have his exclusive service if sales generated were $2,500.00. If higher they were to pay more. Threats of wartime shortages made Bowes afraid to proceed.

In 1960 Wright redesigned the Hunt Foods catsup bottle and worked on many projects for them - caps squeeze bottles, etc. There were many studies for improved packaging.

Wright had a good relationship with Paper Novelty Manufacturing Company in 1949-50. He developed paper Christmas ornaments for them. These were tagged or printed on the ornaments.

Philip Vandoren Storn who worked as an agent for U.S. Plywood organized a group of important designers to submit plans for some "do it yourself" furniture projects. Wright contributed to this in 1955.

Wright had participated in the same sort of group sponsored by the Caseine Company of America's Division of Borden in 1940. Wright's plans, which were sold in coordination with the Stanley Tool Company included a tea cart, cigarette box, hostess tray, bed tray, bookcases which made a wall unit and a drop leaf bedroom vanity combined with a hamper. Tables and lamps completed the units and they all came with directions on how to build and finish with wood, metal, fabric or imitation leather. Advertising included Wright's name and picture.

A streamlined iron designed for Amtra Trading Company in 1946 reverted to Wright when they rejected the design.

A popcorn warmer was designed for Lodge Electric Company and it was later redesigned. No dates are known.

In 1955 Ravenswood contacted Wright and Raymor. Wright felt that his own Spun Aluminum had peaked and he was ready to work with others on aluminum even though it had seemed he owned the market. Both Ravenswood and Raymor wanted Wright to include brass objects but Wright felt brass should be formal. The use of brass was widespread in Europe was well as the Orient and he said the market might be "short" in the United States. He considered it a "vogue" and did not see much hope for success with brass. He had watched the market for 25 years, he said, and he felt brass was priced too expensively. It involved more workmanship and less profit for him would result. He asked for more royalites and, given that, the contract was signed. Some will be stamped with the Ravenswood stamp, but most was unmarked. These facts update our 1985 information but we are still left with questions.

Peerless Electric Company produced a fryer cooker, corn-popper, shis-kabob attachments, and a well and tree serving platter. The files show detailed drawings of an electric broiler and oven. A Bak-O-Matic electric tray was made and a Toto-Chef signed on the top surface would bake, make coffee and cook at the same time. Many technical problems were overcome but Wright proved that he was a designer for industry by taking electrical advice as basic and adding the accoutrements he felt important to those elemental concepts. Some production seems sure.

Sharon Steel requested designs for a baker, broiler and a cart for serving. The president of that company had personally asked for these designs. Date and production are unsure. They were also interested in tubular casual furniture, especially a folding chair and side table. No other information is given.

Extensive advertising accompanied the work done for the Cornwall Corporation in 1958 and the work itself was detailed. Important items were an annodized thermo-electric hot tray 23" x 12" finished in copper, silver or gold. It may be found with either wood or plastic handles. Joining it was an electrical applicance with ceramic insert as a cook and serve unit. Much market research was done by the manufacturer with no detail too insignificant for them to study. Wright's approved items were redesigns of the tray, a well and tree server, a vegetable dish and warming oven. He entered the thermo-tray in the Industrial Design Review, a year-end selection of the best contributions to design from all fields of industry. His association with Cornwall continued until 1961.

The important Wurlitzer Baby Grand Piano was made of walnut with a polished copper trim or ebony with bright chrome hardware. It is the first modern piano made for commerical sales. The back was made adjustable with a folding device and the holder for music slid back and forth for the benefit of the near or far sighted. They keyboard and pieces are extremely low so that the performer's hands could be seen in action. At least two small portable radios were also made for Wurlitzer. All these date from approximately 1934.

For Cresca, a food distributor, some 1961 work was done to redesign their labels, but some product samples were also done. These would include a picnic carrier, a bottle opener, and cork screw. Production is not certain.

For General Electric, the Harker clock as we know it was joined by two other clocks. These were to have involved wood, brass, crystal, aluminum, ceramic or Bakelite. Wright considered them too cost-conscious but they did many surveys and several clocks resulted. None, I believe, is signed with the exception of the Harker clock. There is little information here.

The Baker Lockwood Company asked for hassock designs in 1947. Before work began they wanted Wright's agreement not to design another line of hassocks, hassock chests or hassock record cabinets. He submitted 18 designs and said that his name could be used if he were allowed to approve all selections. No further information is available.

The Samson work was done by the Schwader Brothers Corporation and Wright's contract with them was in 1949-54. It included also some Samsonite luggage and vanity cases. Samsonite card tables are signed on the rim of the table. The chairs were called "self leveling." At least two versions of metal folding chairs were made. The one pictured here is believed to be the redesigned chair and is signed on the back. The other chair is of one color with white arms and legs. These were made in Patio coral, chartreuse, azure and green and were priced at $7.95. His work for Schwader involved many chair studies and some other work may be found. These metal card table chairs are the lawn chairs collectors have found.

Wright also did metal furniture for the Colgate Aircraft Corporation and this included in-house furniture as well as outdoor furniture. Restrictions on this contract would have given Wright ownership of the designs until they had paid him $16,000.00 in royalties. At that time title and possession were theirs. The use of his name was allowed. The date was 1945.

For Sydney Chairs Inc. in 1955 Wright designed four promotional chairs to be sold in pairs, a sectional sofa including a corner piece, a one-piece sofa and matching chair and a mechanical contour-type chair. It is believed that at least the contour chair was produced in 1955. It has the typical 1950's look. Early photographs of Wright's patio and penthouse show metal furniture which he had done for himself and do not represent commercial lines. These show his style, sturdy but not so styled as to deter the eye from the food or the beauty of the surroundings. These pictures emphasize his opinion that outdoor furniture, when not in use, should be hung on outside walls shaker-style to avoid rust or sun fading.

There are places to smile in the Wright lists and I must put one in this list. In 1955 Wright contracted with the Mahama Importing Company to make an adapter for opium lamps, aladdin lamps and designs for lamps to use denatured alcohol. These were to be made in Japan or Hong Kong. He was to enter into a limited partnership with them, each making an equal investment and they were to produce white metal based lamps with upper parts of brass. Of the profits 60% were to go to Wright. Their salesmen were to sell and Wright was to be a

sales consultant. Their 50% of the "seed money" never materialized and Wright went to his attorney who advised him that "opium lamps" raised serious questions and he advised Wright against selling them as such. It was against the law, the attorney said, and no narcotic devices could be made. They might be as innocent as cigarette lighters but Wright was advised not to think up exotic names for them as conversation pieces. The lawyer recommended the establishment of a corporation for Wright's protection (if the other party was forthcoming with their 50%). Wright, accustomed to thinking of innovative names for ordinary things, countered that they were designed for modern outdoor lamps, not a cigarette lighter and certainly not an opium pipe. Mahama did not appear for meetings, did not return his prototypes, did not ask for more examples and did not bank their share. Wright took them to court, or tried to, saying he was owed at least $2,000.00 for the work he had done. Our story ends there with a smile.

Arthur Poulas has written: "He preferred to light his way with a lamp of his own making." It is true. It is also true that he lighted America's way. Our lives have never been the same. The things around us had taken on a new meaning, a richness that had little to do with money. We were elevated and our lives were richer. Easier living had come our way through a man, his book and a teacup. Our way was lighter and his work is a celebration of the better part of our natures.

Cornwall electric tray and its backstamp.

Ad for Cornwall Corporation's electric hot tray.

1930 Wurlitzer radio. Four tube "Supermeter Doyne Compact" wtih automatic volume control to eliminate "fading and blasting." Model M-4-2, rosewood and zebrawood veneer, 10¼" long, 7" high, 4¾" deep.

1932 Wurlitzer Lyric radio, made of Melmac. Redesign of earlier radio.

Cresca labels designed by Russel Wright.

Advertisement for Samson folding armchair designed by Russel Wright.

Russel Wright Chronology

This is to be considered as an incomplete listing. Dates are approximate.

1904	Born April 3 in Lebanon, Ohio
1921-22	Student at Cincinnati Academy of Art
1922-24	Law student at Princeton University
1923	Attended Columbia School of Architecture
1924-31	Engaged in stage and costume design
1927	Married Mary Small Einstein
1930	Established his own factory for the production of first metal serving pieces, Russel Wright Incorporated
1930-31	Experimentation and production of Spun Aluminum
1930-31	Irving Richards and Wright begin working relationship
1932	Lamp work by Russel Wright Inc.
1934	Work done for Wurlitzer
1934	Heywood Wakefield Furniture produced
1935	Conant Ball produced American Modern furniture
1935	Russel Wright Incorporated changed to Russel Wright Accessories
1935	Klise Woodenware made Oceana
1935	Approximate date of Plantene production
1936	Approximate date of Chase chrome work
1938	Designed American Modern dinnerware
1938-39	Steubenville Pottery agreed to produce American Modern dinnerware
1938-39	Attended New York University School of Architecture
1939	Joined with Irving Richards to form Raymor. Exclusive distribution rights for five years on home furnishings designs
1939	World's Fair work
1940	Ellison and Spring linens designed for American Way
1940	Caseine Co. of America/Borden Division Assemble-Yourself furniture kits
1940-41	American Way products shown in stores
1941	American Modern dinnerware received the American Designers Institute award for the best ceramic design of the year
1941	Old Hickory furniture produced
1941	Sprague and Carleton furniture produced
1941	Master Craftsmen furniture produced
1941	War brought metal production to end
1941-42	Silex Coffee items designed
1944	Shenango restaurant ware designed
1944	American Cyanide prototyped Meladur
1944	Raymor exclusive contract expired
1945-47	Century Metalcraft contract for cutlery and glass
1945	Bauer Art Pottery introduced
1945	Colgate Aircraft Corp. furniture
1945	Buffalo Pottery prototyped
1945	Aluminum Manufacturing Goods designed Mirro Stove to Table accessory line
1946	Mutual Sunset Lamp Company design work
1946	Amtra Trading Company streamlined iron work
1946	Iroquois Casual introduced
1946	Chase chrome contract expired
1946	Cohen Hall Marx and Company designed plastic tablecloths and mats
1946	Mary Wright Country Gardens shown at Atlanta trade show
1946	Appleman Art Glass contracted to do bent glass items
1946-48	Acme Lamp contract
1947	Backer Lockwood Company Hassock designs
1947-49	Englishtown Cutlery designed plastic handled flatware
1947	American Crystal assumed glass contract from Century Metalcraft
1947	Popcorn popper produced by Lodge Electric Company
1948	Paden City Highlight dinnerware introduced
1948	Leacock produced American Modern linens
1949	Imperial made Twist footed glass items
1949	Frank and Saden table linens designed
1949	Redesigned swivelite lighting fixture for Amplex Corporation
1949-54	Schwader Brothers/Samsonite Luggage, metal folding furniture

1949-51	Patchogue Mills contract for woven cloth and rugs
1949	Colonial Premier Lamp contract
1949	Conant Ball introduced Birch finishes
1949	Sterling dinnerware produced
1949-50	Paper Novelty Mfg. Co. paper Christmas ornaments
1950	Statton Furniture contract
1950-51	Paper table service for Bowes Industry
1950	Simtex Mills produced Simtex Modern linens
1950	Herbert Honig joined Russel Wright Associates as business manager
1950	American Modern Black Chutney and Cedar Green added to palette
1950	Comprehensive Fabrics drapery fabric
1950-52	Sloan Babcock vinyl flooring and wallpapers
1950	Sterling Instuitional contract dinnerware ended
1950-51	Bowes Industries designed paper table goods
1951	DuPont contract for vinyl products approximate date
1951	Aristocrat Leather produced plastic table linens
1951	Imperial Glass Company made glassware to accompany Iroquois Casual
1951	General American Transportation produced Meladur
1951	Harker White Clover introduced
1951	Paden City White and Green added to Highlight line
1951	"Guide To Easier Living" published by Simon and Schuster
1951	Received Home Fashions League Trail Blazer Award for upholstery fabric and table linen designs
1951	American Modern dinnerware line enlarged
1951-52	President of the Society of Industrial Designers
1951	Simtex Modern linens won Museum of Modern Art award for best design
1951	Patchogue Mills given contract for geometric patterned woven linens
1951	Fairmont Lamp contract
1951	American Modern glassware introduced by Old Morgantown
1951-52	Iroquois Casual dinerware redesigned and new colors added
1951	Highlight dinnerware won Museum of Modern Art Home Furnishings Award and Trail Blazer Award by Home Furnishings League
1952	Museum of Modern Art awarded Harker White Clover its Good Design Award
1952	Mary Wright's death
1952-57	Tilbury Fabric Company tests slipcover fabrics
1953	Paden City Snow Glass discontinued. Pottery items substituted. Additions and redesigns
1953	Wright sold Meladur rights to General American Transportation
1953	Hull produced stainless steel flatware to accompany Highlight
1953	Hull stainless steel won Good Design Award from Museum of Modern Art
1953-54	Hedwin Corporation designed vinyl table coverings
1953	Northern Industrial Chemical contracted to design Residential dinnerware
1953-54	Residential won Good Design Award from Museum of Modern Art in both years
1954	Consideration of Oceana models for use in Lucite called Celomat
1954	Home Decorating Service named to market a variant of Residential
1954	National Silver contracted to design flatware and various serving items
1955	Simtex sold their contract to Edson
1955	Ravenswood Aluminum contract for metal items
1955	Knowles Esquire line introduced
1955	Canteloupe and Glacier Blue added to American Modern dinnerware colors
1955	Assigned by I.C.A. to develop native handcrafts for local use in Cambodia, Taiwan and Vietnam
1955	Sydney Chairs four promotional chairs including lounger
1955	U.S. Plywood Company Assemble-Yourself furniture kits contract
1955	Approximate date of discontinuation Paden City Highlight
1955	Approximate date of discontinuation Harker White Clover
1955	Imperial Glass Co. made Flair tumblers
1956	Seafoam, Chutney and Cedar dropped as American Modern dinnerware colors
1957	Bartlett Collins Glass Company produced large line of decorated tumblers and barware
1957	Ideal dinnerware produced in Fortiflex
1957	SS Sarna contract for 20 pieces of basketry, wood, aluminum
1957	Ideal toy dishes produced
1957	American Olean vinyl flooring contract
1958	Advisor on merchandising and selling to wood and basketry industry in Japan
1958	Cornwell Corporation made small metal and wood table accessory line

1959   Flair dinnerware added to Northern Industrial Chemical line
1959   Patterned Iroquois introduced
1959-61 Southerland Paper made paper table goods
1960   Hunts foods packaging designs
1960   Jewelry case for Arden Jewelry Case Company contract
1960   Involved with U.S. Park Stystem and Nature Conservancy in ecological programs for public lands
1961   Cresca Food Company packaging design contract
1962   Knowles discontinued Wright's Esquire
1964   Duraware Corporation designed thermoplastic serving items
1964   American Made Plastics company assumes Ideal line
1965   Yamato Theme Formal and Theme Informal shown at New York Gift Show
1965   Iroquois line phased out by mid-1960's
1965   Polynesian drawings placed in Sterling files
1965   Chinese drawings placed in Sterling files
1967   Closed Russel Wright Associates Design Studio
1976   Russel Wright's death

Bibliography

"American Way, **House Beautiful,** October, 1940.

Bates, Elizabeth Bidwell and Fairbanks, J.L. **American Furniture 1620 To The Present.** New York: Richard Marek Publishers, 1981.

Battersby, Martin, **The Decorative Thirties.** New York: Walker & Company, 1971.

Bush, Donald J., **The Streamlined Decade.** New York: George Braziller, 1975.

Brody, Barbara, "American Civilization," Master's Thesis, May 7, 1984

Cheney, Sheldon and Cheney, Martha Candler, **Art and The Machine, An Account of Industrial Design in 20th Century America.** New York: Whittlesey House, 1936.

Design Since 1945, Philadelphia Museum of Art, catalog to accompany exhibit, 1983.

"A Designer at Home," **House Beautiful,** April, 1934.

"Designer for All Seasons," Diane Cochrane, **Industrial Design,** March, 1976.

Grief, Martin, **Depression Modern: The Thirties Style In America.** New York: Universe Books, 1975.

Hennessey, William J., **Russel Wright, American Designer.** Cambridge, Mass: The M.I.T. Press, 1983.

Horn, Richard, **Russel Wright: A Pioneer In Modern Design.** New York Times, August 23, 1979.

"Meet Russel Wright, **House Beautiful,** May 1945.

Storey, Helen Anderson. "Aids to Informal Entertaining," **The American Home,** July 1933.

Lucie-Smith, Edward, **A History of Industrial Design,** Van Nostrand Reinhold Co., 1983.

Lynes, Russel, "Russel Wright Revisited," **Architectural Digest,** October 1983.

Pulos, Arthur, "Russel Wright and Industrial Design," panelist at Rochester, New York, June 1983.

Wright, Russel and Mary, **Guide to Easier Living,** New York: Simon & Schuster, 1950.

Wright, Russel, "A Guide to Buying Modern," **Arts And Decoration,** February 1935.

Wright, Russel, "Bed Room Comfort," **House & Garden,** April 1938.

Many phone calls and personal interviews from 1978 to 1988 with Herbert Honig, Ann Wright, Irving Richards, George Ahrents Research Library, Syracuse University, Syracuse, New York. Collection of Wright's business files, contracts, drawings. Files there donated for research purposes by Russel Wright.

Personal photograph files, loaned by Ann Wright.

Price Guide

Spun Aluminum

Condition remains the primary consideration in pricing Wright's metal work. Collectors require perfect pieces, difficult to find. Stains and dark marks are sometimes removed by using his prescription of very careful use of steel wool, rubbing AGAINST the grain. Scratching may respond to this treatment, but it is not a cure-all. Dents and gouged items are worth little since they seldom respond to home remedies.

Original regional distribution still remains a factor in determining rarity/pricing. First time owners have not been as mobile as today's buyers and the concentration of early sales on the east coast makes metal items more available there. With fewer items in the remaining parts off the country, prices are reflected by rarity, at times valued higher than items on the east or west coast.

Groupings of items, Tea Sets, Punch Sets, Beverage Sets and the like tend to have been separated over the years and the value of a grouping is much higher than the same item found singly.

Size still influences pricing, larger items more highly valued than smaller ones.

1990 prices have shown steady increases and we may expect to increase considerably in the future. Spun aluminum adds depth to any Wright collection, but it may add also to its investment value.

Cheese boards, bun warmers, cake salvers and items of less complex design have been offered at prices approaching $100, at least, and larger, but more interesting items start at the $200 mark. Multiple piece sets and premium items are still found at prices seen earlier, however rare. CHASE items are the most sought after of Wright's Metal Work. Consider these items to be worth $200-400 in good condition. Again, multiple parts increase the value of the item.

Bain Marie server	400.00
Beverage set	400.00
Bowls	75.00
Candelabra	200.00
Casseroles	ea. 85.00
Cheese boards	85.00
Cooking items	100.00
Flower ring	125.00
Gravy boat	125.00
Hot relish server	175.00
Ice bucket	75.00
Old Fashioned set	450.00
Portable Bars/serving carts	ea. 2,000.00
Punch sets	ea. 1,500.00
Relish rosette	125.00
Samovar	NPD
Sandwich humidors	ea. 160.00
Serving accessories, large	175.00-200.00
Serving accessories, small	100.00-115.00
Sherry pitcher	250.00
Smoking stand	650.00
Spaghetti set	400.00
Tea set	450.00
Thermo items	250.00
Tidbit tray	85.00
Vase, 12"	110.00
Vases and flower pots, small	85.00
Waste basket	110.00

Furniture

Wright's furniture is still difficult to value. I get as many "I found this at Good Will" as I get reports of pricing in trend-conscious shops. A rule of thumb, not withstanding should be established and my information tends to value small items—end tables, magazine racks, footstools at about $250 and large complex items as high as $1000. If found in a group—Dining Room or Bed Room, each piece would deserve a higher value and the unit could add to $1500 or more. Fewer dealers working with such large items, and fewer collectors of furniture keep comparative values difficult. Very generally, Conant Ball and Slatton items, typical of Wright's blonde maples are the items seen most and these general figures would apply to those lines. NPD would apply to the Old Hickory lines. Heywood Wqkefield items cannot be determined at this time for so little of it has been found. It would be logical for it to be higher in price thany any other of his wood, because of rarity, and not withstanding Wright's own opinion of HW lines.

Lamps

Collectors are somewhat in the dark in pricing Russel Wright lamps. Many of the table-top lamps have gone unrecognized and prices do not reflect their collectability. Large torchier-type lamps, known to be Wright's have been priced from $400.00 but it is reasonable to expect that to increase. Watch for lamps which combine the materials described here to appear as Wright lamps. They are likely to start at $75.00 - for a short time. As we become more aware of Wright's work, we can expect these lamps to appreciate quickly. Table lamps $150.00-300.00. Floor lamps/torchiers $350.00-750.00.

Oceana and other Wood accessories

Collectors should expect that ALL Russel Wright wood pieces are still considered rare. Base lines on Oceana approach double the price which was projected in 1990 and early wood items are reaching double their own pricing then. Any piece of Wright's wood is a prized item in collections and buyers frequently effect pricing by demand. There is still not enough Russel Wright wood to supply examples in many collections. Mary Wright wood items should be valued as very rare also and are begining at $200 for simple items.

Buella shell bowl	500.00-550.00
Centerpiece bowl	500.00-550.00
Frosted Oak bowls	200.00-300.00
Frosted Oak dice shakers	115.00
Frosted Oak platters	225.00-230.00
Frosted Oak relish dishes	200.00-225.00
Jelly jar with tray	200.00-225.00
Leaf tray	250.00-300.00
Nut bowl	200.00-225.00
Salad fork and spoon	250.00-300.00
Serving bowls	200.00-215.00
Snail dish, large	400.00-450.00
Snail dish, small	375.00-425.00
Wave salad bowl	350.00-400.00
Wing shell bread tray	300.00-325.00

American Modern

See additional information at end of chapter.

The Steubenville early success of American Modern still holds its prized position as the most sought after of Wright's dinnerware lines. Patterned American Modern still cannot be valued since so little has been seen. In the regular line, Canteloupe, Glacier, Bean Brown and White command double prices given here. Chartreuse has still not found favor with collectors and must be considered to be at the low end of pricing tables. Cedar, Black Chutney and Seafoam are priced at the high position and Coral and Gray the mid-mark. All pouring pieces, Coffee Pots, Pitchers, Tea Pots are scarce now and some items thought to be easily found are in advanced collections and pricing reflects that disappearance from the market

Canteloupe, Glacier Blue, Bean Brown and White - Double price. Cedar, Black Chutney, Seafoam at high end of scale. Chartreuse at low end of scale.

#301	Bread & butter plate, 6¼"	3.50-5.00
#301	Salad plate, 8"	10.00-12.00
#302	Dinner plate, 10"	8.00-10.00
#303	Cup	10.00-12.00
#304	Saucer	3.00
#305	Lug soup	12.00-15.00
#306	Chop plate	25.00-30.00
#307	Salad bowl*	70.00-75.00
#308	Celery dish	23.00-25.00
#309	Divided relish**	150.00-175.00
#310	Relish rosette**	125.00-150.00
#311	Carafe (stoppered jug)**	150.00-165.00
#312	Covered casserole, 12"	40.00-45.00
#313	Ice box jar**	150.00-165.00
#314	Covered sugar	12.00-14.00
#315	Cream	10.00

#316 Teapot, 6" x 10" 65.00-75.00
#317 Lug fruit..12.00-15.00
#318 Open vegetable bowl 20.00-22.00
#319 Platter, 13¼" 20.00-25.00
#320 Water pitcher* 75.00-100.00
#321 A.D. cup & saucer
      (Child's cup & saucer)* 22.00-25.00
#322 Coffee pot, 8" x 8½"* 130.00-150.00
#323 Salt 7.00
#323 Pepper 7.00
#324 Covered vegetable, 12" 40.00-45.00
#325 Coaster ashtray* 13.00-15.00
#326 Gravy, 10½" 18.00.20.00
#327 Pickle dish (liner for above) 15.00-16.00
#328 Small baker (vegetable
      dish), 10¾"* 25.00-30.00
#329 Hostess set (divided dinner
      plate) with cup** 75.00-85.00
#330 Coffee cup cover** 100.00-150.00

#331 Covered individual ramekin** 140.00-150.00
#332 Divided vegetable dish 75.00-80.00
#333 Stack server* 150.00-165.00
#334 Mug (tumbler)** 55.00-60.00
#335 Covered pitcher** 150.00-175.00
      Cover only 75.00
#336 A.D. coffee pot* 55.00-65.00
#337 Sauce boat, 8¾"* 25.00-30.00
#338 Child's plate** 45.00-50.00
#339 Child's tumbler** 55.00-60.00
#340 Child's bowl** 70.00-75.00
      This bowl doubles duty as the bowl in the
      Covered Ramekin.
#341 Covered butter** 155.00-165.00
      Salad fork and spoon* 85.00-90.00

Notice that several items marked Scarce in 1990 book have slipped into the Rare category.

*   - Scarce
** - Rare

Iroquois Casual Dinnerware

See additional information at end of chapter.

Aqua and Brick Red are double the prices listed. Canteloupe, Oyster, Charcoal 50% above prices listed. Avocado is priced at the bottom of this scale. Patterned Casual has not captured collector's favor and still will be valued at the low end of the listing here. Early Foam Glazes 50% above later refined glaze.

Bowl, fruit 9½ oz., 5½"................................6.00-8.00
Bowl, fruit, redesigned, 5¾"......................6.00-8.00
Bowl, salad, 52 oz., 10"...........................28.00-30.00
Butter dish, half pound*..........................60.00-65.00
Butter dish, restyled, quarter pound**.100.00-125.00
Caraffe wine/coffee**............................115.00-125.00
Casserole, 2 qt., 8".....................................25.00-30.00
Casserole, 4 qt. deep/tureen, 8".............60.00-65.00
Cereal, 5"..7.00-8.00
Cereal, redesigned 5"..................................7.00-8.00
Coffee pot, after dinner, 4½"*.................50.00-75.00
Coffee pot body*.......................................60.00-65.00
Cover for casserole, 4 qt.*.................................20.00
Cover for coffee pot*...20.00
Cover for open divided vegetable...................20.00
Covers for soup and cereal bowls, with or
      without stem opening*.........................18.00-20.00
Cover for water pitcher*............................28.00-30.00
Cream, large family size*...........................22.00-30.00
Cream, redesigned 12.00-15.00
Cream, stacking 10.00-12.00
Cup and saucer, after dinner 75.00-85.00
Cup and saucer, coffee**..........................10.00-12.00
Cup and saucer, redesigned..................................10.00
Cup and saucer, tea 12.00-15.00
Gravy bowl, 12 oz., 5¼".............................10.00-12.00
Gravy cover/ladle slot, 6¾"*....................15.00-20.00
Gravy, redesigned, lid becomes stand** ...85.00-100.00
Gravy stand, 7½"...10.00-15.00

Gravy with attached stand, 16 oz.** 40.00-50.00
Gumbo (flat soup) 21 oz.** 32.00-35.00
Mug, 13 oz.* 45.00-55.00
Mug, restyled, 9 oz.** 70.00-75.00
Pepper mill** 115.00-125.00
Plate, bread & butter 6½"............................4.00-5.00
Plate, chop, 13⅞" 25.00-28.00
Plate, dinner, 10"...8.00-10.00
Plate, luncheon, 9½"......................................7.00-8.00
Plate, party, with cup** 45.00-50.00
Plate, salad, 7½"..8.00-10.00
Platter, oval, 12¾" 20.00-25.00
Platter, oval, 14½" 25.00-30.00
Platter, oval (individual), 10¼"*.............35.00-40.00
Pitcher, water, 1½ qt., 5¼"*....................65.00-70.00
Pitcher, water, restyled, 2 qt.** 115.00-126.00
Salt & pepper, stacking, pair.....................10.00-12.00
Salt, single, redesigned**.........................85.00-110.00
Soup, 11½ oz. 15.00-18.00
Soup, redesigned, 18 oz. 18.00-20.00
Sugar, large family size*............................16.00-18.00
Sugar, redesigned.......................................18.00-20.00
Sugar, stacking 4" 10.00-12.00
Teapot, restyled (replaced coffee pot)** ..125.00-130.00
Vegetable, open, 36 oz., 8⅛" 18.00-20.00
Vegetable, open, divided or
      casserole, 10"...45.00-50.00
Vegetable, open or casserole, 10"..........35.00-40.00

Cookware, redesigned, all rare

Asbestos pad	25.00-30.00	Dutch oven	95.00-110.00
Basketry for cookware	25.00-35.00	Electric serving tray, 17½" x 12¾"	115.00-125.00
Casserole, 3 qt.	80.00-85.00	Fry pan, covered	110.00-125.00
Casserole, 4 qt.	80.00-85.00	Percolator	115.00-125.00
Casserole, 6 qt.	85.00-100.00	Sauce pan, covered	100.00-115.00

* - Scarce
** - Rare

Sterling Dinnerware

See additional information at end of chapter.

Solid colored lines are equally popular with collectors. Patterns which Wright designed should be priced double the prices listed here. Sterling's own patterns are reflected in the lower end of the scale. There are no absolutes, however, and very interesting Sterling patterns have been found, new owners rightly proud of unique, often few of a kind patterns. That prices on Sterling have not reached higher values reflect the number of collectors involved with the line. Prices on this handsome dinnerware can be expected to stretch as more become aware of its fine utilitarian quality.

Ashtray*	65.00-75.00	Plate, dinner, 10¼"	10.00-12.00
Bouillon, 7 oz.	10.00-12.00	Plate, luncheon, 9"	6.00-7.00
Bowl, salad, 7½"*	10.00-12.00	Plate, salad, 7½"	6.00-7.00
Bowl, soup 6½"*	10.00-15.00	Plate, service, 11½"	12.00-15.00
Celery, 11¼"	15.00-18.00	Platter, oval, 7½"	12.00-14.00
Coffee bottle	80.00-85.00	Platter, oval, 10½"	15.00-17.00
Cream, individual, 1 oz.	8.00-10.00	Platter, oval, 13⅝"	18.00-20.00
Cream, individual, 3 oz.	10.00-12.00	Relish, divided, 16½"	50.00-55.00
Cup, 7 oz.	8.00-10.00	Sauce boat, 9 oz.	16.00-20.00
Cup, demi, 3½ oz**	35.00-45.00	Saucer, 6¼"	4.00
Fruit, 5"	5.00-7.00	Saucer, demi	6.00-8.00
Pitcher, cream, 9 oz.	10.00-12.00	Soup, onion 10 oz.	18.00-20.00
Pitcher, water, 2 qt.	50.00-55.00	Sugar, covered, 10 oz.	15.00-17.00
Pitcher, water, restyled	55.00-60.00	Teapot, 10 oz.**	55.00-65.00
Plate, bread and butter, 6¼"	4.00-5.00		

Paden City Highlight

See additional information at end of chapter.

Most collectors have despaired of finding the listed, numbered, restyled serving items which were well documented in Wright's records. For the time being, it seems wise to list them, mark them as not seen and HOPE. All Highlights remains rare to very rare with some collectors proud to own examples. Green is very rare but the other colors seem to have shifted into equal value on the scale given here. Citron, a difficult-to-deal-with color in Wright's chartreuse lines appears to have found equality in the soft treatment of Highlight. High Gloss items are less popular and should still be judged at 20% off the scale. Documented but not found items remain at 1990 prices.

Highlight/Paden City/Justin Tharaud

All rare to very rare. Green found in less amounts. Citron and Nutmeg at lower end of scale. White, Pepper and Blueberry most popular. High gloss items 20% below high end of scale.

Bowl, oval vegetable	55.00-60.00	Pitcher, covered*	95.00-100.00
Butter dish*	100.00-125.00	Plates, bread and butter	8.00-10.00
Casserole (Bain Marie)*	75.00-100.00	Plates, dinner	25.00-30.00
Cover for soup	35.00-40.00	Platter, large (oval)*	35.00-40.00
Cream	25.00-30.00	Platter, small (oval)*	45.00-50.00
Cups	18.00-20.00	Platter, small (round)	55.00-60.00
Cups and saucers, after dinner*	50.00-55.00	Relish server*	55.00-60.00
Dish, divided vegetable*	35.00-40.00	Shakers, pair (2 sizes)	45.00-50.00
Dish, round salad or vegetable	50.00-60.00	Soup/cereals (2 sizes)	25.00-35.00
Gravy boat*	30.00-35.00	Sugar bowl	25.00-30.00
Mug	30.00-35.00	Teapot*	95.00-110.00

* Indicates items not found

Late (1953) Pottery Additions
Late Paden City items produced when Snow Glass was dropped

Covers for vegetable bowls	30.00-35.00	Saucers	8.00-10.00
Cover for sugar bowl	25.00-30.00	Sherbet or fruit dishes	15.00-20.00
Plates, salad	25.00-30.00		

Snow Glass Items Completing Paden City High Light Production

Bowl, salad/vegetable, round	155.00-165.00	Sugar cover/tray	55.00-65.00
Candleholders	150.00-200.00	Tumbler, ice tea, 14 oz.	115.00-125.00
Dish, sherbet/fruit	55.00-65.00	Tumbler, juice, 5 oz.	115.00-125.00
Plates, salad	45.00-55.00	Tumbler, water, 10 oz.	115.00-125.00
Saucers	28.00-30.00	Vegetable, oval, cover/tray/platter	110.00-130.00
Shakers, pair	55.00-65.00		

Harker White Clover

See additional information at end of chapter.

All items scarce to rare. Charcoal has shown to be color favorite. Decorated items more desirable than plain ones, as Wright had predicted.

Ashtray, clover decorated	28.00-30.00	Gravy boat, clover decorated	22.00-25.00
Casserole, covered, clover decorated, 2 qt.	45.00-50.00	Pitcher, covered, clover decorated, 2 qt.	60.00-65.00
Cereal/soup, clover decorated	12.00-14.00	Plate, barbecue, color only, 11"	15.00-18.00
Clock, General Electric	45.00-50.00	Plate, bread and butter, color only, 6"	5.00-6.00
Creamer, clover decorated	12.00-14.00	Plate, chop, clover decorated, 11"	18.00-20.00
Cup, tea	8.00-10.00	Plate, dinner, clover decorated, 9¼"	12.00-14.00
Dish, fruit, clover decorated	12.00-14.00	Plate, jumbo, clover decorated, 10"	14.00-16.00
Dish, vegetable, covered, 8¼"	40.00-45.00	Plate, salad, color only, 7⅝"	7.00-9.00
Dish, vegetable, divided, clover decorated	35.00-40.00	Platter, clover decorated, 13¼"	25.00-30.00
Dish, vegetable, open, 7½"	18.00-20.00	Salt and pepper, either size as set	20.00-25.00
Dish, vegetable, open, 8¼"	22.00-25.00	Saucer, tea, clover only	3.00-4.00
		Sugar, covered (individual ramekin)	18.00-20.00

Knowles

See additional information at end of chapter.

Alliance and Sovereign pottery not found in sufficient amounts to determine values. Grass has emerged as favorite with collectors. Knowles continues to attract those who identify with Design and Art interests. Hard to sell when it was designed, the Knowles patterns have proved to be hard to care for. Watch for distinct pattern and good gold markings. Avoid knife-marked, scratched pieces.

Grass, Antique White, Fontaine and Mayfair at high end of scale.

Dinner plate, 10¾" 12.00-15.00
Salad plate, 8¼" 8.00-10.00
Bread and butter plate, 6¼" 5.00-6.00
Fruit, 5½" 7.00-8.00
Soup/cereal, 6¼" 8.00-10.00
Cup, 7½ oz. 8.00-10.00
Saucer 3.00-4.00
Open oval serving bowl, 12¼" 25.00-28.00
Round serving bowl, 9¼" 20.00-22.00
Cover for above 18.00-20.00
Oval platter, 13" 16.00-18.00

Oval platter, 14¼" 20.00-22.00
Oval platter, 16" 25.00-30.00
Cream pitcher 12.00-14.00
Covered sugar 18.00-20.00
Shakers (each) 10.00-12.00
Pitcher, 2 qt. 65.00-70.00
Deep compote, 7" x 12½" 65.00-70.00
Divided vegetable bowl 55.00-60.00
Sauce boat 25.00-30.00
Centerpiece/server, 22" 65.00-70.00
Teapot 100.00-125.00

Bauer Art Pottery

See additional information at end of chapter.

Bauer Art Pottery is difficult to price, commanding premium prices on either coast, only slightly less in the mid-section. Values have sky-rocketed. Be aware that Wrights Bauer is sought after by three classifications of collectors, Art Pottery enthusiasts, Bauer collectors and Russel Wright collectors. Wright Bauer was difficult for HIM to find and many collectors wish for examples. Prices listed here may be considered base values and these figures can be expected to rise steadily.

#1A Pillow Base 350.00-500.00
#2A 8½" vase 275.00-375.00
#3A 5" Corsage vase 200.00-250.00
#4A 9" Irregular jug vase 500.00-550.00
#5A 22" Tall vase 600.00-800.00
#6A 10½" Vase 450.00-500.00
#7A 17" long, 9" wide centerpiece 500.00-600.00
#8A 6½" Ash Tray Pinch 250.00-275.00
#9A 24" long Mantelpiece Bowl 800.00-850.00
#10A 5½" Square Ash Dish 250.00-275.00
#11A Irregular 13" large centerpiece bowl 800.00-1000.00
#12A 4½" Flower Pot Square 175.00-250.00

#14A Now known to be candlesticks about 10" tall, unmarked but recognizable by glaze and similar irregular bottom 600.00-750.00
#15A Long centerpiece bowl/candle stick
    ends 600.00-700.00
#16A 7½" tall Vase/planter $400.00-600.00
#17A 17" Long low bowl Half egg
    shape 400.00-450.00
#18A 12" Vase, oval 600.00-900.00
#19A 8½" Bowl, round, deep Bulb bowl .. $450.00-500.00
#20A 20" Square Vase 600.00-800.00

Stainless Steel

Pinch, the Highlight line, is rare - and it is the most easily found line. I had "off the charts" pricing in response to questions on pricing Pinch. Most agree that "what the market will bear" is just about right for this very desirable stainless. Realistic pricing is very high. Consider $75.00-80.00 for each fork, spoon and salad fork. Soup spoons, ice tea spoons and butter spreaders should be at the higher mark. Knives and serving pieces should start at $100.00 and go up. Even at these prices, collectors would stand in line for pieces of Pinch. The new lines described in the text cannot be evaluated. Any and all of these items are extreme rarities.

Plastics

All rare and difficult to find in good condition, Wright's plastic lines have not become as collectable as early buyers hoped. They remain the best designed in the plastic field, however. His work in this field may gain a position of favor when Melmac becomes more collectable than it is at this time.

Meladur

All are rare and difficult to find.

Cereal, 9 oz. 8.00-9.00	Plate, dinner, 9" 6.00-8.00
Cup, 7 oz. 7.00-8.00	Plate, salad, 7¼" 6.00-8.00
Fruit, 6 oz. 7.00-8.00	Plate, service, 10" 8.00-10.00
Plate, bread and butter, 5¾" 4.00-5.00	Saucer 2.00-3.00
Plate, compartmented, 9½" 8.00-10.00	Soup, 12 oz. 8.00-9.00
Plate, dessert, 6¼" 4.00-5.00	

Home Decorator, Residential, and Flair

Add 25% for Copper Penny and Black Velvet. These are VERY rare colors.

701	Cup 5.00-6.00	709	Oval vegetable, deep 12.00-13.00
702	Saucer 2.00-3.00	710	Platter 15.00-18.00
703	Dinner plate 4.00-5.00	711	Creamer..8.00-10.00
704	Salad plate 4.00-5.00	712	Covered sugar 11.00-13.00
705	Bread and butter plate....................2.00-3.00	713	Covered vegetable bowl 25.00-30.00
706	Lug soup.............................10.00-12.00	714	Divided vegetable bowl 16.00-18.00
707	Fruit** 11.00-13.00	715	Tumbler 13.00-15.00
708	Oval vegtable bowl, shallow 10.00-12.00	716	Covered onion soup, each piece 12.00

Ideal Ware Adult Kitchen Ware

All rare.

Bowl, salad 14.00-16.00	Dish, salad/dessert 6.00-8.00
Bowls, leftover, 2 sizes with covers, ea. .. 15.00-18.00	Jug, water, large 20.00-25.00
Butter dish and cover.......................35.00-45.00	Salad servers, fork and spoon, pair........22.00-25.00
Decanter, juice 20.00-25.00	Tumblers, 2 sizes 20.00-25.00
Dish, freezing....................................18.00-20.00	

Ideal Children's Toy Dishes

Boxed sets 125.00-150.00	Serving items, each.......................15.00-20.00
Plates, cups and saucers, each 6.00-8.00	

Glassware

Glassware is still a treasure to add to a dinnerware set and some of Russel Wright's glass has increased in value approaching treasures. Coral is the most popular color, Smoke and Crystal the least favored. The Chartreuse glassware is so delicately colored that there has been no dislike for it despite the usual objection to that color in the dinnerware.

Iroquois glassware is found less often than American Modern and should bring $30.00 to $35.00 for each tumbler. Those with "off colors" should be considerably less. Red and Canteloupe tumblers now may be considered as prototyped tumblers and that puts them into the "name your price" category. Twist has been on the collecting scene for only a short time and no pricing has been established. Much interest would seem to translate into high prices, but those must wait until they are established.

Yesterday there were many Bartlett Collins Eclipse pieces but they have disappeared. The suggested pricing puts these in the $10.00 to $15.00 range with the ice bowl or other drink accessories slightly higher. These prices do not reflect correct pricing for a carrier-tray with a set in place. Such a unit should bring a higher price. Condition should enter into pricing as the gold trim and gold "moons" on these glasses may show wear or dish washer abuse. Be careful when you buy Eclipse and when you care for it. At first we believed the bargains would be found in the Bartlett Collins line, but that hope is all but gone. If you want these and find them within this price range, it would be well to buy them for they are quickly identified today and their value has been realized.

Flair glasses follow the same principal. They seemed more plentiful than they have turned out to be. Flair is a glassware example of the same sort of phenomena that we see with the plastic Idealware line and the flawed Bauer line difficult to find, expensive when found.

Appleman work has been so seldom found that pricing on it cannot be judged. Paden City Snow Glass is discussed in the Highlight chapter and the Theme Formal and Informal are considered in the chapter devoted to that subject.

The addition of a sticker to a piece of glassware is important and could add $5.00 to an item. That it adds no more can be explained by the fact that most collectors want to use these glass items. If you find yourself with that problem, do what you can to save the sticker. There are those who prize them.

Old Morgantown/American Modern

American Modern Old Morgantown, Coral and Seafoam, are most difficult to find and should be at the top of the scale.

Tumblers:
Ice tea, 5", 13 oz. 25.00-30.00
Juice, 4", 7 oz. 26.00-30.00
Pilsner, 7" (rare) 85.00-100.00
Water, 4½", 11 oz. 25.00-30.00
Double Old Fashioned................................40.00-45.00

Stems:
Cocktail, 2½", 3 oz. 25.00-30.00

Cordial, 2", 2 oz. 35.00-38.00
Goblet, 4", 10 oz. 35.00-40.00
Sherbet, 2½", 5 oz. 25.00-30.00
Wine, 3", 4 oz. 25.00-30.00

Chilling bowl, 3" tall, 5½" wide, 12 oz. ..95.00-100.00
Dessert dish, 2" tall 35.00-40.00

Iroquois Pinch

Tumblers:
Ice tea, 14 oz..30.00-35.00
Juice, 6 oz. 30.00-35.00
Water, 11 oz. 30.00-35.00
300% Value for Red and Canteloupe

Imperial Twist Footed Items
No Price Determined
Ice tea
Juice
Old Fashioned
Water

Measurements not available

Imperial Flair

Ice tea, 14 oz. 50.00-65.00
Water, 11 oz. 50.00-65.00
Juice, 6 oz. 45.00-50.00

Sizes as found, variation in sizes may be noted and a 3 oz. glass may exist.

Bartlett Collins/Oklahoma Shape
Eclipse and other patterns
All sizes 10.00-15.00

Cocktail, 3"	Old Fashioned, 3½"
Double Old Fashioned, 3¾"	Shot glass, 2"
Highball, 5"	Zombie, 7"

Linens

Not all those who helped with these prices felt that they had seen enough of these linens to value them with objectivity. Identity, condition, availability and interest all influence prices. I am hopeful that this writing will increase the accuracy of identification and create interest in Wright's linens.

Condition is of primary consideration as we view these cloth pieces and we should not be tempted to overspend for an abused example. It is reasonable to suppose that a cloth in good condition would be priced at $60.00-65.00. Napkins, more rare than the cloths should start at $15.00. Runners, scarfs, and mats should start in the $25.00 range. Any group, such as cloth and napkins together should be considered as more valuable than these prices. Tags or labels add to values. Sizes seem not to be important considerations. Mary Wright cloths should begin at $50.00, in good condition, and go up to whatever you are willing to pay for them.

Mary Wright Items

Most of those who helped with this pricing agree that Mary Wright items are too rare for established prices. With the not-produced Country Garden line recognized more readily than other of her works, the facts speak for themselves. We should remember that even though a set of Country Garden may seem an impossible dream, collectors hope for ex- amples. Any other items described here should be treasured. Not many were made and it seems that the fragile materials used in linens, basketry and leather would leave few items in good condition. Demand is high among collectors who expect that these items will be expensive.

Country Gardens plates 65.00-75.00
Cups and saucers 75.00-100.00
Serving items ....150.00+

Theme Formal and Theme Informal

See additional information at end of chapter.

Prices are comparative only. Think of the Paden City lines and go UP. Theme Formal glasses have been priced at $150.00-$200.00 for some time. Teapots have been priced at $650.00. Bakelite, seldom seen, has been reasonable but will not be so again. Bakelite items have been priced at $250.00. Other Theme Formal rare and no price determined. None of the Theme Informal glass has been reported, nor has the wood been found. So little of these lines has been seen, so little offered for sale, that it is not possible to determine definitive values. All items in Theme Informal are more difficult to find than Formal. Place settings have been offered at $425.00 per six item setting. Mugs $85.00-100-.00, rice bowl $350.00-375.00.

Advertising/Ephemera

Pottery ashtrays, frequently made as Christmas Greetings by potteries and sent to their customers have been seen in Iroquois and it has been pictured in this book. With a personalized message this advertising piece would have value for Russel Wright collectors, those who collect work done by the pottery and also for advertising collectors. These may be priced at $110.00-125.00.

Original cartons vary according to the information they convey. A carton from the American Modern line should be worth $30.00-35.00. This would include starter set boxes as well as those to be used to contain special group promotions. Iroquois cartons are less decorative and may be at the lower end of the scale. Residential boxes should be in the same price range. Other dinnerware boxes are found less often and values would increase because of that. Think of them as being at $35.00-40.00.

Brochures and price lists should begin at $35.00 for American Modern and the other lines should be priced higher. This higher price should include glass brochures as well.

Large display signs used to demonstrate Iroquois Cookware are complicated pieces and they are valued at $300.00 plus if complete and in good condition.

The pricing for full page ads has not been determined. There was a great deal of this sort of advertising and it may never realize the value which has accrued to other dinnerware lines. Time and demand will establish those values.

Copies of the Wright book, Guide To Easier Living are very sought after. Often libraries have deacquisitioned these and they are difficult to find, very difficult to own. Think of them in terms of $50.00-75.00.

These advertising items are just beginning to be collectible. Look for steady increases.

Photo Credit List of Adam Anik Photographs

P. 34   Spaghetti Set photo and Punch Set photo
P. 35   Bain Marie electric server photo
P. 36   portable bar
P. 72   Centerpiece bowl
P. 78   Both photographs
P. 80   all except stoppered jug carafe
P. 81   all photographs
P. 82   Rare American Modern patterns. (bottom of page)
P. 89   all photographs
P. 90   all except Iroquois advertising ashtray
P. 91   all except Restyled water pitcher
P. 98   1) Dinnerplate; 2) Sauceboat 3) Ashtray
P. 99   all except 1) After dinner cup and saucer, rare & 2) Teapot - Chinese
P.102   bottom photo only
P.106   Sugar & Vegetable
P.110   1)Fruit; 2)White Clover plates
P.111   Water pitchers
P.116   all photos
P.117   all photos
P.118   Snowflower tidbit
P.125   all photos
P.133   Meladur plates & bowls
P.134   all photos
P.135   color photo only
P.136   Ideal Salad Bowl
P.139   all photos except upper left photo
P.145   Imperial Pinch Tumblers
P.152   all color photos
p.154   all color photos
p.169   Theme Formal Shinko Shikki
P.173   Cornwall Electric Tray

Books on Antiques and Collectibles

Most of the following books are available from your local book seller or antique dealer, or on loan from your public library. If you are unable to locate certain titles in your area you may order by mail from COLLECTOR BOOKS, P.O. Box 3009, Paducah, KY 42002-3009. This is only a partial listing of the books on antiques that are available from Collector Books. All books are well illustrated and contain current values. Add $2.00 for postage for the first book ordered and $.30 for each additional book. Include item number, title and price when ordering. Allow 14 to 21 days for delivery.

BOOKS ON GLASS AND POTTERY

1810	American Art Glass, Shuman	$29.95
2016	Bedroom & Bathroom Glassware of the Depression Years	$19.95
1312	Blue & White Stoneware, McNerney	$9.95
1959	Blue Willow, 2nd Ed., Gaston	$14.95
2270	Collectible Glassware from the 40's, 50's, & 60's, Florence	$19.95
2352	Collector's Ency. of Akro Agate Glassware, Florence	$14.95
1373	Collector's Ency. of American Dinnerware, Cunningham	$24.95
2272	Collector's Ency. of California Pottery, Chipman	$24.95
3312	Collector's Ency. of Children's Dishes, Whitmyer	$19.95
2133	Collector's Ency. of Cookie Jars, Roerig	$24.95
2273	Collector's Ency. of Depression Glass, 10th Ed., Florence	$19.95
2209	Collector's Ency. of Fiesta, 7th Ed., Huxford	$19.95
1439	Collector's Ency. of Flow Blue China, Gaston	$19.95
1915	Collector's Ency. of Hall China, 2nd Ed., Whitmyer	$19.95
2334	Collector's Ency. of Majolica Pottery, Katz-Marks	$19.95
1358	Collector's Ency. of McCoy Pottery, Huxford	$19.95
3313	Collector's Ency. of Niloak, Gifford	$19.95
1039	Collector's Ency. of Nippon Porcelain I, Van Patten	$19.95
2089	Collector's Ency. of Nippon Porcelain II, Van Patten	$24.95
1665	Collector's Ency. of Nippon Porcelain III, Van Patten	$24.95
1034	Collector's Ency. of Roseville Pottery, Huxford	$19.95
1035	Collector's Ency. of Roseville Pottery, 2nd Ed., Huxford	$19.95
3314	Collector's Ency. of Van Briggle Art Pottery, Sasicki	$24.95
2339	Collector's Guide to Shawnee Pottery, Vanderbilt	$19.95
1425	Cookie Jars, Westfall	$9.95
2275	Czechoslovakian Glass & Collectibles, Barta	$16.95
3315	Elegant Glassware of the Depression Era, 5th Ed., Florence	$19.95
3318	Glass Animals of the Depression Era, Garmon & Spencer	$19.95
2024	Kitchen Glassware of the Depression Years, 4th Ed., Florence	$19.95
2379	Lehner's Ency. of U.S. Marks on Pottery, Porcelain & Clay	$24.95
2394	Oil Lamps II, Thuro	$24.95
3322	Pocket Guide to Depression Glass, 8th Ed., Florence	$9.95
2345	Portland Glass, Ladd	$24.95
1670	Red Wing Collectibles, DePasquale	$9.95
1440	Red Wing Stoneware, DePasquale	$9.95
1958	So. Potteries Blue Ridge Dinnerware, 3rd Ed., Newbound	$14.95
2221	Standard Carnival Glass, 3rd Ed., Edwards	$24.95
1848	Very Rare Glassware of the Depression Years, Florence	$24.95
2140	Very Rare Glassware of the Depression Years, Second Series	$24.95
3326	Very Rare Glassware of the Depression Era, Third Series	$24.95
3327	Watt Pottery - Identification & Value Guide, Morris	$19.95
2224	World of Salt Shakers, 2nd Ed., Lechner	$24.95

BOOKS ON DOLLS & TOYS

2079	Barbie Fashion, Vol. 1, 1959-1967, Eames	$24.95
3310	Black Dolls - 1820-1991 - Id. & Value Guide, Perkins	$17.95
1514	Character Toys & Collectibles 1st Series, Longest	$19.95
1750	Character Toys & Collectibles, 2nd Series, Longest	$19.95
1529	Collector's Ency. of Barbie Dolls, DeWein	$19.95
2338	Collector's Ency. of Disneyana, Longest & Stern	$24.95
2342	Madame Alexander Price Guide #17, Smith	$9.95
1540	Modern Toys, 1930-1980, Baker	$19.95
2343	Patricia Smith's Doll Values Antique to Modern, 8th ed	$12.95
1886	Stern's Guide to Disney	$14.95

2139	Stern's Guide to Disney, 2nd Series	$14.95
1513	Teddy Bears & Steiff Animals, Mandel	$9.95
1817	Teddy Bears & Steiff Animals, 2nd, Mandel	$19.95
2084	Teddy Bears, Annalees & Steiff Animals, 3rd, Mandel	$19.95
2028	Toys, Antique & Collectible, Longest	$14.95
1808	Wonder of Barbie, Manos	$9.95
1430	World of Barbie Dolls, Manos	$9.95

OTHER COLLECTIBLES

1457	American Oak Furniture, McNerney	$9.95
2269	Antique Brass & Copper, Gaston	$16.95
2333	Antique & Collectible Marbles, 3rd Ed., Grist,	$9.95
1712	Antique & Collectible Thimbles, Mathis	$19.95
1748	Antique Purses, Holiner	$19.95
1868	Antique Tools, Our American Heritage, McNerney	$9.95
1426	Arrowheads & Projectile Points, Hothem	$7.95
1278	Art Nouveau & Art Deco Jewelry, Baker	$9.95
1714	Black Collectibles, Gibbs	$19.95
1128	Bottle Pricing Guide, 3rd Ed., Cleveland	$7.95
1751	Christmas Collectibles, Whitmyer	$19.95
1752	Christmas Ornaments, Johnston	$19.95
2132	Collector's Ency. of American Furniture, Vol. I, Swedberg	$24.95
2271	Collector's Ency. of American Furniture, Vol. II, Swedberg	$24.95
2018	Collector's Ency. of Graniteware, Greguire	$24.95
2083	Collector's Ency. of Russel Wright Designs, Kerr	$19.95
2337	Collector's Guide to Decoys, Book II, Huxford	$16.95
2340	Collector's Guide to Easter Collectibles, Burnett	$16.95
1441	Collector's Guide to Post Cards, Wood	$9.95
2276	Decoys, Kangas	$24.95
1629	Doorstops, Id. & Values, Bertoia	$9.95
1716	Fifty Years of Fashion Jewelry, Baker	$19.95
3316	Flea Market Trader, 8th Ed., Huxford	$9.95
3317	Florence's Standard Baseball Card Price Gd., 5th Ed.	$9.95
1755	Furniture of the Depression Era, Swedberg	$19.95
2278	Grist's Machine Made & Contemporary Marbles	$9.95
1424	Hatpins & Hatpin Holders, Baker	$9.95
3319	Huxford's Collectible Advertising - Id. & Value Gd.	$17.95
1181	100 Years of Collectible Jewelry, Baker	$9.95
2023	Keen Kutter Collectibles, 2nd Ed., Heuring	$14.95
2216	Kitchen Antiques - 1790-1940, McNerney	$14.95
3320	Modern Guns - Id. & Val. Gd., 9th Ed., Quertermous	$12.95
1965	Pine Furniture, Our Am. Heritage, McNerney	$14.95
3321	Ornamental & Figural Nutcrackers, Rittenhouse	$16.95
2026	Railroad Collectibles, 4th Ed., Baker	$14.95
1632	Salt & Pepper Shakers, Guarnaccia	$9.95
1888	Salt & Pepper Shakers II, Guarnaccia	$14.95
2220	Salt & Pepper Shakers III, Guarnaccia	$14.95
3323	Schroeder's Antique Price Guide, 11th Ed.	$12.95
3324	Schroeder's Antique & Coll. 1993 Engag. Calendar	$9.95
2346	Sheet Music Ref. & Price Guide, Pafik & Guiheen	$18.95
2096	Silverplated Flatware, 4th Ed., Hagan	$14.95
3325	Standard Knife Collector's Guide, Stewart	$12.95
2348	20th Century Fashionable Plastic Jewelry, Baker	$19.95
2349	Value Guide to Baseball Collectibles, Raycraft	$16.95

Schroeder's ANTIQUES Price Guide

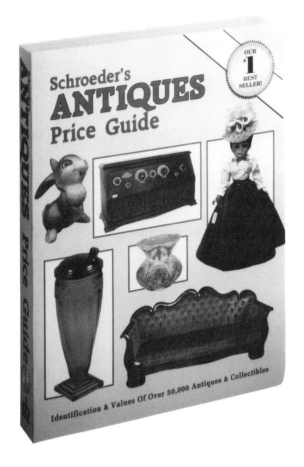

Schroeder's Antiques Price Guide is the #1 best-selling antiques & collectibles value guide on the market today, and here's why . . . More than 300 authors, well-known dealers, and top-notch collectors work together with our editors to bring you accurate information regarding pricing and identification. More than 45,000 items in almost 500 categories are listed along with hundreds of sharp original photos that illustrate not only the rare and unusual, but the common, popular collectibles as well. Each large close-up shot shows important details clearly. Every subject is represented with histories and background information, a feature not found in any of our competitors' publications. Our editors keep abreast of newly-developing trends, often adding several new categories a year as the need arises. If it merits the interest of today's collector, you'll find it in Schroeder's. And you can feel confident that the information we publish is up to date and accurate. Our advisors thoroughly check each category to spot inconsistencies, listings that may not be entirely reflective of market dealings, and lines too vague to be of merit. Only the best of the lot remains for publication. Without doubt, you'll find Schroeder's Antiques Price Guide the only one to buy for reliable information and values.

8½ x 11", 608 Pages   **$12.95**

COLLECTOR BOOKS

A Division of Schroeder Publishing Co., Inc.